W9-BYF-566

From a child in North Korea to her journey into adulthood in South Korea and on to America, the mission of Dr. Hak Ja Han Moon has always been to bring peace and unity among all people. After you read her life's story you will agree that Dr. Moon is the Mother of Peace. — **Pastor Dr. Mark Abernathy**, *Connect Point Christian Center, National ACLC Co-President, USA*

I wish to commend the founder, Dr. Hak Ja Han Moon, for setting up the Sunhak Peace Prize to recognize works that make the world a better place. The ideals that you stand for—a world where we live in peace with one another—is not only the decent thing to do, it is the moral imperative. — **Dr. Akinwumi A. Adesina**, *President, African Development Bank, Nigeria*

A life well lived in service to others. A good read for reflection and emulation. — **Hon. Dr. Jean Augustine**, *PC, CM, CBE, Member of Parliament, Canada (1993 - 2006)*

Mother Moon is a woman of indomitable spirit, profound love and incredible humility. She has cemented herself in history as a visionary leader for her contributions to a better, more peaceful world. — **Hon. Margarett R. Best,** *Member of Provincial Parliament, Ontario, Canada (2007-2013)*

Mother Moon is bringing God's message to the world, and works to help marriages and families survive during these troubled times, bringing all nations and religions together to achieve world peace. We know of no one in the past or the present that has worked harder than Mother Moon to achieve these goals. — **Hon. Dan Burton**, *US House of Representatives (1983-2013); International Co-Chairman, International Association of Parliamentarians for Peace &* **Dr. Samia Burton M.D.,** *American Board certified in Internal Medicine, USA*

Unity is the one element most central in Dr. Moon's work. We need unity and God's blessing so the world's religious leaders, parliamentarians and professionals in every field can overcome the challenges and barriers to building a world of lasting peace. — **Hon. John T. Doolittle,** *US House of Representatives (1991-2009); Chairman, IAPP-North America, USA*

Mother of Peace awakens readers on the journey of the "Only Begotten Daughter" extending parental love worldwide. A blessed exemplification of holiness in the culture of heart. — **Bishop Jesse Edwards**, *National ACLC Evangelist &* **Rev. Dr. Tanya Edwards**, *Co-Pastor, Pentecostal Apostolic Church, New York; National Executive Committee member of American Clergy Leadership Conference, USA*

Dr. Moon has impressed us in how she continues the efforts of her husband to bring the message of peace and the blessing of marriage to the nations of the world. — **Dr. Willem van Eekelen**, *former Minister of Defense &* **Mrs. Hanneke van Eekelen**, *The Netherlands*

I am confident that this autobiography depicting the unprecedented life story of Dr. Hak Ja Han Moon will provide any contemporary reader with an abundance of valuable and profound wisdom. — **H.E. Ambassador Tetsuya Endo,** *former Ambassador of Japan to the International Organizations in Vienna and New Zealand, Japan*

The whole world is now looking to North and South Korea in East Asia where Mother Moon has been so ambitious to apply new methods to foster peace. — **Dr. Werner Fasslabend,** *Minister of Defense (1990-2000); Member of Parliament (1987-1990, 2000-2007); President of the Austrian Institute for European and Security Policy, Austria*

I want to assure you that my prayers are with you for the success of the work that your late husband started and that you have nobly undertaken. May God be with you and prosper the work of your hands. — **Cardinal Kelvin E. Felix,** *Dominica*

Mother Moon's endless work for peace is an example to follow, especially her constant struggle for preserving the traditional family unit, teaching our children moral and spiritual values and putting God, love and peace at the center of our everyday life. — **Hon. Maria Fernanda Flores,** *First Lady, Nicaragua (1999–2002)*

Dr. Hak Ja Han Moon is the Peace Herald for all humanity. — **Professor Eliezer Glaubach-Gal,** *President of the Jerusalem Peace & Security Forum; former Councilman, City of Jerusalem, Israel*

You experienced firsthand the ravages of communism in your youth, so the reality of the Venezuelan people is not foreign to you. A great movement of hope that seeks the reunification of Korea and other sister nations is a source of inspiration for our people. — **H.E. Juan Guaidó,** *President, National Assembly, Venezuela*

We politicians don't always succeed in fulfilling our commitments. Dr. Moon is not a politician; she is a private person. Thus, she could have chosen a very comfortable life; however, she chose to act. — **H.E. Dalia Itzik,** *President (2007), Israel*

Together with your husband, Rev. Dr. Sun Myung Moon, you have served the people of Sri Lanka through the works of the Religious Youth Service, a project of UPF, every year for 21 years. On behalf of Ambassadors for Peace of Sri Lanka, I would like to extend my sincere congratulations on the publication of your autobiography. — **H.E. D.M. Jayaratne,** *Prime Minister of Sri Lanka (2010-2015)*

The story of Dr. Hak Ja Han Moon is one of a life lived in total devotion to God and humanity. It comes at a time when our fragmented world is in dire need for a comprehensive view of world peace. The book is a must read for all who are advocates for a peaceful world. — **H.E. Dr. Goodluck Jonathan,** *GCFR President, Nigeria (2009-2015); Chairman, International Summit Council for Peace (ISCP) Africa*

The Father has always provided illumination in the darkest times of our lives, so we thank Him for inspiring this memoir, Mother of Peace, authored by His luminary, Mother Moon. This book of hope is a must-read in this trepid season!
— **Bishop Noel Jones**, *Senior Pastor, City of Refuge Church, Los Angeles, CA, USA*

You and True Father show that one can learn about the realities of life only by living it in person. Your teachings of taking care of the people who are suffering and loving and comforting the poor, elderly and sick (who are generally rebuked and loathed by the society) have a deep influence on the lives of the people.
— **Hon. Bhubaneswar Kalita**, *Member of Parliament; Chairman, International Association of Parliamentarians for Peace-India*

Mrs. Moon's life and achievements have earned her immense respect and reverence. The difficulties and trials that this amazing woman had to go through are hard to imagine. Despite it all, her heart remains unchanged in her kindness, sincerity and desire to change the world for the better.— **H.E. Leonid Kravchuk**, *the first president of Ukraine (1991-1994); Chair of the Ukrainian Peace Council*

My knowledge of the gracious Lady Hak Ja Han Moon was through my grandfather, Grand Mufti Sheikh Ahmad Kuftaro. I feel she is able to carry this big message and fight for it and help the women of the world to improve their situation and eradicate poverty, ignorance and suffering.
— **Mrs. Asmaa Kuftaro**, *Women's Advisory Board, UN Special Envoy, Syria*

True Mother has been a strong tower and fortress for me in my spiritual walk with ACLC. I am so grateful for her model leadership and guidance, which are so beautifully described in her memoir, *Mother of Peace*.
— **Archbishop Sulanch Lewis-Rose**, *Pastor of Little Rock Zion Deliverance International Ministries; ACLC National Co-President, USA*

The Founders of the UPF recognize that living for others and for the public interest is the basis of development in an interdependent world. With this perspective the Africa Summit was held, chaired by my brother and friend, Macky Sall, President of Senegal, and the Heavenly Africa project was launched by UPF's co-Founder, the Mother of Peace Dr. Hak Ja Han Moon. Niger is changing because we carry the values and ideals that are in line with those carried by UPF. — **H.E. Issoufou Mahamadou**, *President of the Republic and Head of State of Niger*

May the memoirs of Dr. Hak Ja Han Moon allow her to be rightfully recognized as one of the most important and inspirational women leaders of our time.
— **Hon. Patricia Lalonde**, *former Member, European Parliament, France*

The Korean Peninsula remains a fulcrum around which the tensions for peace seek to be resolved and where the leadership of Mother Moon is a shining light of hope.
— **H.E. Sir James Mitchell**, *Prime Minister of Saint Vincent and the Grenadines (1984–2000)*

The work of UPF in peacebuilding is so much needed in the world today, not least in the Balkan region where I live. I have no doubt that Mother Moon's autobiography will shed light and hope and give deep insight and inspiration to those who read it.
— **H.E. Alfred Moisiu**, *President of Albania (2002-2007)*

I would like to deeply commend Mother Moon and her strategy for world peace through ideal families. I salute her efforts for peace in the world.
— **Hon. Mathole Motshekga**, *Minister and Advisor to His Excellency President Emmerson Mnangagwa, Zimbabwe*

Mother Moon is working to create a world of interdependence, mutual prosperity and universally shared values. A world in which all people live together loving and respecting each other as brothers and sisters: one human family under God! Let us join her in this divine endeavor! Let us support this noble cause!
— **Prophet Dr. Samuel Mbiza Radebe**, *Founder of the Revelation Church of God, South Africa*

Dr. Moon's initiatives bring together all the actors of the international community and of social and family life around the ideals of peace, harmony and shared prosperity. She is truly recognized as the mother of peace.
— **H.E. Brigi Rafini**, *Prime Minister and Head of the Government of Niger*

With their many accomplishments as husband and wife, they are indeed without a doubt fulfilling the role of the global True Parents of all humankind. … I am therefore very much honored to be able to greet Mother Moon on the occasion of publishing her autobiography, and I encourage all peace-loving people to have a copy and read this historic book. — **H.E. Mahinda Rajapaksa**, *President of Sri Lanka (2005–2015)*

During these extraordinary times when divisiveness, hate, and a climate of fear threaten global unity and international discourse, Dr. Hak Ja Han Moon is a beacon of hope to those who continue to believe that long-lasting peace is an attainable goal and not just a dream. — **H. E. Leni Robredo**, *Vice President of the Philippines*

This inspiring memoir reveals the Divine heart within our beloved True Mother, the only begotten Daughter, and describes her true love in building the Holy Community on earth. — **Dr. Luonne Abram Rouse**, *National Co-Chairman, American Clergy Leadership Conference, United Methodist Pastor, Retired &* **Minister Marie L. Rouse**, National ACLC Executive Committee Member, USA

Mother Moon's tireless efforts to bring peace to this troubled world have inspired millions of women of all ages around the globe. It is the right time for all of us to rise and honor her for her mission of Peace, Social Justice and Hope.
— **Dr. Rima Salah**, *former Assistant Secretary General of the United Nations; Faculty, Child Study Center, School of Medicine, Yale University, USA*

For many years, Dr. Hak Ja Han Moon has been motivated by a deep heart and wonderful impulse of generosity, and has dedicated much time and effort to contribute to peace and the welfare of humankind. She has a unique ability to care for people while also bringing comfort to others to build a community of love and solidarity. — **H.E. President Macky Sall**, *President of the Republic of Senegal*

Unique to Dr. Moon's vision is her appreciation for the contribution of faith leaders and Godly principles as cornerstones in the foundations for peace. What has been most special in this work over the years is the intentional effort to bring heads of state and members of parliaments together with faith leaders and break through racial and cultural barriers to see the solutions that are possible.
— **Hon. Matt Salmon**, *Vice President of Government Relations, Arizona State University; US House of Representatives (1995-2001 and 2013-2017)*

Dr. Moon has been a role model for women around the globe as she has worked for world peace. Her dedication to re-establishing the family as the most important building block of strong and peaceful societies may be her most important and lasting legacy. — **Hon. Ellen Sauerbrey**, *former Assistant Secretary of US State Department's Bureau of Population, Refugees and Migration*

Dr. Hak Ja Han Moon is the epitome of a consecrated life that speaks with holy boldness to summon forth the best in all of us to make this world a better place.
— **Archbishop George Augustus Stallings, Jr.**, *Patriarch & Founder, Imani Temple African American Catholic Congregation; North America Director - Interreligious Association for Peace and Development (IAPD)*

We congratulate Dr. Hak Ja Han Moon for deepening and enlarging the late Reverend Moon's sustained commitment and tireless efforts in promoting peace, reconciliation and unity, interfaith dialogue, strengthening marriage and family, and many other critically needed initiatives in Asia and in the global community. — **Hon. Jose de Venecia,** *former Speaker of the House, Philippines; Founding Chairman and Chairman of Standing Committee, International Conference of Asian Political Parties (ICAPP); International Co-Chairman, International Association of Parliamentarians for Peace (IAPP)*

I want to commend Dr. Moon and her beloved husband for founding *The Washington Times* in Washington, DC I support their work in part because *The Washington Times* is strengthening the resolve of America's leaders to achieve peace and, God willing in time, freedom for the entire Korean Peninsula.
— **Amb. R. James Woolsey, Jr.**, *Director of US Central Intelligence (1993-1995)*

The personality and teaching of Rev. Dr. Sun Myung Moon, a global citizen who loves peace, is transparently reflected in Dr. Hak Ja Han Moon, with the qualitative complement of being a woman, wife and mother.
— **H.E. Jaime Paz Zamora**, *President of Bolivia (1989-1993)*

Over her 50 years of public ministry, Hak Ja Han Moon, known as the "Mother of Peace," has dedicated her life to God and the realization of peace.

With the heart of true parents, she and her husband created a global faith community, non-profit organizations, businesses, conferences, and awards. This work addresses so many facets of society and culture, aiming to resolve historical wounds and finding solutions to the world's critical challenges.

At the root of all their initiatives is a path to strengthen families and prevent the breakdown of society through the Marriage Blessing movement.

As the only woman spiritual leader operating on such a global level, her powerful message, compassion, and empathy have inspired millions to transcend national, racial, and ideological boundaries.

As a reader of this book, we invite you to stay updated and connect with these initiatives. We'd love you to join the conversation and become part of the community. Look for our reader's guide and free offers.

Please join our exclusive reader's list at:

MotherOfPeace.com/readers

MOTHER OF PEACE

MOTHER OF PEACE

And God Shall Wipe Away All Tears from Their Eyes

❧

A Memoir by

Hak Ja Han Moon

Copyright © 2020
The Washington Times Global Media Group
3600 New York Avenue, NE
Washington, DC 20002
(202) 636-4840

This is the English edition of Dr. Hak Ja Han Moon's memoir,
originally written in Korean. With Dr. Moon's express permission,
effort has been made to render some passages in a way that makes them
more understandable to readers unfamiliar with Korean language,
history and culture, or with the Unification movement and its teachings.

Distributed in the USA by
HSABooks, 4 West 43rd Street, New York, NY 10036

First edition published in Korean by
Gimmyoung Publishing Co., Republic of Korea

Cover and Interior creative: Jonathan Gullery Design

Library of Congress Control Number: 2020940902

ISBN Paperback 978-0-9601031-2-6
ISBN Hardcover 978-0-9601031-1-9
ISBN EPUB 978-0-9601031-3-3
ISBN Kindle 978-0-9601031-4-0
ISBN Audiobook 978-0-9601031-5-7

Printed in the United States of America

CONTENTS

PREFACE

Ｓão Tomé and Príncipe, an island nation of Africa that lies directly on the equator, is very special to God and to me. It is the first heavenly nation, a nation where Heavenly Parent prepared the president and the people to receive the Holy Marriage Blessing, and the youth to make the Pure Love Pledge. After conducting these events, I took a little rest on the tiny island nation of the Seychelles.

The crashing waves—
The refreshing breeze—

I walked along the shore of an emerald green sea whose dancing waves smiled and greeted me. The white sand between my toes was soft and warm. I felt truly at peace, enveloped in a cloudless sky, touched by cool rhythmic breezes and warm sunshine. I saw the beauty God created for us in the beginning, intact and untouched. I communed with God, the One who gives this blessing.

You freely gave the creation to us, Your children, and You hoped to dwell with us in joy and peace. You wished for nothing more than to be the Heavenly Parent sharing the beauty of creation with Your son and daughter. You created them to grow to maturity, marry with Your Blessing, and become True Parents of their own children. When they fell away, You, and we, lost everything.

We commonly say that when we lose a child, we bury a piece of our heart. Suddenly losing a beloved child, for whom we would willingly give our own life, brings pain and anguish beyond imagination. Our God, You lost humankind, Your family. As You pushed Your way through history, You must have been like a traumatized parent who had lost his senses, his entire being in shambles. You were not a God of joy and glory; You were a heartsick Parent filled with mourning and sorrow over Your lost children.

Nonetheless, as Jesus said in the Parable of the Lost Sheep, You could not abandon even the least of Your children. As the God of love, You pushed forward to one day find us, embrace us into Your bosom, and realize with us the world of peace that You envisioned at the beginning.

You want us to know You as our Heavenly Parent, the One who is the love of Heavenly Father and Heavenly Mother. You want us to live as heavenly individuals, heavenly families, heavenly tribes, heavenly peoples and heavenly nations in a heavenly world. The fallen world lost Your ideal of man-woman oneness, and worshiped an incomplete image of the Heavenly Father rather than welcoming and attending Heavenly Parent. Men took the dominant position and shaped Western civilization through the Hellenic and Hebraic traditions. Neither men nor women understood the feminine heart of Heavenly Mother and the perfect eternal love of Heavenly Parent. Lacking this existential awareness, the feminist movement that erupted in the West could not but degenerate into a one-note movement blaming men for all problems.

For this reason, I am investing everything to restore to You Your original position as our Heavenly Parent. I travel to the north, south, east and west in order to teach the truth of Heaven's providence to those who have ears but have not heard, and those who have eyes but have not seen. With a desperate and urgent heart, as if searching for a needle in the midst of a sandstorm while unable to see an inch in front of me, I proclaim the truth of Heaven's providence.

Like a person who is beside herself with desperation, I embrace the world again and again, loving all Your children as my own. With my whole heart I embrace even those among Your children who, unaware of the truth, have misunderstood and even persecuted me. As I do, You heal the wounds that they inflict.

During the last 40 days of 2019, despite challenges to my health and sometimes physical exhaustion, I continually traversed the earth. I had pledged to complete this path within my lifetime, and I did not break my promise to You. Political and religious leaders lowered their guard, responded, and embraced each other. People began referring to me as the Mother of peace.

Now Your true sons and daughters who share my passion are appearing. Our skin colors are irrelevant. I have filial children with black skin, yellow skin and white skin, sons who are Muslim leaders and daughters who lead large Christian churches. I have sons and daughters who lead nations. All of these mother-child ties came about in Your name. My children ask me to bless their nations and religions. Before them and their peoples, I talk about You, our Heavenly Parent. I talk about Heavenly Mother, hidden behind Heavenly Father, and explain that if there is an only begotten Son, there is an only begotten Daughter.

Without parents, there can be no harmony in the family. This is because parents are the center and origin of the family. Likewise, without You, the Parent of humankind, there can be no true peace in this world.

To this cause, I have devoted my life. At its center is Korea, the nation that gave birth to the only begotten Son and the only begotten Daughter.

You have blessed and chosen the Korean people. This is Your doing, of which the world is now becoming aware. Our Pacific civilization must learn from the Atlantic civilization's mistakes. The Atlantic civilization could not realize its own Christian ideals. It degenerated time and time again into conquest and exploitation. In contrast, the Pacific civilization must display a maternal heart. It must grow as an altruistic culture based on true love, as the Holy Community of Heavenly Parent, setting the standard of living for the sake of others that uplifts all peoples. This is Your wish, and I am offering the remainder of my life to realize it fully.

I am weaving the golden strands of Your love into a story of shared historical suffering. I look back upon my life as an unrelenting mission to attend God as our Parent from the position of His only begotten Daughter. Not being able to memorialize everything into one volume, I will share more in the future.

As I complete this book, one person I dearly miss at this moment is my beloved husband, Father Sun Myung Moon. We spent our lives together to convey and accomplish God's will, and he and I experienced much more together than I can share at this time. In September of 2012, he ascended to Heaven. If he were here to witness the publication of this book, his face would shine with a joy greater than that of anyone else. The sparkle in his eyes is dancing in my heart today. I hope that this book will reveal a taste of our life spent together for God's will.

Lastly, I would like to express my sincere gratitude to all those who devoted their time and expertise to accomplish this book's publication.

Hak Ja Han Moon
February 2020
Hyojeong Cheonwon
Seorak, Republic of Korea

CHAPTER 1

MY CHERISHED LIFELONG WISH

❧

A woman shouts "Mansei!" for independence

It was the first day of March 1919, the beginning of spring by the lunar calendar's marking of seasons. The temperature remained below freezing, and the people of Anju, a village in Pyong-an Province of what is now North Korea, were experiencing biting frost. A woman braved the cold to cook her family's morning meal. She lit the wood fire and set rice on the stove, and then her attention shifted from the morning routine. She lifted her arms and, from the back of a cupboard, carefully took out an item wrapped in a plain cotton cloth.

By the light of the fire and a ray of sunshine shining through a crack under the door, the woman untied the cloth to reveal another, larger and more substantial cloth, one with a red and blue yin-yang symbol on a white background. As she laid it out on the table, the design on the larger cloth came into full view. It was a Korean flag. This emblem of her people was always in this woman's mind, even in her dreams. Feelings of sadness and deep emotion rushed into her heart. Hearing the soft cries of her daughter who was awakening, she rolled up the flag, wrapped it again, and returned it to the back of the cupboard.

With their 5-year-old daughter on her lap, this village woman shared breakfast with her husband, who had returned from his early morning work in the fields. She then busied herself cleaning the kitchen, living room, porch and yard. A little after noon, trying to appear nonchalant, she left the house with an expectant heart, her daughter on her back and the flag in her bosom.

A narrow gravel path to the Anju market meandered through her village. It joined a larger road, on which she met others making their way—a farmer leading a cow, a young man carrying a heavy load on an A-frame carrier, a mother with a bundle on her head…. Some were walking at a leisurely pace, others quickly, all heading for the market.

Arriving at her destination, the woman stopped in front of a vegetable stand centrally located in one of the most crowded areas of the market. Her child awoke from her afternoon nap taken on her mother's back. Turning her head, the mother quietly looked at her beloved daughter and smiled. To this daughter, her mother's smile was the most beautiful sight in the world.

Suddenly, a loud shout burst through the quiet of the market: "Korean independence! *Mansei!*" As if she were a runner hearing the sound of the starting gun, the woman quickly pulled the Korean flag from her bosom. Waving it vigorously, she joined the crowd, shouting *"Mansei*, victory for ten thousand years!" With all her strength, she shouted, "Korean independence! Mansei!"

The first shout had been a signal, and all at once, people in the market were taking out Korean flags and vigorously waving them high above their heads. From every corner of the open market, cries of "Korean independence! Mansei!" reverberated. This woman's voice was the loudest of all. Shocked by the sudden melee and scores of Korean flags bursting into view, market-goers unprepared for the uprising had to decide what to do. Some fled in fear of possible consequences. Others, the ones who believed in their nation's independence, joined the ranks of the demonstrators.

The woman had been eagerly awaiting this day. She had stayed up many nights with her daughter, sewing her nation's flag, her hands shaking. Sitting under a kerosene lamp, she spoke to her daughter about Korea, its people, its faith, its ageless traditions, and the meaning of the Mansei Independence Movement. Listening to her mother, the little girl nodded her head, taking in everything. Now, clinging to her mother's back, she heard the shouts of *mansei*. She felt the innocence and righteousness of her countrymen and women, dressed in white, ready to lay down their lives for the sake of their nation's right to exist.

The March First Independence demonstrations took place not only in Anju; they occurred simultaneously in Seoul and across the nation. At most sites, they included a public reading of the Korean Declaration of Independence. This public outcry was not futile symbolism; it was an act of peaceful, non-violent protest, an acclamation that the Korean people will cherish for eternity.

Within moments, the demonstrators' ears were assaulted by the sound of whistles and boots. With batons and rifles, dozens of policemen converged upon the market. They mercilessly struck everyone in their path. Right and left, people were beaten to the ground, bloodied. The policemen did not distinguish between man or woman, young or old. Desperate to protect her daughter, this mother had no choice but to hold back her tears and retreat. Although she was filled with the resolve to stand to the last, she knew that God's wish is for human fellowship, and that bloodshed would only increase the burden of pain in God's heart.

And there was something else. Something told this mother that it was not yet time for her nation to rise. It told her that in the future of Korea, a woman would be born with an unprecedented destiny, a woman who would break the mold of this fallen world. With this light of hope in her heart, she endured the humiliation of that afternoon.

In accordance with God's providence and the absolute faith and love of Christian believers since biblical times, what that woman conceived in faith entered the world 24 years later. To her lineage, the only begotten Daughter of God was born, as the one called to fulfill that woman's dreams.

⁓

Anju was my birthplace. It was an epicenter of Korean patriotism, and it is no coincidence that it was an area in which Christianity was first introduced to Korea. That woman was my grandmother, Jo Won-mo, and she continued her support of the independence movement, and she engaged her daughter—my mother—and me in her activities.

I was just two years old when my nation's history took its next turn, liberation from Japanese occupation. On that day, August 15, 1945, my grandmother Jo Won-mo again had a child on her back while she shouted, "Mansei!" But this time, the child was me. And this time my grandmother was shouting and waving our national flag with joy and delight for our nation's newfound freedom.

God chose our family, a family of three generations of only daughters. Jo Won-mo, my grandmother, a woman who committed her heart to the Independence Movement, was an only daughter. Hong Soon-ae, my mother, a woman who single-mindedly committed her flesh and blood to fulfill her faith that she would meet Christ at his Second Advent, was her only daughter. I was her only child, the only daughter

4

of the third generation. Among the oppressed people of the Korean Peninsula, God's only begotten Daughter was born.

Hak Ja Han as a middle school student with her grandmother Jo Won-mo who joined demonstrations for Korean independence in 1919

As I write these words in 2019, the centennial of the March First Independence Movement, I am pursuing my forebears' dream, the dream of the ages, the completion of God's providence of salvation throughout the Earth.

Thank you! Mother, please take care of everything!

Moon, moon, bright moon, the moon
with which Lee Tae-baek used to play,
Far away on that moon,
there is a cinnamon tree.
I cut it down with a jade axe
and trimmed it with a gold axe,
To build a small cottage
where I attend my mother and father.
I want to live with them forever;
I want to live with them forever.

While laden with sadness, this traditional Korean song also stirs and uplifts the heart. The wish to live forever with one's mother and father conveys the heart of filial piety. We are orphans, far from the Heavenly Parent whom we have lost, and we have to find our True Parents and our original homeland. Nothing leads to greater happiness than being able to attend the beloved parents for whom we long, be it in a palace or a small hut.

Everything and everyone loves the sun. Only with the sun can life flourish. The moon, on the other hand, bestows something else. The sun represents splendor, the moon tranquility. When people are far from home, they tend to think about their hometown and long for their parents while looking at the moon, not at the sun. I have fond memories of gazing at the moon together with my husband. We watched it with many members during the Korean Chuseok harvest festival, and at the first full moon of the new year. Nonetheless, those moments were rare. My husband and I could not immerse ourselves in such tranquility.

"After this work is done …," my husband would always say, and so would I: "After this work is finished and we have a bit of free time, we'll be able to take a break." Over our years of ministry, one would think there would have been brief moments to relax after completing an urgent task. But for us, free time never materialized. Spurred on by the thought of my grandmother Jo crying "Mansei!" for the independence and salvation of our nation, I burned with a youthful passion for saving humanity and building a peaceful world.

I have always held high the banner of peace, inheriting the March First Independence Movement's noble spirit of non-violence and self-determination. Because I lived with this sense of urgency, I found myself accomplishing what I would never have imagined possible. Throughout my life, I have done my utmost to fulfill all the tasks that have come to me. I have striven to dedicate myself to living for the sake of others with one heart and one will. I have never given my body the rest it needs. Many were the times I neglected to eat or sleep.

My husband, Rev. Dr. Sun Myung Moon, who is often known as Father Moon, was the same. He was born with a strong physique, and had he taken better care of his health, he would have had more time to work for a better world. But he too followed God's will with unflinching devotion, and this damaged his health, ultimately to the point of no return. Up to four or five years before his ascension in 2012, he was in continual motion, living each day as if it were a thousand years. His work was strenuous, both physically and spiritually. For example, he often spent entire nights in a small fishing boat on rough seas. He did this for the sake of others, setting an example for our Ocean Church members as well as leaders who accompanied him. He wanted to help them cultivate patience and the spirit to overcome hardship.

Father Moon constantly traveled between continents, and it usually was between east and west, which takes a much greater toll than traveling between north and south. Considering his age, he traveled far too often between Korea and the United States. He should have limited such trips to once every two to three years, but he would not consider it. The year before his passing at age 92, he traveled between Korea and America at least eight times. This was a complete self-sacrifice, offered solely for God and humankind.

Father Moon's daily schedule itself was grueling. Every morning he would rise at 3:00 a.m., exercise, pray and study. At 5:00 a.m. he led *hoondokhae*, which means "gathering to read and learn," with followers. It was a time of devotional scripture reading, prayer and instruction. During hoondokhae, my husband had so much to share that it was not uncommon for it to continue for up to 10 hours, skipping breakfast and lunch. No sooner would he conclude the session than he would grab a quick bite and depart to visit a movement project. In the final years, while in Korea, he would travel by helicopter to Geomun Island or Yeosu, where we were developing fishing, recreational and educational facilities.

Into his seventies, Father Moon could handle this physically, but in his last decade it would wear him out, and he would end up with a cold or worse. Of course he would ignore the symptoms. And then, during the summer of 2012, he caught a deep chest cold that was particularly alarming. We should have gone to the hospital immediately, but he kept postponing it, saying over and over, "We can go after this is done."

Eventually, the decision was non-negotiable; he had to go to the hospital. His body was already in a very fragile state. He was hospitalized for a short time, but as soon as his medical examinations were finished, he stubbornly insisted on being discharged. We tried to persuade him to stay longer, but he wouldn't listen.

"I still have a lot of work to do; I can't just sit here in hospital!" he said, scolding the people who advised him to stay. There was no choice but to discharge him. That was August 12, 2012. We arrived home, and all of a sudden he said, "I want to have breakfast sitting opposite you, Omma." The members who heard this weren't sure they heard him right, because I always sat next to my husband during meals, not facing him. And then, when the food was served, my husband seemed uninterested in eating. He just gazed at me as if he were trying to engrave my face in his heart. I smiled and placed a spoon in his hand and something from the side dishes on his plate. "These vegetables are delicious, so take your time to eat," I said.

Father and Mother Moon, East Garden, Irvington, New York

The next day, the sun was unusually strong, even for mid-summer. In the oppressive heat, Father Moon toured parts of our Cheonwon complex on the shores of Cheongpyeong Lake, accompanied by an oxygen tank larger than himself. Upon his return to our home, Cheon Jeong Gung, he asked me to bring a voice recorder. With the recorder in his hand, he fell into deep thought for 10 minutes, and then little by little, began recording his thoughts.

He stated that when we transcend the history of the Fall and return to the original Garden of Eden, following only God, we can then move in the direction of the kingdom of heaven. He also proclaimed that we can restore nations through fulfilling the mission of guiding our tribes. It was a soliloquy and prayer that embraced the beginning and the end, the alpha and omega. "Everything has been accomplished! I offer everything to Heaven," he said in closing. "Everything has been brought to its consummation, completion, and conclusion."

⁓

This turned out to be True Father's final prayer. With it, he brought his life to a close. Breathing with some difficulty for a moment, he squeezed my hand tightly. "Mother, thank you! Mother, please take care of everything. I'm so sorry and I'm truly grateful," he said, struggling to get the words out. Again and again he said those same words. I held his hand more and more firmly, and with warm words and loving eyes, holding back the tears, I reassured him that everything would be all right. "Don't worry about anything."

On September 3, 2012, my husband, Rev. Dr. Sun Myung Moon, ascended into God's embrace. He was 93 years old, by the Korean way of counting, and was laid to rest in the *Bonhyangwon*, which means the garden in the original hometown, beside a pond on Mount Cheonseong. I have often slipped into deep thought gazing at the moon rising above Mount Cheonseong. "*I cut it down with a jade axe and trimmed it with a gold axe, to build a small cottage where I attend my mother and father. I want to live with them forever.*" I repeat this poem to myself, over and over.

Wildflowers smile on a mountain path

"It's been raining a lot and the path will be slippery," my assistant informed me. "Why don't you just rest today?" Of course she was concerned for my safety, and I thanked her but continued my preparations.

In autumn, we have heavy rainstorms, and snow falls in the winter. There are countless reasons and excuses to stay inside. Regardless, after his passing, I departed my room each day at dawn for prayer at my husband's tomb, and upon returning, I prepared his breakfast and dinner.

As I walked along the path up the hill to the Bonhyangwon and back, he and I shared many heart to heart conversations. My husband's thoughts became my thoughts, and my thoughts became his.

Korean bonsai pines lined the path to the Bonhyangwon, and underneath them, clusters of wildflowers bloomed in the spring. During the winter, wildflowers disappear, but in spring they bloom profusely, as if competing with each other. I would stop on my way up the steep incline to take a closer look at the grasses and flowers. They displayed their colors beautifully in the spring's bright morning sun, whether I was there to admire them or not. I would become intoxicated with their beauty, caressing the wildflowers before resuming my ascent up the path. The walk was difficult but my heart would be as serene as the flowers.

When I would reach my husband's tomb, I would carefully check to see whether any weeds had sprouted among the blades of grass, or whether animals had left any traces. The lawn on the grave became greener and greener as time went by. Sitting alone in front of his tomb, I would pray for everyone in the world to be as beautiful as wildflowers, to have minds as strong as pine trees, and to always live prosperous lives as green as a summer lawn. On my way down I would say farewell to the flowers and pine trees, "My friends of the natural world, I will meet you again tomorrow."

The path I would walk was the same each day, but the weather was never the same. There would be days when I felt the warm rays of the sun; there were windy days, rainy days when thunder roared and lightning struck, and snowy days covering everything in white.

During this three-year period of devotions, I also retraced my husband's travels throughout the United States, traveling nearly 4,000 miles as my husband had done in 1965, and visited the 12 mountain peaks we had toured in the Swiss Alps to pray and meditate. Through these devotions, our spiritual oneness deepened into eternity.

In traditional Korea, offering such filial devotions in remembrance of one's deceased parents was expected. Representing the family, the first son would build a small hut just to the west of his father's or mother's tomb, and live in it for three years, regardless of the weather, even if unable to eat properly or make a living through this period. Those three years represent the three years after we are born, when we receive our father's and especially our mother's full love and care, without which we would not have survived. This time of devotion is a time to acknowledge, show gratitude and return that love and kindness.

Today, there are too many people who forget their father's and mother's kindness. From those who lack filial piety toward their own parents, comprehension of Heavenly Parent and the True Parents, who have shed tears over humanity's suffering, cannot be expected. People today live without any connection to the True Parents, not knowing that they are here on earth.

To awaken people who have eyes but cannot see, as my husband's wife, I offered devotions in remembrance of True Father every day for three years, on behalf of all people. With this depth of commitment, I promised my husband and all the members of our worldwide movement: *I will bring us back to the spirit of the early days of our church, and I will create a revival through spirit and truth.*

I dream of a church that feels like a mother's warm embrace, a church that is like a home, where people always want to come and stay. This is my husband's dream as well. Honoring him, I made the decision to dedicate myself to God and all of humankind even more than before. Since that hour, I have never fully rested.

Then, in 2015, moved by my husband's unchanging heart, I prepared his gift for humanity. May the Sunhak Peace Prize stand forever as an expression of his eternal commitment to peace.

The Sunhak peace culture

Looking into the hazy summer sky, I queried what the weather was going to be like the next day. "There'll be showers in the morning," I was told, "with lots of clouds." With a smile on my face, I accepted that that was how it was going to be. Rain has poured down during many of our Unification Church events. It was more than 40 years ago that heavy showers and strong winds swept through our Yankee Stadium rally in New York. Heavy rain also fell all day long during the International Blessing of 360,000 couples, as well as during the inauguration of the Women's Federation for World Peace at the Seoul Olympic Stadium. I have grown to accept rain at such times with gratitude, as a gift.

So it rained on August 28, 2015, the day of the first Sunhak Peace Prize Awards Ceremony. That day, hundreds of guests converged on our hotel in Seoul, moving quickly through the downpour, summer's last cleansing gift. Thankfully, when the doors opened, the skies cleared, and this felt like God's joyful welcome to our guests. These were special people, leaders from all fields, gathered from throughout the global village, many traversing long distances, for the sake of peace.

Everyone desires peace, but peace does not come easily. If it were as commonplace as stones on the side of a country road or trees on a mountainside, we would never have experienced the terrible wars and conflicts that plague the human world. But bringing peace demands that everyone invest sweat, tears and sometimes blood. That is why, even though we long for peace, we seldom achieve it. To experience true peace, we must first practice true love without expectation of reward. My husband and I walked this path and, continuing on it, I prepared the Sunhak Peace Prize as a gift for the world from Father Moon.

August 28, 2015: The first Sunhak Peace Prize Laureates –
President Anote Tong of Kiribati and Dr. Modadugu Vijay Gupta of India,
leader of the "Blue Revolution"

Despite the rain on this first day of the awards ceremony, none of the guests could suppress their excitement. They were like little children about to receive a special gift. Everyone was wide-eyed as they greeted the person beside them, one saying, "There are so many kinds of people here! I've never been to a more diverse gathering," and the other, "It's unbelievable! I wonder where *that* attire is from."

The event was an exhibition of the world's ethnicities; the hall was alive with the rushing flow of various languages. Everyone's eyes showed gratitude on behalf of the entire human family. People seeing me for the first time focused on the stage to get a good look, wondering, "Who is this Dr. Hak Ja Han Moon?" Then they would tilt their heads quizzically. Perhaps they considered my clothes to be no finer than theirs, and that I looked like a typical mother.

As I prepared the Sunhak Peace Prize project, my utmost concern was that people would understand its fundamental root. To embrace the future, we must expand the scope of vocations that can herald the coming of peace. Even though we may never meet our descendants, we must make sure that all their activities will harmonize in peaceful societies and nations. After serious consideration and discussion, the Sunhak Foundation determined its overarching orientation, the peace that transcends the present and builds the future.

True peace certainly requires that we resolve the current conflicts between religions, races and nations. The even greater challenges that we face, however, include the destruction of the environment and demographic trends. The world's leading peace awards focus on solving the problems of the present generation. Yet we must solve the problems of the present in a way that is integrated with a practical vision for a happy future. I founded the Sunhak Peace Prize as a bridge bringing us out of this world's maelstroms of conflict and as a compass pointing to a future homeland of peace.

The oceans are a treasured resource

In every era of recorded history, humanity has experienced incredible pain. The most tragic period was also the most recent—the twentieth century. Wars raged ceaselessly across the global village, and countless good people lost their lives in that savagery. I was born during the Japanese occupation of Korea, and I experienced the aftermath of World War II and the Korean War. I still cannot forget the terrible things I witnessed as a small child.

Those times have passed, and now we are waging war against a complex enemy, the temptation to forget our responsibilities to our families and the natural environment and seek only personal comfort and convenience. Fortunately, we have a deep moral sense and wisdom, and practical methods by which we can work together to achieve God's ideal.

All people hope that we can recover and sustain the oceans as the Heavenly Parent created them. Covering 70 percent of the Earth, the oceans contain immense resources. Like hidden treasures, they hold solutions for the dilemmas confronting the human race. I have emphasized the importance of the ocean on many occasions and have, together with my husband, suggested various approaches we might take. Accordingly, "The Ocean" was chosen as the theme for the first Sunhak Peace Prize. The Peace Prize Committee oversaw a strict process to select righteous, achievement-oriented leaders in this arena. Those selected as our laureates that year were Dr. M. Vijay Gupta of India and President Anote Tong of Kiribati, a small island nation in the South Pacific.

Dr. Gupta is a scientist who, concerned over persistent food shortages, led the "Blue Revolution" by developing fish farming technologies. He greatly contributed to relieving hunger among the poor by widely distributing these technologies in Southeast Asia and Africa.

President Anote Tong is a leading global advocate for the intelligent preservation and management of the marine ecosystem. It is predicted that much of his nation of Kiribati could be submerged in less than 30 years due to the rising sea level. In the face of such a crisis, President Tong took the lead toward protecting the ecosystem by creating the largest protected marine park in the world.

For decades, my husband and I took on the task of ensuring that humanity moves into a future assured of abundant food supplies and pleasant, healthy environments. We advocated the free exchange of technology across national borders, and shared our vision that the oceans are a gift from God and the ultimate source of the world's nutrition. Stable food sources and pure air, land and water are essential to world peace and the salvation of humankind.

Not confining ourselves to theoretical explanations, we devoted significant resources to practical projects in the real world. For half a century, Latin America was a major site for this investment of true love and human resources.

In the mid-1990s, with serious hearts, Father Moon and I traveled to the Pantanal region. The Pantanal is a vast wetland straddling the borders of Paraguay and Brazil. It is located precisely on the opposite side of the globe from our home country. There, we worked hand in hand with farmers and fishermen. Putting an end to food shortages begins by getting your hands dirty. Rather than give sermons from an air-conditioned pulpit, we worked under the scorching sun, neglecting to eat or rest. I vividly remember pondering environmental issues as I wiped beads of sweat from my face.

We launched various initiatives in the Pantanal region, and we have carried out countless other projects for the sake of humankind over the past 60 years. My nature compels me to give everything I have for the happiness of others, with no desire for recognition. I know who I am, the True Mother, the Mother of peace and God's only begotten Daughter, and my mission is to live this way. To end Heavenly Parent's sorrow I have dried the tears of strangers in need, considering this to be connected through threads of fate to the salvation of humanity.

Everyday heroes

The end of winter can be bitterly cold, but no matter how cold it is, when spring comes and its warmth envelops the Earth, we quickly forget that there ever was a winter. The bitter cold of humanity's winter is receding and as Heavenly Parent's warmth envelops the Earth, it will be forgotten. We feel this warmth at our Sunhak Peace Prize events, such as its second bi-annual convention that took place in Seoul on February 3, 2017.

That very busy day began by my personally welcoming hundreds of guests. These men and women hailed from 80 countries, representing various races, speaking many languages and following different paths of faith. I tried to create an environment in which everyone would freely greet the strangers around them and quickly become friends.

The warmth of spring was the setting in which I reminded my guests that many people in the world are friendless and hungry. Many families have been driven from their homelands. As a child refugee myself, I know there are no words to express the misery of being forced to flee one's home due to the devastation of war. The Sunhak Peace Prize is an initiative through which I can issue the call for solutions to the painful plight of refugees and prevent livelihoods from being destroyed. I look for righteous but unheralded pioneers of peace, honor them, and strongly encourage them. The second set of Sunhak Peace Prizes, presented in 2017, went to two such people. Dr. Sakena Yacoobi and Dr. Gino Strada do not look like celebrities. They look like everyday people.

A gentlemanly middle-aged European with ruffled hair is a gifted surgeon and founder of an international medical relief organization. Dr. Gino Strada from Italy is a surgeon and humanitarian whose work over the past 28 years provided emergency medical care for more than 9 million refugees and victims of war in the Middle East and Africa.

A motherly woman with a sun-weathered face framed by a black hijab has brought thousands of young women hope. Dr. Sakena Yacoobi of Afghanistan is an educator, referred to as the "Afghan Mother of Education." She has worked in Afghan refugee camps for more than 20 years, helping refugees and displaced people resettle. She has risked her life to teach, encouraging people to hope for a better tomorrow, even in the face of enormous obstacles. In response to her award, Dr. Yacoobi wrote to me in her clear handwriting, expressing her heartfelt gratitude:

It is really, really wonderful, the award itself is really big, it's comparable to the Nobel Peace Prize.... My life is in danger all the time. In the morning, I get up; in the evening, I don't know whether I will be alive or dead.... Knowing that somebody values you in your work helps a lot. Also, I want to say to Mother Hak Ja Han Moon that I am really thankful to her because she gives me credit for what I do.... It means a lot to me.

Korea is a country that I admire because you have been to war, you have suffered but with your determination, hard work, sincerity and wisdom, you have accomplished a lot in a really short time. I hope and pray that someday my country can use your country as a role model.

Putting her own life in danger, Dr. Yacoobi continues to fight for women and children. While we are comfortably at home, eating warm meals, many are being driven from their homes. Uprooted, they live in pain and anguish, their lives completely shattered. This is the time to bring this sad tragedy to an end.

Give us this day

When Jesus' disciples asked him to teach them how to pray, his answer was clear: "Give us this day our daily bread." Two thousand years have passed since Jesus taught us that prayer; however, there are still so many people, more than we imagine, who do not have daily bread.

Africa is the birthplace of human civilization. Yet some African people live in circumstances so poor that their primary goal is having enough to eat. This fundamental human need is often not met, and the opportunity for basic education is also limited. Many face this situation. Each time I visit Africa, I seek solutions to these issues, which I take very personally. When the Sunhak Peace Prize Committee announced its 2019 theme, Human Rights and Human Development in Africa, I was delighted because it addressed the task I have always set for myself.

Akinwumi Ayodeji Adesina, president of the African Development Bank (AFDB), and Waris Dirie, a woman's rights activist, our 2019 laureates, are examples of what I have always thought of as "righteous people of action."

Dr. Adesina was born to a poor farming family in Nigeria. From a young age, he researched methods to modernize farming and nurtured the dream of making Africa a land of abundance. After earning his Ph.D. in agricultural economics from Purdue University in the United States, he returned to Africa and for the last 30 years has worked on agricultural innovation, helping millions of people overcome the problem of hunger.

February 9, 2019: The Third Sunhak Peace Prize Laureates –
Waris Dirie (Founder, Desert Flower Foundation) and
Akinwumi A. Adesina (President, African Development Bank)

In February 2019, during his visit to Korea to receive the Sunhak Peace Prize, Dr. Adesina said that there was still much for him to do to make the world a better place. "Nothing is more important," he said, "than eliminating hunger and malnutrition. Hunger is an indictment on the human race. Any economy that claims growth without feeding its people is a failed economy. Nobody has to go hungry, white, black, pink, orange or any color you can think of.... That's why I am fully dedicating the whole of the $500,000 award of the Sunhak Peace Prize to my foundation, the World Hunger Fighters Foundation." Dr. Adesina's dream of peace is to discover the actual means to bring it about. I encouraged him never to give up his noble work.

The other Sunhak Peace Prize laureate for 2019 was Ms. Waris Dirie, an African woman of remarkable willpower, who has overcome many virtually insurmountable obstacles. Ms. Dirie was born into a Somali nomad family. While her childhood was fraught with civil war, hunger and oppression, she had big dreams and challenged herself and her circumstances. Eventually, she became a celebrated supermodel.

In 1997, she revealed her own experience of genital mutilation (FGM), and her life changed. On behalf of millions of African women, she took up the cause of eliminating the practice of FGM. The United Nations appointed her Special Ambassador for the Elimination of Female Genital Mutilation. She supported the Maputo Protocol, which prohibited FGM and was ratified by fifteen African countries. Also, in 2012 she played a significant role in introducing a UN resolution prohibiting FGM, which gained unanimous approval by the General Assembly. Ms. Dirie did not stop there. She founded the Desert Flower Foundation, which mobilizes doctors in France, Germany, Sweden and the Netherlands to treat victims of FGM. In several locations in Africa, she runs educational institutes that help women stand on their own feet.

Female genital mutilation is neither a religious nor an ethnic tradition; it is nothing other than a violent abuse of girls. This abuse of removing part of the external genitals of young girls is not only a means of oppressing women, but it is also life-threatening. Waris Dirie has devoted her life to eradicating this heinous custom, and global organizations have responded to her efforts. One can only imagine how difficult a path she traveled.

Waris Dirie's goal has also been to help women in Africa, and to see women empowered. In Africa, women are on the front lines in the battle for life as they strive to protect their families. They also play a central role in their nation's economy. We should therefore be deeply aware how this violence against young African girls injures them physically and often cripples them emotionally.

The African peoples are tremendously good-natured. They love their families, respect their neighbors, and live in harmony with nature. Nonetheless, as it has everywhere in the world, western modernization has brought Africa mixed blessings. Its prosperity comes at a cost of destroying family and tribal traditions. I believe that Heavenly Parent's love will strengthen indigenous African values that support interdependence and mutual prosperity, and will wipe away Africa's tears.

The Sunhak Peace Prize is painting a beautiful picture of the new century, by honoring men and women who represent the best we can be. It embraces all people as one human family. The Prize is a stepping-stone into a better future. It is a friend to righteous people who labor with a true heart. It is planting seeds of peace that will grow into beautiful trees of life and knowledge bearing nourishing fruit in this home we call Earth.

In this chapter I have presented to you, the reader, the scale of my life, from my grandmother's struggle for liberty among a colonized people, to the last days of my God-sent husband's glorious life, to my years of mourning, to the new global horizons that he and I are opening today. Now I invite you to wend your way through this story as it unfolded, breathing its air with me, tasting the bitter and the sweet, finding the needles in the sandstorms, and discovering with me our Heavenly Parent's hand in every moment.

CHAPTER 2

I CAME INTO THIS WORLD AS THE ONLY BEGOTTEN DAUGHTER

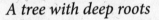

A tree with deep roots

When I gently closed my eyes and listened to the harsh winds blowing through the cornfield, it sounded like thousands of horses running in the wilderness. It captured the dynamic spirit of Goguryo knights galloping powerfully across the continent. At other times, if I listened quietly, I would hear another kind of sound, the affectionate "Hwoo! Hwoo!" of scops owls in the high branches of trees deep in the mountains.

I remember those summer nights when I fell asleep holding my mother's hand, with the sound of hooting owls echoing in my ears.

More than 70 years have passed, but the beautiful scenery and sooth-
ing sounds of Anju remain in my heart. My hometown holds many
beautiful memories for me, and I want to go back there. One day I will
certainly return home.

～⁓

When I was born, my father, Han Seung-un, had a dreamlike vision. He
saw bright sunlight beaming into a thick grove of pine trees. The light
fell on two cranes that were dancing together in harmonious affection.
He decided to name me "Hak Ja," which means "crane child."

I am a member of the Han clan of Cheongju in North Chungcheong Province, the clan's historical birthplace. "Chungcheong" means
"center of the heart that is pure and clear," and Cheongju means "clear
village." When the water in a river or the sea is clear, one can see the
fish swimming all the way to the bottom. Living in the pure and clear
environment of Cheongju, I could see the bright spirits of my pure and
humble ancestors.

The Chinese character for my family name, "*Han*" (韓), has various meanings. It can mean "one," symbolizing God. It also can mean
"big," as in large enough to embrace all created things in the universe,
and "full," meaning overflowing abundance. The founding father of the
Han clan, Han Lan, was honored as a loyal patriot of the Kingdom of
Goryeo. The king of Korea would recognize persons of civic virtue, and
reward them with land and a perennial stipend. The court recorded
their names in a book of honor, and there is an entry for Han Lan.

Han Lan's story is this: He built a bureau for agricultural administration in a district of Cheongju called Bangseo-dong and turned a
large expanse of land into productive farmland. When a war between
Korean rulers broke out, Wang Geon—a nobleman and military general—passed through Cheongju on his way to do battle with Gyeon
Hweon, the king of Hu-baekje. Han Lan greeted Wang Geon, fed his
army of 100,000 soldiers, and joined him on the battlefield. Once Wang

Geon became king, he declared Han Lan a loyal patriot. Han Lan's reputation as a "founding contributor" to the kingdom has endured through the ages.

Thirty-three generations after Han Lan, I was born of his lineage. The numbers 3 and 33 are significant. Jesus asked three disciples to pray with him in Gethsemane. He prophesied that Peter would betray him three times before the cock crowed. Rejected of men, Jesus was crucified at the age of 33—yet he promised to return. He was one of three who were crucified on that day, to one of whom he said, "Today you will be with me in paradise." On the third day, Jesus rose from the grave. The number three signifies Heaven, Earth and humankind. It signifies the perfect fulfillment of both heavenly law and natural law.

The Korean people are descended from the Dong-yi race, a wise people who studied the stars and were able to ascertain heavenly fortune. They developed a prosperous agriculture-based culture, worshiped God and loved peace from the time before Christ. The Dong-yi people established kingdoms based on the name "Han." Some people, including my husband, cite records that show that the Han people pre-date the Gojoseon era, which is considered to be the first Korean kingdom. Korea's founding legend, called the Dangun legend, says we were chosen as the descendants of Heaven according to the deep will of God.

Our people are also called the Baedal race. The Chinese characters for *bae* and *dal* signify brightness and brilliance. That attribution recognizes our reverence for God and love of peace and serenity. To this day, Korea is known as "the land of the morning calm."

Still, the Korean people's 5,000-year history is filled with deep sorrow. Foreign powers constantly marched through Korea, trampling us like wild grass and leaving us stripped like the bare branches of a tree in the coldest of winters. But we never lost our roots. We overcame foreign invasions with wisdom and patience and survived as a nation, and of this we are proud.

One cannot help but wonder why God allowed this people to suffer such great hardships. I believe it was to prepare a people to whom He could entrust a great mission. We learn from the Bible that God's chosen people always endure great adversity. On the foundation of Noah, Abraham and other providential figures, God prepared the people of Israel as the ones to whom He could send the Messiah, Jesus Christ. Facing rejection, God had to allow Jesus to suffer great trials and hardship, and to finally offer his life on the cross.

Two thousand years later, God chose the Korean people and entrusted to them His only begotten Son and only begotten Daughter, the ones who can receive God's first love. God needed a man and a woman who could endure suffering and rejection while continuing to forgive and love all people, thus revealing God's heart of parental love. So too, God needed a nation capable of enduring suffering for the sake of all nations. God prepared the Korean people for this. Many peoples have suffered and disappeared from history, but the Koreans endured. Thus God entrusted this people with a noble mission.

As a hen embraces her brood

When I was born, Earth was groaning with anguish as a battleground in which people shed each other's blood. People dwelled in extreme confusion and darkness and heartlessly exploited each other. As part of this wretched mosaic, the Korean Peninsula suffered indescribable torment under a Japanese occupation that lasted 40 years, from the 1905 Eul Sa Neung Yak, a protectorate treaty between Korea and Japan, until our liberation in 1945. I was born during that period of oppression.

I was born in 1943 in Anju, South Pyong-an Province of what is now North Korea, at 4:30 am on February 10 of the solar calendar and the sixth day of the first lunar month of that year. I remember clearly the address of my home, 26, Sineui-ri Anju-eup, which has been renamed Chilseong-dong, in what is now the city of Anju. My home was not far from the center of the village, and the surrounding neighborhood had a very warm and cozy feeling, as if we were chicks cuddled under a mother hen.

Unlike the thatched-roof houses nearby, my house had a tile roof and a big front porch. Behind it rose a small, verdant hill covered with chestnut and pine trees. Beautiful flowers bloomed and colorful leaves fell with the rhythm of the seasons, and I heard every kind of bird singing and chirping together. When spring warmed the earth, yellow forsythias smiled brightly between the fences, and azaleas bloomed red on the hill. A small stream flowed through our village, and, except when it froze solid in midwinter, I could always hear the laughing sound of the water. I grew up enjoying the happy sounds of the birds and the stream, as if they were a choir of nature. Even now, thinking of life in my hometown is like snuggling into a cozy and heartwarming mother's embrace. This memory brings tears to my eyes.

Between our house and the hill, we had a small cornfield. When the corn was ripe, the husks would crack and yellow kernels of corn would appear through the long, silky hair. My mother would boil the ripened corn, put a generous number of cobs in a bamboo basket and call our neighbors to come and eat. They would come into our house through the gate built from sticks, sit in a circle on our porch and eat cobs of corn with us. I remember wondering why their faces did not look very bright, even though they were gratefully eating a delicious meal. Thinking about it years later, I realized these people were impoverished due to the severe exploitation of the occupying government.

I would squeeze in between the grown-ups and try to eat the kernels off a small cob of corn, but, as a small child, I was never successful. Noticing me, my mother would smile gently, break off some yellow kernels from her cob and put them into my mouth. I remember the sweet corn kernels rolling around in my mouth as if it were yesterday.

The Dallae Bridge legend

"Mother, why is where we live called Pyong-an Province?" I was full of curiosity, and whenever I had a question about something, I ran to my mother and asked her for the answer. Every time my mother responded kindly. "Well, dear," she replied, "it is called that because the *Pyong* part is the first character of Pyongyang and the *An* part is the first character of Anju."

"Why do they take one character from each name?" I asked.

"It's because both of them are big districts," she said. Over time, Anju had grown into a large town. It was surrounded by expansive plains that were ideal for farming, and there was normally plenty to eat.

My father, Han Seung-un, was born on January 20, 1909. He was the eldest of five children of Han Byeong-gon and Choi Gi-byeong of the Cheongju Han clan at Yongheung village, by the city of Anju. My father entered Mansong Public Primary School in 1919, when he was 10. He had to leave after finishing the fourth grade, but his desire to learn led him to enter a private school, Yukyong School, in 1923, from which he graduated in 1925 at age 16. He then became a teacher at his alma mater, Yukyong School, for ten years. During the chaotic period from Korea's liberation until 1946, he served as the vice principal of his other alma mater, Mansong Primary School.

I lived with my father for only a brief time, but his gentle nature and features are engraved in my mind. He was meticulous and thrifty, and he was very strong. One day he was out for a stroll on a local road when he saw some people struggling to clear a big rock from a rice field. He went over, lifted up the rock and moved it out of the way. He was a devout Christian and follower of Rev. Lee Yong-do, pastor of the New

Jesus Church. Because of my father's work as a teacher and his active life of faith, he was rarely at home. He lived a life of service to God, even though the government tracked and persecuted Christians from independent churches such as his.

My mother, Hong Soon-ae, was born on March 18, 1914, in Chongju, North Pyong-an Province. That is the town where my husband, Father Moon, also was born. She and her younger brother (my uncle) were born to a devout Christian couple, Hong Yu-il and Jo Won-mo.

My maternal grandmother, Jo Won-mo, was a direct descendant of Jo Han-jun, a wealthy scholar of the Joseon Dynasty. Jo Han-jun lived in a village of tiled roofed houses in Chongju, a community of people who held government positions. Not far from his home was a bridge across the Dallae River. It once was a sturdy bridge made of neatly piled, large stones, but over time it had deteriorated to the point that no one could cross it. No one had the time or resources to fix the bridge, and one day a flood swept it away and buried its stones in the riverbed.

As did everyone else, Jo Han-jun knew the prophecy that had been passed down for generations:

If a rock carved like a totem pole standing beside the Dallae River bridge is buried, then the nation of Korea will fall, but if that rock is clearly exposed to the people, then a new heaven and earth will unfold in Korea.

The Dallae River bridge was important for another reason as well. In order for Chinese envoys to make their annual trek to the seat of Korea's government in Seoul (then named Hanyang), they had to cross that bridge. Now it was gone, and the government did not have money to rebuild it. In desperation, officials posted a bulletin calling upon the citizens to rebuild the bridge. Grandfather Jo Han-jun accepted the call and rebuilt the bridge using his personal wealth. The sturdy new stone bridge was now high enough for boats to pass under.

Grandfather Jo Han-jun spent his entire fortune on this task, and when it was done, all he had left were three brass coins. These were just enough to pay for the new straw sandals that he needed in order to properly attend the bridge dedication ceremony the next day. That night, he had a dream of a grandfather in white clothes who came to him and said, "Han-jun, Han-jun! Your sincere devotion has moved Heaven. I was expecting to send a Son of Heaven to your family. However, because you bought the sandals, I will send to your family the Princess of Heaven."

Grandfather Jo Han-jun awoke from that dream and found that a stone statue of the Maitreya Buddha suddenly had appeared near the bridge. Over the years, this miracle created such an atmosphere that all those who passed that Buddha would get off their horses to offer a bow before proceeding on their way. The people of the village marveled at this sign from God and built a shelter over the statue so that it would not be exposed to rain or wind.

On this foundation of devotion and loyalty, generations later, in the family line of Jo Han-jun, God sent my maternal grandmother, Jo Won-mo. We three women—Grandmother Jo Won-mo, her daughter (my mother), and I—all had a very deep Christian faith. We were also the only daughters born into our families over three generations.

The providence to bring about the birth of God's only begotten Daughter on the Korean Peninsula was based upon countless conditions of devotion that started long ago with my ancestors Han Lan and Jo Han-jun and continued through the generations to this time.

God is your Father

"My sweet child, shall we go to church?"

When I heard those words, I would run to my mother. She would take my hand in hers, and we would walk to church. I think the long walk with my mother was why I liked going to church. One Sunday, as we arrived back at our village after church, my mother stopped in her tracks. She plucked a wildflower blooming shyly on the roadside and tucked it into my hair, right behind the ear. She kissed my cheek and whispered to me with a delicate, loving voice, "How pretty you look, my one and only daughter of the Lord!"

Mother's eyes always looked the same. They were clear and deep, almost as if her irises were one with the blue sky. As I returned her gaze, I could glimpse traces of tears but, not knowing her deep heart, I was only excited and delighted by the words, "one and only daughter of the Lord." Mother often called me "precious daughter of the Lord" with emphasis, as if she were praying. Throughout her life, this was the term that she used when she prayed for me, her only daughter.

In this way, I grew up feeling honored that I was the daughter of God, the daughter of the Lord. My maternal grandmother, Jo Won-mo, also looked into my eyes and told me clearly, "God is your Father." Because of that, whenever I heard the word "father," my heart would burst in my chest. For me the word, "father" brought to mind not my own father, but our Heavenly Father. Because of such love in my home, I never worried about my life. Despite our poverty, and despite my father not being with us, I always was content. This was because I knew that God was my Father, that He was my reason for being alive, and that He was always right there by my side, taking care of me. I sensed that God was my real Parent from the moment of my birth.

I realize now that I had a sensitive spiritual intuition. My husband recognized this in me, and complimented me for my insight into things that were taking place. He did so sometimes during his talks to members.

My grandmother and mother taught me the duties of heavenly love, and not to obsess over what I was going through personally. They set the example for me, obeying God absolutely and wholeheartedly. For Him, they did not mind carrying out exhausting endeavors that seemed to melt their very bone marrow. They offered their devotions of prayer most earnestly and carefully, almost as if they were building a tall stone tower. They also made other extraordinary conditions that I didn't fully understand. They would bow before Jesus hundreds and even thousands of times in a day. They cooked meals for Jesus and sewed clothes for him, as if he were living in our house with us, and then they did the same for the Lord whom they expected to return to Korea. They shared their faith with everyone they met and their meager food and resources with anyone who needed it. Their generous and happy spirits moved me and shaped my character as I grew up.

Several times a day, I would stand at the edge of our front porch and look up at the clear sky. It was astonishing how often I saw three or four beautiful cranes in flight. I would continue my gaze at the sky even after the cranes were out of sight, my arms wrapped tightly around my chest to contain my heart, which I felt was about to burst out of me and join the cranes in the heavens.

One day, out of the blue, my mother asked me, "Do you know how you cried when you were born?"

"I was a little baby," I replied, "so I must have cried, 'Waah.'"

"No, you didn't," she said. "You cried, 'La-la-la-la-la' as if you were singing! Your grandmother said, 'Perhaps this child is going to grow up to become a musician.'" I engraved her words in my heart, for I thought they might symbolize my future. However, my mother was not done telling me about my infancy.

She said that after she ate her first bowl of seaweed soup, the traditional meal for a mother after childbirth, she cradled me in her arms and fell asleep. As she dreamed, she saw Satan, a monstrous demon, appear before her. He shouted so loudly that even the mountains and streams rang with his fearsome voice. "If I let this baby be, the world will be in danger," he yelled. "I must do away with her right now." Suddenly he made as if to strike me. My mother held me closely and cast upon him all her energy to declare his defeat.

"Satan, be gone at once!" she said fiercely. "How dare you try to hurt her, when she is the most precious child to Heaven! I cast you out in the name of the Lord! Get out of my presence! You have no right to be here! Heaven has claimed this child and your days of power have come to an end!"

Mother was shouting so loudly that my grandmother rushed into the room and shook her. She collected herself, looked deeply into my face and searched her heart for the reason Satan was trying to strike me. She took this experience as a sign that I was destined to strike the head of the serpent. And this was the answer to her and my grandmother's prayers. "I must raise this child with complete devotion," my mother vowed to herself. "I will raise her to become a pure and beautiful girl for the Lord, and protect her from the pollution of the secular world."

About a month later, she had another dream. This time, a heavenly angel dressed in shimmering white came to her on a sunlit cloud. "Soon-ae," the angel spoke; "I am sure you must feel incapable to prepare this baby for the service that our Heavenly Father has in mind, but don't be. This baby is the daughter of the Lord and you are her nanny. Please devote all your energies to raising her with absolute faith, love and obedience."

Satan, however, did not give up. Until we left North Korea, he would appear in mother's dreams, looking hideous and voicing threats both dramatic and subtle. Mother fought hard to protect me over a number of years. When I heard about these dreams from my mother, I became very serious: "Why was Satan trying to hurt me? And why did he keep stalking me?" I wondered.

Hak Ja Han with her mother Hong Soon-ae,
a devout Christian who prepared for the Lord's return

My father played an essential role

"Alright, from now on, you should wear these when you go out," my maternal grandfather told me. I looked at the strange footwear and asked, "What *are* these?" "They are called high heels," he said.

During the Japanese colonial rule in rural Korea, Western fashions such as high heels were almost never seen in rural areas. My grandfather, Hong Yu-il, however, was an enlightened gentleman who welcomed modern things. He personally had gone into the city and bought high heels for all the women in his family. He was tall, friendly and handsome, and everyone highly respected his progressive thinking. Even though he had grown up in a household of strict Confucian tradition, he was ahead of his time. Interestingly, when I met Father Moon for the first time, I thought in my heart that he resembled my grandfather. That was one reason I could feel at ease with Father Moon when I first met him, even though I was only 13. He was not a stranger to me.

My maternal grandmother, Jo Won-mo, was a petite woman with beautiful features. In addition to being a devout Christian, she was industrious and active. She made a living by running a small business, called the Pyong-an Store, selling and repairing sewing machines. At the time, sewing machines were expensive, and they were considered the most important part of a bride's trousseau. Townspeople admired my grandmother for giving big discounts to the families of new brides and for setting up payment plans, something unheard of back then. Grandmother used to go from village to village to collect the monthly payments, carrying me on her back. I first experienced the wider world on those excursions.

My grandfather's family moved from Chongju, which is my husband's hometown, and crossed the Cheongcheon River to the town of Anju—to be precise, Shineui, a village in the town of Anju. My mother inherited Grandmother Jo Won-mo's devout faith; they attended a local Presbyterian Church in Anju until she was age 19. The pastor of that church actually gave my mother her name, Hong Soon-ae. My mother studied at Anju Grade School and, in 1936, graduated from a Christian mission school called Pyongyang Saints Academy.

My parents were married in the New Jesus Church on March 5, 1934, and I, their first and only child, was born in 1943, nine years later. That unusually long interval elapsed not because my parents were infertile but because they were living separately, each engrossed in their lives of faith and, for my father, his career as an educator. He taught in Yeon-baek County, Hwanghae Province, which was some distance from my maternal home, and my mother did not want to move there. My mother's intense devotion to Jesus led her to focus all her time and attention on her church work. There was another reason as well. My maternal grandparents, the Hongs, wished to make my father, Han Seung-un, their heir, but he did not accept it. As the eldest son of the Han family, his parents did not allow him to put his roots down in his wife's home. So she would not move in with him, nor him with her. But God wanted me to be born, and so I arrived in my grandparents' home in Shineui-ri, Anju. I grew up there, and came to accept God quite naturally.

In 1945, when Korea regained its independence, the great powers divided our peninsula at the 38th parallel, and soon the joy of having our country back turned into despair. The Russians put the Korean communist party in charge, and it implemented policies backed by brutal oppression. I was four years old when my father suddenly appeared at our home to announce, "Conditions are not going to improve here. I cannot have my family live in North Korea. Let us go south."

My mother could not help but think hard about my father's unexpected request. While she had been living with the sole purpose of meeting the Lord at the Second Advent, she actually did not know what she would do when she met him. Her husband's request tore her in two: "Would it be better to stay here and walk the unknown path of God's will? Or should I elect to live as an ordinary housewife?" She pondered these things and then made up her mind. "I will not succumb to the communist persecution," she said. "I will stay here and continue to walk the path of faith to receive the Lord." My father was dumbfounded, but he left as he had determined to do.

My mother was not the only person to remain in the North out of faith that Jesus was going to appear there. Pyongyang was called the "Jerusalem of the East," and Christianity was in full bloom there. It was a holy place where churches were making preparations to receive the Messiah at the Second Coming. Though mainstream Christians said he would come on the clouds, the spirit-led groups in Pyongyang believed he would come in the flesh. My mother along with my grandmother believed that completely. They were now attending the New Jesus Church, one of the most fervent churches in the city. My mother resolved to remain in Pyongyang and continue her mission as a member of the faithful household of the Messiah.

Though my father did his best to fulfill his duties as husband and father, God's providence broke up our family in the end. Watching him as he left through the gate, I thought, "This will not be the last time I see my father." However, I was wrong. That was the last time I saw him.

Except for when I was very young, I lived my life without my father, Han Seung-un. Sometimes I would wonder where he was and what he was doing, but I never set out to find him. This was because of the words I had heard from my grandmother and my mother from the time I was a little girl, "Your Father is God." I grew up knowing those words to be the unchanging truth. Since I was born as God's daughter,

I firmly believed He is my true Father. That is why I did not harbor any hurt over my father's departure.

I was molded from my conception to be the True Mother who would devote her life to God's purposes. I see everything from that perspective—the Japanese colonial rule and Korean War, my childhood full of hardships, my family consisting of my maternal grandmother and mother, the Christian love that enveloped us day and night. I treasure it as a growing period designed by Heaven. When all is said and done, my father played an essential role.

I later learned that my father dedicated his life to education in South Korea, teaching in more than 16 schools over a period of 40 years and retiring as a principal. He was peacefully taken into God's embrace in the spring of 1978. A long time later, when our Unification movement was building its international headquarters on Cheongpyeong Lake, I learned that my father had taught at the Miwon Elementary School in the village of Seorak, a few kilometers from our complex. As I live at this location now, I take it that God's plan was to unite my father and me together in the end.

God calls those whom He chooses

On the foundation of 6,000 turbulent years of God's providential history, the only begotten Daughter came to this earth. Innumerable people waited impatiently, ignorant of what it was they were waiting for, having no concept of the only begotten Daughter from the teachings of the world's religions.

It was my husband who discovered that for God to bring forth His only begotten Daughter, He needed to find a nation that had endured injustice for over 5,000 years and was now filled with devout Christians. That nation is Korea. From ancient times, Koreans loved peace and wore white clothing out of reverence for God and their forebears.

The spirit of filial piety, loyalty and chastity, which are the fundamental virtues of human life, lives and breathes in the history of Korea. Moreover, historically speaking, Korea is a place where the world's religions have borne fruit. Even though its history of Christianity is not long, God chose it as the nation and people to whom He would send His only begotten Daughter. Father Moon realized that God would work through a family in which the hearts of three generations of only daughters were connected in sacrificial faith. The Holy Spirit guided Father Moon to discover this in the Bible—no one else saw it. As these conditions were fulfilled, only then could the Mother of peace, destined to bring about a peaceful world, be received on this earth.

Every one of us needs to feel deeply grateful for being born. There is not one person whose birth is meaningless. Moreover, no person's life is his or hers alone. Heaven, earth, and all things in the universe interconnect through lines of latitude and longitude. Peace means that all the energies in the entire world, and in the entire universe, are in harmony. Therefore, no one should belittle his or her life. We should deeply realize that everyone is a precious being, born through the sacred workings of the universe.

As for me, I was born in the midst of a world consumed by chaos, in which no light of hope was to be seen. The Second World War, set in motion in the autumn of 1939, was growing ever more intense. German fascism and Japanese imperialism were staining Europe and Asia with blood. With the exception of Britain, most nations in Europe had been trampled by Hitler. And even Britain was suffering constant air raids from Nazi Germany.

The plight of Korea, a Japanese colony, was just as wretched. My warm childhood experiences notwithstanding, Koreans endured a tremendous struggle just to survive and find food to eat and clothes to wear. As the end of the war approached, Japanese soldiers raided

Korean homes and confiscated everything metal, even the brassware used in ancestral rites, to create weapons. All rice went to feed Japanese soldiers, with the Korean people left to starve. Farmers who harvested rice with their own hands did not get to eat even a morsel of that rice.

Japan went as far as to ban the use of *hangeul*, the Korean alphabet that encompasses the spirit of its people, and to force us to renounce our Korean names and adopt Japanese names. All young Korean men were drafted, either to fight on battlefields far from home or to work long hours in coal mines and factories.

Even in the midst of such hardships, our people set forth to reclaim our nation. In 1940, Koreans set up offices of the Provisional Government of the Republic of Korea in Chongqing, China, and established the Independence Army. These patriots believed that the expropriation of Korea was only temporary, and had a firm resolve to liberate their fatherland.

While the war raged on, in April 1941, Korean independence movement organizations abroad came together at the Christian Academy in Kalihi in Honolulu, Hawaii. At a Rally for the Korean People, representatives from nine organizations, including the Korean National Association in North America, the Korean National Association in Hawaii, and the Korean National Independence League, pledged with one heart to fight the Japanese military for the liberation of their homeland.

On January 1, 1942, one year before I was born, representatives of 26 allied nations gathered in Washington, DC. They signed a declaration pledging to end the war and then work together toward peace. This created the opportunity for Korea, which had been invaded and colonized by Japan, to regain its independence. From the viewpoint of God's hand that rules history, this was His preparation to insure that the only begotten Daughter would grow to maturity in a nation with its own sovereignty.

Decades earlier, in March 1919, Grandmother Jo Won-mo took to the streets carrying my mother, Hong Soon-ae, then five years old, and desperately cried out for independence. She did so knowing only by faith that she was making preparations for the birth of the only begotten Daughter. The world and its people endured great suffering in the year 1942 for the same purpose. In a late spring week that year, my father and mother finally spent some time together, and I was conceived.

Christianity and the only begotten Daughter

From the moment of the Fall, God worked His providence to send His beloved only begotten Son and Daughter to humankind. After many foundations were laid—some bearing fruit, others claimed by Satan—His plan developed dramatically in Korea. From the early 1900s, spiritual fires flared up among Pentecostal Korean Christians who received guidance about God's providence. Many groups believed that the returning Lord would appear in Pyongyang. Exemplary among these was a particular lineal succession of churches: the New Jesus Church, led by Rev. Lee Yong-do; the Holy Lord Church, led by Rev. Kim Seong-do; and the Inside-the-Womb Church, so named to emphasize that the returning Lord would be born of a woman, led by Rev. Heo Ho-bin. All three overcame oppression, on one side from the non-Christian government and, on the other, from the mainstream denominations. Amid such pressures, these churches completed the Christian foundation to receive the only begotten Son and only begotten Daughter.

The eastern Korean Peninsula, upon which the sun first rises, is a region of mountains, and the western peninsula, where the sun sets, is a region of valleys. Following the principles of geomancy, spiritual works led by men unfolded in the mountains of the east, at Wonsan in Hamgyong Province, and spiritual works led by women unfolded in the valleys of the west, at Cholsan in Pyong-an Province. Representative among such women were Kim Seong-do of the Holy Lord Church and Heo Ho-bin of the Inside-the-Womb Church. Representative among the men who ignited spiritual works were Evangelist Hwang Gook-ju, Rev. Baek Nam-ju and Rev. Lee Yong-do of the New Jesus Church.

My mother grew up in the mainstream Presbyterian Church, but my grandmother connected to various Spirit-led groups and, when the time was right, introduced her spiritual life to my mother. Long before Korea's liberation in 1945, my grandmother and mother both offered fervent devotions, lived a life of self-sacrifice, and served others with perseverance, with their sole focus being on receiving the Lord at his Second Advent.

In those days, Hwang Gook-ju, with some 50 followers, set out from Jindao, northeast China, on a pilgrimage across the Korean Peninsula. They witnessed to their faith, ate nothing but flour mixed with water, and performed miracles at revival meetings. The Holy Spirit often came to the evangelist's sister, Hwang Eun-ja. She, as well as Rev. Lee Yong-do, a local pastor whom she had met at one of their revivals, deeply impressed my mother, who joined their pilgrimage. Mother walked with them on their witnessing journey, from Anju all the way to Shineuiju near the border with China. They preached God's word as they went. Politically speaking, it was a fearful age, for anyone who so much as alluded to the existence of the "Korean people" could be arrested by the Japanese police. But the group's services were so powerful that even police detectives sent to spy on the meetings would be deeply moved.

The witnessing journey was not a pleasure trip; it was a course filled with hardships. They had nothing but the clothes on their backs, and the residents of the villages were just as destitute. Nonetheless, these believers walked as many as 40 kilometers every day and night, and lit the fire of the Holy Spirit in every village they visited. My mother made the journey through Shineuiju, and on to Ganggye, arriving there on the 100th day of their pilgrimage. At that point the witnessing team sought to cross the border with China into Manchuria, but this proved to be impossible and they returned home.

By the time they returned to Anju, Rev. Lee Yong-do had established a congregation called the New Jesus Church. My mother decided to join that church and invest in her revitalized life of faith. Rev. Lee Yong-do, formerly of the Presbyterian Church, was not a healthy man. He sometimes would vomit blood and collapse during revival meetings. He created the founding council of the New Jesus Church in Pyongyang, but before he could do more, he passed away at the young age of 33, in Wonsan. After his funeral, the New Jesus Church began again under the leadership of Rev. Lee Ho-bin.

For three years, beginning in 1933, my grandmother and mother practiced their life of faith at the New Jesus Church in Anju. With the belief that she needed to be pure to receive the returning Lord, my mother repented tearfully every day. Then one day, she received a revelation from Heaven: "Rejoice! If your baby is a boy, he will become the king of the universe, and if a girl, she will become the queen of the universe." She was sitting under a moonlit sky, early in the spring of 1934, just 21 years of age. Although it was a revelation from Heaven, her actual circumstances were not such that she could easily embrace such words. Nonetheless, she calmed her heart and accepted it serenely. "Whether You give me a son or a daughter," she replied to God, "I will consider the child to be as great as the universe, and will raise the child with care as Heaven's prince or princess. I will completely dedicate my life for Your will." A few days later, Rev. Lee Ho-bin matched my mother to another member of his church, Han Seung-un, a young man of 26. On March 5, Rev. Lee officiated their marriage. After the marriage, Han Seung-un continued to work as a teacher, and my mother kept house while working hard for the church.

My mother kept God's revelation about the child she was to bear in the forefront of her mind. She came to realize that even though the baby would be born into the world through her body, he or she was God's child more than it was hers. She believed that, just as a child was given unto Mother Mary, a child would be born unto her to govern the universe as God's begotten Son or Daughter. My mother read the Gospels from that viewpoint, and determined that, unlike Mary, she would support her child's heavenly mission with body and soul.

My grandmother and my mother believed that something great would take place in their church before long, but three years passed, and nothing changed. At that time, my grandmother journeyed to Cholsan in North Pyong-an Province and participated in a gathering held by a women's spiritual sisterhood led by Mrs. Kim Seong-do. There she received much grace. She also learned that Kim Seong-do was ministering even though her husband beat her every time she went to church. Mrs. Kim's followers, who were holding meetings in their homes, received the name the Holy Lord Church. Around 1936, my mother joined my grandmother on her journey to Cholsan for the first time. As she met Kim Seong-do, she knew that God was opening the next chapter in her life of faith.

At this point I will introduce my maternal uncle, Hong Soon-jeong. He was not a part of my life in North Korea, but he later played a major role in determining my family's fortunes. He was my mother's younger brother, and was very studious and attended Pyongyang Teachers' Academy. Every year, he would travel a long distance to visit our family during the holidays. He took the Gyeongui Line train to Charyeong-wan Station, from which he had to walk for half a day. My mother was always overjoyed to meet her brother, who had come such a long way to see her. However, she was unable to enjoy much time chatting with him because of her witnessing work.

Thanks to the active witnessing of its followers, the Holy Lord Church expanded from Cholsan to Chongju, Pyongyang, Haeju, Wonsan and even Seoul, opening more than 20 churches. In 1943, the Japanese police imprisoned Kim Seong-do and ten or so of her followers. They were released three months later, but Kim Seong-do passed away in 1944 at the age of 61.

My mother and grandmother, who had been attending her church in Cholsan for eight years, believing that they were about to restore the Garden of Eden, were at a loss. Together with all of the church members, they asked God, "Whom should we follow now?" This question weighed on everyone's hearts. Responding to the prayers of this flock seeking a shepherd, the Holy Spirit chose one among them, Mrs. Heo Ho-bin.

Mrs. Heo had devotedly attended Kim Seong-do and was well respected by the entire Holy Lord Church. God guided her to found a new church, which came to be known as the Inside-the-Womb Church, and gather followers. God taught her how to purify herself and also how to raise children after the Lord comes. Just as God had prepared for Jesus before he was born in the land of Israel, Heo Ho-bin made thorough preparations for the Lord of the Second Advent, who she firmly believed would be born in the land of Korea.

In pursuit of this mission, one year later Heo Ho-bin summoned my mother. "We need to make sets of clothes for the Lord of the Second Advent, so that he will not be embarrassed when he appears in front of us. You should finish making a set of clothes before the end of each day."

Every day, mother sewed for dear life, for she was making the Lord's clothes. While doing so, she thought to herself, "I will have no regrets in my life if I can meet the Lord at his Second Advent before I die, even if only in a dream." As she sewed one day, she quietly dozed off.

In her dream, she saw a robust man in the room, sitting to the east of her with a small table in front of him, a headband around his head. He had been studying, but he turned to look at her. "I am studying this hard just to find you." Those words moved her to tears of gratitude and appreciation.

She awoke from the dream and realized that this man was the returning Lord. In this way, long before she could meet him in the flesh, my mother had had profound, spiritual communication with Father Moon, who came as the Lord at the Second Advent. That dream gave her confidence to persevere through the long and precipitous path of faith that separated the dream from the reality.

During that interim, my grandmother and mother were focused with yearning and impatience for the Lord, the only begotten Son. They, along with the entire Christian world, were unaware of the providential plan for the advent of the only begotten Daughter. Father Moon himself was the only one who understood this. As this illustrates, God unfolds the providence step by step, not disclosing the providence of restoration except to those who need to understand and who have set the conditions to do so.

As was expected to happen sooner or later, the World War finally came to an end with Japan's defeat. Korea enjoyed the liberation its people had long desired, but North Korea soon fell under communist rule. The communist oppression of religion knew no bounds. There are always people who betray others—even Jesus had a treacherous disciple. The Inside-the-Womb Church was not spared. One of its members accused the group of amassing wealth, and the communist police took Heo Ho-bin and many of her followers to Daedong Police Station in Pyongyang. Security agents interrogated Heo Ho-bin harshly and mocked her. "When is this 'Jesus' who is inside your womb going to come out?"

Heo Ho-bin boldly answered, "He will come out in a few days!"

Though white-clad members of the church offered prayers every day in front of the prison gates, even after a year the prisoners had not been released. That was the time that Father Moon, who had been living in Seoul, journeyed to Pyongyang. It was in August of 1946 that he opened a meeting room in the Gyeongchang-ri district of the city and began witnessing. The police accused Father Moon of being a spy for South Korean President Syngman Rhee, and imprisoned him in the jail in which Heo Ho-bin and her followers were being held.

The sad fact is that the imprisoned members of the Inside-the-Womb Church failed to recognize that Father Moon was the returning Lord. During his imprisonment of a hundred days, he contacted Heo Ho-bin several times, but she refused to listen to him. Father Moon was eventually thrown out on the brink of death due to severe torture. Most members of the Inside-the-Womb Church died under the same torture. Those who survived scattered when the Korean War broke out in 1950, some remaining in the North, some fleeing to the South.

This history illustrates the fate of those who receive Heaven's revelation and do not fulfill their responsibility. The sole purpose of those groups was to welcome the Lord at the Second Advent, and they knew this was their mission and declared it. For that purpose, this group, to which my mother belonged, had endured unbelievably difficult hardships, but they failed when their concept of the Lord blinded them to the reality of the Lord.

Participating wholeheartedly in such groups, my grandmother and mother lived with devout faith in order to receive the Lord. For long years, they sincerely believed the prophecy that "The only begotten Son, the savior of the world, will come to the land of Korea." They offered single-minded devotion with unsurpassed zeal and purity. They never compromised with the world or stayed comfortably at home; they served God with heart and soul.

Participating in my grandmother and mother's walk on the path of suffering to receive the Lord, I inherited the essence of their faith.

Because they made whatever sacrifice was needed on the path of God's will, the only begotten Daughter, for whom Heavenly Parent had long waited and yet of whom the world was ignorant, was born on this earth in the third generation of their family. I was born into this intensely spiritual family in an intensely spiritual milieu, and grew up in constant rapport with God, who taught me the mission that was unknown to them: the mission of the Mother of the universe.

Worlds divide at the 38th parallel

"You came here to see your mother?" The guard asked this question as a formality; he knew why I was there, because I came every day.

"Yes, sir," I would respond in my soft voice.

"Wait here," he would say, in a fatherly tone. "I'll call her for you. Would you like a candy?"

In 1948, when the oppression of religions by North Korea's Communist Party was at its height, my mother and grandmother were imprisoned for nearly two weeks for being members of the Inside-the-Womb Church. I was five years old at the time, and I would go to the prison to see my mother. The guards were nice to me because I was polite and well-behaved. Even those ruthless communists gave me fruit or candy when they saw me.

I cannot explain why the authorities released both of them, as the Party was increasing its suppression of religious activities. Perhaps it was out of their concern for me. The good result was that the imprisonment convinced my grandmother that to live a peaceful life, let alone a life of faith, they had to go to South Korea. Since Heo Ho-bin was still in prison, my mother was of two minds about it, but Grandmother persuaded her to go.

"If we stay here," she reasoned, "we will die before we meet the Lord. Once we are in South Korea and have met up with Soon-jeong, the right way will appear." The mention of her younger brother, my uncle Hong Soon-jeong, who was preparing to be a medical practitioner in the South, swayed my mother. She mounted a last protest as she gave in: "How can we go there with no destination? We don't even have a place to stay."

Grandmother took a deep breath and said firmly, "We still must go. God will protect us."

My grandfather did not join us. Like many, he had received the revelation that Pyongyang was the "Palace of Eden," and he was determined to remain there to guard it. Nonetheless, he encouraged his wife and daughter to leave for the South. Because her purpose in life was to meet the Lord at the Second Advent in Pyongyang, my mother had to pray for several days and nights before finally agreeing to go to South Korea, and she went on the condition that it would be temporary.

As good luck would have it, we received the news that uncle Soon-jeong had completed his studies in Japan and in Seoul, and had joined the South Korean Army. My uncle was an intellectual and a dapper young man. Moreover, he was very strong-minded. My grandmother missed her only son and wished very much to see him. In addition, she wanted to protect me, her granddaughter, at all costs. She wanted to prevent my being taken by the cruel communists and made to suffer at their hands. She was sincere when she told me repeatedly over the years, "You are God's true Daughter." Her mission in life was to protect me from the misfortunes of the world.

Along with most people in the North, my family believed that North Korea's Communist Party would not last long. We expected that after a short stay in South Korea, we would see the downfall of the communists and be able to return home. As history shows, this dream was not to be realized. After we crossed the 38th parallel, we never considered returning to the North. Looking back, I believe that God worked through my grandmother's affectionate heart for her son and granddaughter. When all is said and done, a mother's parental heart reflects God's motherly heart.

———

"It is dark now," my mother whispered. "Let's go."

It was the autumn of 1948, and we left our home in the middle of the night, my mother carrying me on her back and my grandmother carrying a couple of bundles. It is quite a distance from Anju to the 38th parallel, 200 kilometers (125 miles) as the crow flies. We had to walk for days and days to cover that distance. And we took every step on that journey with anxiety, fearing for our lives. At night we slept in empty houses, and when the morning dew fell we would start again. Our shoes were flimsy and the roads were rough, and so our feet ached from the very start. What was hardest to endure was the hunger. We would knock on the doors of shabby cottages and give them something from our bundles in exchange for food, which was usually a cup of boiled barley and rice. Undergoing such hardships, we walked and walked endlessly southward.

The communists had plowed the fields and broken up the shoulders of roads to make such a journey even more difficult. Our feet sank into mud as we walked through the fields, and we shivered all over with cold. Still, we continued on, looking only at the starlight.

North Korean People's Army soldiers were blocking the 38th parallel, and they easily captured my mother, grandmother, and me. They locked us up in a shed, together with other frightened people who had the same intention as we did. The soldiers were rough with the men, but they did not treat women and children harshly.

One day, one of the adults asked me to take food to the soldiers standing watch. Though my heart trembled inside, I forced a smile and handed the food to the soldiers. After I had done so several times, the soldiers' hearts softened, and one night they set my family free. They instructed us to return to our hometown, and we walked out of their sight in that direction. And then, as we stood at the crossroads between life and death, night fell, and we waited, and Heaven sent a young man to guide us on the path of life. Under the cover of darkness, we followed him across the 38th parallel.

As we crossed, I was so happy that I said to Mother, "We don't have to sing songs praising Kim Il Sung anymore, do we? I will sing a song from the southern part of Korea!" This too was God's intervention, for on the South Korean side soldiers also were keeping a strict watch. I sang a few lines of the song with a joyous heart. At that moment, we heard a rustling in the bushes in front of us. We were surprised and stood frozen in place, fearful that we would be captured by North Korean soldiers once again. Soldiers emerged from the bushes—South Koreans. At the sight of them, we almost wilted in relief. Those South Korean soldiers told us that they had heard us as we approached and had been about to fire upon us. When they heard the voice of a child singing, they had lowered their weapons. They welcomed us and comforted us.

One soldier said, "It must have been difficult for you to make it all the way here with this beautiful young child. This isn't much, but please take it." We were so grateful to this soldier, whom God moved to give us money, enough to get us to Seoul.

Looking back, if I had not sung at that moment, those young soldiers probably would have mistaken us for North Korean soldiers and shot us dead. In this way, once again, God protected us. We arrived safely in South Korea after undergoing hardships such as these. Yet, in making that journey, we parted from my grandfather, whom we never saw again.

⁓

South Korea was a strange place to us. Having never been to Seoul, we had no idea how we could survive, and we were getting lost constantly. We also had lost the moorings of our faith; the hope to meet the returning Lord was indeed floating in the clouds. We had no money and no skills by which to make a living. We camped in a shabby, empty house and barely made it through each day. All we could do was talk to people.

Our most urgent task was to find my maternal uncle Soon-jeong. He was the only person we could depend on in South Korea, and we were hoping he was somewhere in Seoul. My mother pleaded in prayer, "What should I do to find my younger brother?" She prayed most earnestly every day to find her brother on whom she could rely. We devoted ourselves to this search by visiting clinics and pharmacies.

Then we received an unexpected blessing from God. We met a man on the street who turned out to be a friend of my uncle's. This was indeed God's providential help. His friend told us that Uncle Soon-jeong was serving at the Army Headquarters in Seoul's Yongsan district. After returning from Japan, he had graduated from the College of Pharmacy in Seoul and then received training as a pharmaceutical officer in the Korea Military Academy. He was currently serving as a first lieutenant.

This kind man took us to Yongsan, and what a reunion it was! Soon-jeong was delighted to see his mother, sister and niece. He had no idea of the conditions in the North and was so distressed to hear of what we had gone through to get to Seoul. He immediately rented a small room for us in Hyochang-dong.

Our life in the South soon stabilized. I entered Hyochang Primary School and, in the free land of South Korea, began going to school for the first time. I loved going to school with my bag of books every day. The older residents of the neighborhood would pat me on the head, and the neighborhood children also liked me very much. Looking back, I find it interesting that our rented room was close to Cheongpa-dong, the neighborhood in which, seven years later, we would end our search for the Lord at the Second Advent. Until that day arrived, however, we endured many twists and turns on our odyssey.

While at Hyochang-dong, we heard the news that Jeong Seok-cheon, the eldest son of the founder of the Holy Lord Church, had settled in South Korea. We took it as a miracle and prayed that God would guide us to meet him. All in all, we praised God that my uncle was serving as an army officer, and that Jeong Seok-cheon's family from the Holy Lord Church had come to the South. Without doubt, our Heavenly Parent prepared a path to protect the one called to serve humankind as the only begotten Daughter, the one to whom He would entrust the providence. Now that our physical pilgrimage had reached an oasis, it was time to renew our spiritual pilgrimage.

A blue flash of death

It was early on a hot summer morning. Red balsam flowers blossomed on one side of our courtyard, and thick, old willow and sycamore trees stood along the street. I was seven years old, but I remember the moment clearly, as a frantic neighbor burst into our living room with the words, "War has broken out! The North Korean army has crossed the 38th parallel!"

Apprehensive residents gathered in the alley in groups of two and three. I had been getting used to settled life in the South, but when the North Korean People's Army launched their invasion, our short respite was over. Everyone was frightened, government reports mingled with rumors, and no one knew for sure what was going on.

What happened was that the South Korean interim government packed up and moved to the city of Daejeon, 90 miles to the south of Seoul. The government ordered the South Korean army to blow up the Han River Bridge, the only bridge across the Han River on the south side of Seoul. They expected North Korean troops to arrive in Seoul soon, and they had no means to protect the city. Their strategy was to prevent the communist army from crossing the river. They could do little or nothing to help the city's residents, who were crying out for Seoul's defense.

Two days later, my mother woke up at dawn and began packing our clothes in a bundle. Awakened by the rustling noise, I kept my eyes shut and listened to her conversation with my grandmother. "We have to seek refuge," my mother said. "After the communists get here, they'll kill us."

"I know they are bad," my grandmother responded, "but do you think they would treat women harshly?"

"If they find out we have escaped from the North," my mother reasoned, "they probably will kill us on the spot."

On the evening of June 27, 1950, two days after the start of the Korean War, Seoul residents streamed out of the city's ancient neighborhoods under a gentle summer rain. The more they realized that they were not the only ones seeking to escape, and that they all had to cross the same bridge, the more serious and desperate they became. This was war. My grandmother, mother and I joined the exodus with our bundle, following the throng moving toward the Han River Bridge. When its dim shape appeared in the dark, something told me to stop, and I grabbed my grandmother's skirt. She stopped in her tracks, and my mother turned and asked her, "Mother, what's wrong?"

Grandmother looked up at the sky and then glanced down at me. Then she turned her head again in the direction of our house. "Soon-jeong may come," she said with a steady tone, speaking of her son, my uncle. It seemed senseless to turn around when everyone else was fleeing the city, but she was firm. "Let's go back in case he does."

My mother understood. The three of us made our way back home, fighting the crowds. When we got home, I spread out my blanket and lay down to sleep, but it was not long before I was awakened by the noise of a three-quarter-ton truck. Its headlights illuminated our room as the door suddenly burst open. There was my uncle in his military uniform. My grandmother and mother gasped sighs of relief and hope. I thought to myself, "We can leave now," and felt at ease.

"Hurry," he barked. "We have to move now!" Uncle Soon-jeong, based in the army headquarters as a military medic, was aware of the progress of the war. As soon as he heard that the South Korean army was preparing to destroy the Han River Bridge, he requisitioned a truck and sped to our home, knowing his family was in danger. He had left the truck with its engine running in our foggy alley. We climbed in with our already-packed bundle, and he drove toward the bridge. In the pre-dawn hours, crowds of refugees were swarming there from all directions, creating total chaos.

We moved forward at a snail's pace on the congested street. As an army officer, my uncle had the official pass necessary to take a vehicle across the bridge. Honking the horn, he inched the truck through the crowd. Held in my mother's arms, I clung to her and gazed at the people fleeing their homes, their fear and confusion increasing by the minute.

As soon as we had crossed the bridge, my uncle shouted, "Get down in your seats!" As I squeezed down on the floor at my mother's feet, a huge explosion behind us shook our truck. There was a blue flash and a deafening sound. My uncle set the emergency brake and turned off the engine. Together we jumped out of the truck and clambered down into the ditch at the side of the road. I turned my face to the bridge and witnessed the next explosion. I saw a light like a demon's burning eyes piercing the night. Countless civilians as well as soldiers and policemen who were crossing the bridge were thrown about like plastic toys, flying everywhere, cast into the river below. For us, a few meters proved to be the difference between life and death. Our lives had been spared.

I closed my eyes, and many thoughts flashed across my mind. Why would anyone start a war? Why did innocent people have to die? Why is God permitting such pain and suffering? Who can bring an end to this madness? I could not conceive of any answers. When I reopened my eyes, I saw that the bridge was cut in half. The military had accomplished its mission, at the cost of hundreds of lives. What remained amid the corpses, the screaming wounded, and the dazed survivors, was an ugly skeleton of steel, smoldering in the dark.

The Han River Bridge was blown up at 3:00 a.m. on June 28, 1950. Even though the South Korean government had announced that it would defend Seoul, it severed the only link to safety, even before the North Korean People's Army came into the city. Hundreds of people, fleeing the city, were killed. Amid this desperate crisis, through the help of my uncle, my life and the lives of my family were preserved. At that critical moment, God guided me and protected us from danger.

Even today, whenever I cross a bridge over the Han River, I see that blue flash and hear people's agonized screams echoing as if they still are burning in hell. My heart aches at the sound. At a young age I directly witnessed the horror of war and experienced the wretched life of a refugee. The simple and innocent were killed like flies. Children who had lost their parents were crying and wandering in the streets. I was only seven, but I became so serious that war has to vanish forever from this world. It took place 70 years ago, but my throat still tightens when I recall the night the Han River Bridge fell.

Left by my uncle, who had to return to military duty, barely able to keep ourselves in one piece, my grandmother, mother, and I walked and walked on unfamiliar paths heading south. Once in a while we got a ride in a passing car. Presenting a document as to my uncle's position as a medic, we finally gained shelter in a refugee camp for military families.

As the tide of the war shifted, on September 28 we returned to Seoul. The South Korean military had driven out the communists and reconstructed a passable bridge across the river. We lodged in an empty house, one that the soldiers from the North had occupied, to which the owners did not return.

Then the tide of war turned again. Half a million communist Chinese troops invaded Korea across the Yalu River. On January 4, 1951, the South Korean army again abandoned Seoul, and we again had to escape. This time we were able to board a train for the families of soldiers, and we safely arrived in the city of Daegu.

The day-after-day sights and sounds of our year-long wilderness course from the North to the South defy description. I saw countless dead bodies—adults, children, victims of freezing, starvation, disease and battle. My family and I also teetered on the brink of death, but somehow, throughout this journey for survival, I felt God was with us. There was a greater power protecting our family as we escaped the North and found refuge in the South. Heavenly Parent gave me more than a sense of meaning and value. He provided me with a scale by which to measure my purpose in life.

The way of God's will

By God's hand, on our way to Daegu we met Jeong Seok-cheon, a member of the Holy Lord Church, to which my family had belonged in Cholsan. He was very pleased to see us, and we all felt as if we were meeting long-lost relatives. The Holy Lord Church was the church in which my parents were married, and Jeong Seok-cheon's mother, Kim Seong-do, was its founder. She was one of many female church leaders in the northern part of Korea whose devotion to Jesus was unparalleled and who had received revelations of what was to come.

The Holy Lord Church had withered due to Japanese persecution, and the Communist Party's brutal oppression had put an end to it and all churches in the North. Escaping to the South, Jeong Seok-cheon continued to worship God. With scattered Holy Lord Church members who had found each other, he created a prayer group in Daegu. He maintained his ardor to accomplish God's will and prepared himself to meet the returning Lord. He also worked diligently and had a good livelihood managing mining, rice and oil businesses. Mr. Jeong organized our lodging in Daegu.

My mother made a simple request of him. "When we were in North Korea," she said, "we received much grace through Mrs. Heo Ho-bin, and there were great works." Mr. Jeong knew of Rev. Heo, whose congregation had prepared food and clothes for Jesus, as well as for the Second Coming Lord. "As the Lord will return to Korea soon," my mother said to Mr. Jeong, "please, let us pray very hard to welcome him."

One morning, during the Daegu group's intense prayer, my mother received a revelation from Heaven. God told her that she had to live a life of greater devotion if she wanted to meet the Lord at the Second Advent. "Prayer alone is not enough," she was told. "You have to eat your food uncooked." My mother began to subsist on pine needles, which would have been digestible had they been steamed, but she ate them raw, even though they badly damaged her teeth.

My mother had come from a relatively well-to-do family. Her father had owned a large farm, and Grandmother Jo had a sewing-machine shop, so they were able to pay for my mother and her brother to attend high school. My maternal grandfather always taught my mother, "No matter how hard things may be, you must never be indebted to others." Abiding by his words, there in Daegu my mother opened a small shop, thinking that it would provide enough money to enable her to re-enroll her only daughter in elementary school.

Daily subsistence of two meals of kimchi broth, raw pine needle tips and peanuts, plus taking care of her shop, exhausted my mother's physical frame. A normal person would have eased off that discipline, but for my mother, her mind only became clearer. When I saw her serene countenance, while feeling sympathy for her, I could not help but be amazed.

"How can she run a business while consuming so little?" I asked myself. "It is nothing less than a miracle." My mother maintained a near-starvation diet, and her shop did not bring a profit for three months. Most people would have given up, but her faith was deep and, with supreme confidence that she was upholding God's dream, she persevered unconditionally. She did not compromise with reality. With the Holy Spirit, she created her own reality.

No matter her plight, my mother surrendered her mind to her search for Jesus at his return. Now, as I began to mature, she added to that the task of providing her daughter a spiritually safe environment. She wanted me to reach maturity in an environment of internal and external purity, and she considered how to separate me as much as possible from the influence of the secular world.

I was attending Daegu Elementary School in a neighborhood called Bongsan-dong. As time passed, not only my face but also my bearing became attractive. I was good at my studies, so I soon became popular among my friends, and I was well-liked by many adults as well. One afternoon, I was playing alone on the narrow street in front of the shop, with my mother inside. A Buddhist monk walked by and I caught his eye, and he stopped. I returned his gaze, and I remember his piercing eyes. My mother came out and bowed politely to him. Pointing to me, he asked, "Is she your daughter?" Hearing her affirmative answer, his eyes turned warm and deep. As I turned to look at my mother, the holy man spoke.

"You live with only one daughter, but don't envy someone who has ten sons. Please raise her well. This daughter of yours is going to be married at a young age. Her future husband may be older than she is, but he'll be a great man with outstanding ability that transcends the sea, the land and the skies."

My mother took the ascetic's words seriously. Acting on her intention to rear her only daughter in the most serene and secure surroundings, in 1954 my mother moved us to Jeju Island off the southern coast of the Korean Peninsula, to the town of Seogwipo. She wanted to leave the crowded city streets and allow me to mature in the pristine countryside. We spent our first nine months on Jeju with the family of Jeong Seok-jin, the younger brother of our Holy Lord Church friend, Jeong Seok-cheon.

***

On Jeju, as she had everywhere, my mother led me on the path of sainthood for the Lord, with no thought of worldly matters, and this fit my emerging personality very well. I read biographies of holy women and devoted myself to the ideal of complete purity in preparation to receive my calling as the Daughter of God. Once settled in Seogwipo, I enrolled in Shinhyo Elementary School as a fifth-grader. At the age of 11, while my classmates were running around and playing, I lived a rigorous and strict life of faith. With my grandmother and mother, I devoted myself to prayer, study and worship.

My mother soaked flattened barley in water and added it to radish kimchi for her raw food diet, while I ate millet porridge. Even though weak due to nutritional privation, when she saw farmers working the barley fields, my mother could not resist helping with the plowing. If she saw someone having difficulty carrying a load, she would volunteer to carry it for them. Without her saying a word, people were filled with admiration. "I've never met such a thoughtful person," one village woman would say to another, who would respond, "That's what I'm saying. I heard she's a regular churchgoer, but still, she is so different from the others."

My mother lived the exemplary life of an authentically religious person, always putting her faith into practice by helping others. She studied the Bible and shared with me the teachings of the Holy Lord Church and the Inside-the-Womb Church that Jesus would return as a man in the flesh, just as he had come 2,000 years ago, that he would find his holy bride and hold the marriage supper of the Lamb, as the Bible prophesies, and that all this would take place in Korea. From her I learned the meaning of Jesus' Second Advent and could imagine it and taste and touch it. And from my mother, I learned the meaning of true discipleship.

My uncle, who had rescued us at the outbreak of the Korean War, married at the end of that war, and Grandmother Jo went to live with him and his new bride in Seoul. Within a few months, she was longing to see her daughter and granddaughter, and she came to visit us on Jeju Island. While she was with us, my uncle was posted to the city of Chuncheon, some 50 miles northeast of Seoul. He sent us an abrupt but clear message: "Please wrap up your life on Jeju and move to Chuncheon." Grandmother Jo urged us to comply, saying softly, with the pleading eyes of a loving matriarch, "My only pleasure in life is to have Hak Ja nearby and take care of her every day."

That was it. In February 1955 we all three departed Jeju, bound for Chuncheon. My mother rented a small room for us in the Yaksa-dong neighborhood, and my grandmother lived with my uncle's family nearby. I enrolled in Bongui Elementary School and soon entered the sixth grade. On the school grounds stood a big sycamore tree, its circumference greater than I could reach around. I read books under its abundant shade in the hot weather. There was a coal briquette factory next to the school, and my shoes would be covered with black soot when I walked past. All this springs out fresh in my memory. In the next year, 1956, I graduated from elementary school. I was 13 and received my graduation certificate after having attended four different schools. Though I had been a student at Bongui but one year, I was honored at the graduation ceremony with an award for doing well in my studies.

God finally responded to my mother's ceaseless prayers and pleadings. His care for her once again was extended through Jeong Seok-cheon, our friend from the Holy Lord Church. Mr. Jeong remembered the last words of his late mother, the Holy Lord Church founder, Rev. Kim Seong-do: "If someone fails to accomplish what God has entrusted him to do, it must be accomplished through someone else. The group to which the Lord is coming will be accused and slandered as a sex cult. Its members will be persecuted and imprisoned. If you hear of such a church, know that it may be the true church, and that you should personally investigate it and decide for yourself."

So Mr. Jeong diligently traveled the country to participate in revival meetings. He did not find what he was looking for until May 1955, when he read in the *Dong-A Ilbo*, a Seoul newspaper, about an incident at Ewha Womans University. Five Ewha professors had been fired from the faculty for joining a group called the Unification Church, led by a man they called Teacher Moon, and fourteen students had been expelled from the same school for the same reason.

Sensing the spirit of his prophetic mother, Mr. Jeong sent a letter with the newspaper clipping to his older sister in Busan. His sister took a look at the clipping and, without thinking twice, booked passage to Seoul with her daughter. They arrived and found their way to the Jang-chung-dong headquarters of the Unification Church, but were unable to meet its leader at that time. The members told her the location of the

Unification Church in Busan, and she returned home. From there, she informed her younger brother what had happened and that there was another Unification Church branch in Daegu.

Jeong Seok-cheon visited the church in Daegu, listened to Divine Principle lectures, accepted its teachings and joined. Then out of the blue, ten days later, the local group was sent reeling. On July 4, Teacher Moon and several of his church members were incarcerated at Seodaemun Prison in Seoul. Mr. Jeong traveled to Seoul to visit Teacher Moon in prison. In that visit he received inspiration and encouragement. Mr. Jeong knew that he had found the one whom Jesus had sent.

Some three months later, on October 4, Teacher Moon was acquitted of all the charges for which he had been imprisoned. At that point, Mr. Jeong secured his family's support in Daegu and moved to Seoul to devote himself full time to God's will.

After his release from Seodaemun, Teacher Moon visited Daegu. At that time, I was 12 years old, living with my family in Chuncheon, several hours north of Daegu. One morning, my mother told me that she had a dream of cuddling a white dragon in her arms. She did not know what the white dragon symbolized, nor what it meant to cradle it in her arms, but she said that something earth-shaking was about to transpire. That very day she received a letter from Mr. Jeong about his meeting the Divine Principle movement, and meeting Teacher Moon in prison, and who Teacher Moon is, and that Teacher Moon was in Daegu. My mother left for Daegu immediately, only to find that Teacher Moon had returned to Seoul.

My mother felt deep regret, and while staying overnight in Daegu she had another dream. In it she saw a pair of golden dragons prostrating themselves in the direction of Seoul. With this vision carved into her heart, she took the train to Seoul the next morning and proceeded to the Unification movement's newly purchased headquarters church in Cheongpa-dong. It was early in December 1955. There, she met the teacher of the Unification Church for the first time.

The moment she greeted him, she realized that the white dragon in her dream represented none other than him, and that he was the one she had been seeking. She was deeply moved to meet, in her lifetime on earth, the Lord at the Second Advent, for whom she had suffered and sacrificed for three decades. She stayed at Cheongpa-dong to study the Principle, and heard teachings that put together what she had learned in the Holy Lord Church and Inside-the-Womb Church. With each lecture, her eyes were opened and her initial inspiration was confirmed. At times she pondered the meaning of her dream of the pair of golden dragons. Not coming up with anything, she put that out of her mind.

Despite my mother's admiration of him, and in contrast to his affectionate openness with everyone else, Teacher Moon related to my mother in a formal and reserved fashion. As a result, she felt empty and a little bit isolated, with a feeling of lack of love lodging in her heart. She invested in prayer silently, without rest, erasing from her soul all the concepts and expectations she may have had about whom she was going to meet.

Then one Sunday, Teacher Moon preached a sermon about the heart of Jesus. He said, "The people of Israel did not welcome Jesus, who came as their True Father. They allowed him to die on the cross," and asked the congregation, "Do you know how great was the sin they committed?" Upon hearing this, my mother withdrew into a corner of the church. There she wept, crying her heart out for the remainder of the service. Teacher Moon viewed this, and after the service he called to my mother and consoled her, saying, "A person anointed by God must pass the test of Satan as well as that of Heaven."

At that, like the snow melting in springtime, all sorrow disappeared from my mother's heart. Her faith in God became stronger than it ever was. Soon thereafter, she returned to Chuncheon to commence pioneer work for the Unification Church.

CHAPTER 3

THE MARRIAGE SUPPER
OF THE LAMB

The true meaning of sacrifice

My mother officially joined the Unification Church in Seoul on December 15, 1955. Early in the following year, a small yet historic first step was made as the Chuncheon Unification Church convened its first public Sunday service at a home in Yaksa-dong. I was a young girl of 13 who had just graduated from Bongui Elementary School.

One day when the sun was shining brightly, my mother said to me, "Let's go to Seoul for the day." Without knowing why we were going, I followed her. That was the day I first met Father Moon. Cheongpa-dong Church, where we met, was a small, two-story wooden house. The Korean government had categorized it as "enemy property" because it had been owned by the Japanese during their occupation of our country. It was more like a home than a church.

I greeted Father Moon politely, and as he returned the greeting, he asked my mother, "Who is this child?"

"This is my daughter," she replied.

With a look of surprise, Father Moon gazed at me as he said to my mother, "You have such a pretty daughter." He then closed his eyes as if in meditation, and asked my name.

I politely replied, "My name is Hak Ja Han."

As if struck by something, Father Moon spoke very softly to himself, "Hak Ja Han has been born in Korea. Hak Ja Han has been born in Korea. Hak Ja Han has been born in Korea." After saying this three times, he began expressing gratitude to God, saying, "You sent such a magnificent daughter, named Hak Ja Han, to Korea. Thank you." Then Father Moon spoke to me as if he were asking me to gather my resolve: "Hak Ja Han, you will need to make sacrifices in the future."

"Yes!" I replied, surprised at my own forwardness.

On the way home on the train, my mother and I thought the encounter was curious. "How strange," she said. "Why would he repeat that you were born in Korea three times?" As we fell into silence, I contemplated the word "sacrifice." The word Father Moon used took on a meaning different from what I had learned in textbooks. What he was alluding to was a higher dimension of sacrifice, a nobler and more complete sacrifice. What you sacrifice is important, but why you make that sacrifice is even more important.

As I listened to the rhythmic rumble of the train and looked out the window at the scenery as it slipped by, I couldn't stop thinking about what Father Moon had said. I thought about what I might need to sacrifice for. From that day, the word "sacrifice" was engraved in my heart. Thinking back as the person called to live as the Mother of peace, I realize that, over time ,"sacrifice" became a name I could call myself.

God is my Father

From the time I could understand words, my maternal grandmother, Jo Won-mo, consistently taught me one thing: "God is your Father." She went so far as to say, "Your mother is like your nanny who is raising you as God's daughter." Since I had been surrounded by an atmosphere of faith even while in my mother's womb, I accepted this without a second thought. When I heard the word "God," my heart would open unreservedly and fill with warmth.

*1956: Together with classmates from her art class
in Seongjung Girls' Middle School (at back, center)*

My mother did not mind investing herself body and soul for the purpose of raising me to reject secular life and follow God's way. She lived with single-minded devotion in absolute unity with and obedience to God. After joining the Unification Church, our family moved to Seoul, where she worked even harder to protect me from the world's temptations. As a result of her dedication, God allowed me to see myself as a noble crane.

Even as an adolescent in middle school, I poured my heart into quiet reading and study. I attended the Seongjung Girls Middle School, located in Sajik-dong of Seoul's Jongno district. Situated at the southern foot of Mount Inwang, it was a small school that seemed always bathed in sunlight. From the moment of its founding, that school shared in the suffering of the Korean people. It was established in May 1950, but had to close less than a month later due to the Korean War. After the war, its doors reopened and, true to its mission, the school prepared many girls to become talented women who would help build a prosperous country. In 1981, the school moved to the Eunpyeong district of Seoul, and in 1984, its name was changed to Sunjung Girls' Middle School. Our Tongil Group acquired this school in 1987 and brought it into the Sunhak Academic Foundation. I have continued to give it support and attention.

In middle school I spoke little and developed a calm personality. I studied hard and always ranked at the top of my class. I was pretty and modest and, as I was also quiet and well-behaved, I received love and attention from my teachers. My school life was uneventful; I only remember that I missed a day or two of school in the first year when I became quite sick. In my second and third years, I received an award for earning the highest grades in my class. I preferred to read in a quiet spot and listen to music rather than engage in social life or sports. My hobby was drawing. I enjoyed art and had some talent, but set aside the possibility of becoming a professional artist.

For all three years of middle school I was the class representative on the student council, and in the third year I was the head of the student activities committee. I led many student activities, and this awakened my leadership abilities. One day when the entire school was gathered, I went to the podium and announced the decisions of the student council. The teachers complimented me on my poise and confident attitude. After witnessing this side of me, which they had not seen before, the teachers commented, "Hak Ja seems gifted …I thought she was just quiet and docile, but actually she shows good leadership skills."

During adolescence, I didn't worry about my life or losing my way. I credit this to my grandmother and mother instilling in me a deep faith in God and the habit of living in attendance to Him. My mother, in particular, strictly guided my life of faith. Yes, there were times when I thought it difficult and wearisome, but I am grateful now, for it prepared me to blossom as the only begotten Daughter of God who one day would meet the only begotten Son of God.

Within that atmosphere, I grew roots of unshakable faith. I read a lot. I enjoyed reading tales of the saints, and particularly *The Good Earth,* by Pearl S. Buck. The characters in that book struggle against nature and fate. The story helped me realize that ultimately we must return to nature's embrace, represented in that book by the earth. It is human nature to cling to God's embrace. I earnestly wished to be together with God, and for that reason I devoured songs and novels about the love of one's hometown.

I knew from a young age that God is my Father, and naturally connected everything I read to God. I cut off entirely from the harsh secular world and lived a chaste life as if I were a nun. I was aware that a higher power was guiding me, that my path had been prepared in Heaven.

Especially during this time, the Bible was my close companion. I cried myself to sleep many nights after reading about God's history of creation, the tragic Fall, and God's work of salvation carried out through histori-cal figures who took responsibility at the behest of Heaven. I learned how they sacrificed themselves, and realized that God created us so He could love us as His children. After reading God's bitter history and His desire to embrace us, even though we give Him only pain and sadness, it was not just once or twice that I lay awake, unable to sleep, my heart aching for Him. I naturally continued to ponder ever more deeply what Teacher Moon had said to me about sacrifice. The question, "What can I sacrifice for God?" was shaping my life.

Without sacrifice and service, one cannot even begin to think one is living for the sake of others rather than for oneself. As I strictly culti-vated my faith from a young age, I cherished a dream deep within my heart. That dream was to liberate my Heavenly Father who, through-out history, gave Himself for the salvation of humanity. I wished to free Him from the chains of our fallen history.

We cannot meet God from a position of reigning over others. He finds us when we are silently working for the sake of those in greater difficulty than ourselves. I came to know that when we think about God's will from the lower position, the position of offering and self-sac-rifice, God's bitterness washes away and He will come to us.

During the postwar years, the streets of Seoul were full of the wounded. Numerous children, including war orphans, were suffering from hunger and disease. Few people were able to get timely treatment when they became sick. I wanted to heal people's injuries, relieve their pain, and guide them to a brighter world. As it was time for me to enter high school, in the spring of 1959 I entered St. Joseph's Nursing School.

Heavenly and earthly phoenixes

In the late 1950s, it wasn't easy for a single mother. My mother managed to make ends meet by doing any odd job that came her way. She did not rest even a moment in her devoted life of prayer, and in that way she triumphed over those hardships and tribulations. One day, however, she announced to her small family, "I've been living meaninglessly; I must live a life of greater value."

1959: Hak Ja Han (left), a student at St. Joseph's Nursing School

She left my maternal grandmother and me in the care of my aunt and moved into the Cheongpa-dong Church, and dedicated herself completely to church activities. She chose to take on the most menial of tasks. People would try to dissuade her, but she pursued such work with a joyful and grateful heart. She had lived a life of devoted faith in

North Korea, greater than anyone, but started at the bottom in the Unification Church.

She overworked herself, however, and her body grew weaker and weaker until she became seriously ill. Luckily, a church member she knew from the Inside-the-Womb Church took her in. This person, Mrs. Oh Yeong-choon, was like a sister to her. They lived together in the Noryangjin neighborhood, and as they cared for each other, my mother gradually recovered her health.

While at nursing school, I attended Cheongpa-dong Church every Sunday. One day, when my mother saw me there, she took me to a corner and softly whispered, "A few nights ago, I had a dream that was hard to understand."

"What did you dream?" I asked.

"There were women from church wearing white holy robes and standing there holding pink flowers," she said. "Then I saw you walking toward Teacher Moon." At that time, we called Father Moon "Teacher." "All of a sudden, thunder roared and lightning crashed from the sky and struck one spot. There you were, and other women all looked at you enviously." She paused, collecting her thoughts. "That's when I woke up. I think it means that something will happen that will shake the world."

"I think so, too," I replied. "I'm sure it is a prophetic dream, but I don't want to guess more than that."

My mother did not imagine that this dream was a revelation from God, a prophecy that her only daughter would be called to become the True Mother who would give her life for the world. But I had been thinking constantly about the word "sacrifice" and had determined to live a life of sacrifice for God. This dream fit with that, and I had a sense of its meaning.

In the late autumn of 1959, Father Moon conducted a national missionary workshop at the Cheongpa-dong Church, and I participated with my mother. I was on one side of the overcrowded church, busy with the workshop, but could see that on the other side, elder sisters were quietly working on another important matter. A few months earlier, senior grandmothers of deep faith had begun preparations for Father Moon's marriage. They were considering which among the women of the church could be God's choice to be his bride. As I was only a schoolgirl and so much younger than Father Moon, my name would not have come up.

Then one day, one of the sages among the grandmothers sought out Father Moon to tell him about her dream. "I saw many flocks of cranes flying down from the heavens," she told him, "and even though I kept trying to shoo them away, they came and covered Teacher Moon." Father Moon provided no interpretation, so the elder sister continued with confidence: "I believe my dream is revealing God's will, that your bride's name will include the Chinese character for *hak* (crane)."

Shortly after I heard that, my mother told me another revelation she had received in prayer. A phoenix flew down from heaven, and another flew up from the earth to meet it. The phoenix from heaven was Father Moon. It brought to her mind her dream from years before, when she went to Daegu to meet Father Moon; the dream in which a pair of golden dragons bowed down in the direction of Seoul.

My mother thought about what all this might mean, and then one morning at dawn she received a heavenly message. She had just taken a cold shower, and it came as she was reciting the Pledge prayer. "The phoenix descending from heaven represents the True Father," she announced, "and the phoenix rising from the earth represents the True Mother." My mother was happy with this understanding, but she continued quietly with the workshop and didn't speak about it.

In the months following my 16th birthday, I matured quickly, and it caught people's attention at church. Members would mention that I looked elegant and neat. I would hear someone say, "Hak Ja is peaceful and virtuous. She is like a crane, befitting her name." And another, "She's also very polite, and if you watch, you will see she is very observant and has clear judgment." I stood out when I was with members of the congregation. People commented that I had an untainted purity, that I was one with God's will, and that I had embraced the virtue of obedience through the difficulties I had endured in North Korea. Hearing such comments, I disciplined myself not to feel proud or act carelessly.

More than anything else for his bride-to-be, Father Moon was looking for a person with a sacrificial and devoted heart of living for others. He did not care about family background, economic status, or appearance. She had to be a woman with absolute faith who could love the world. She had to be a woman who could conceive of saving the world. Because he had been unable to find such a woman, there had been no marriage of the Lamb. He still did not fully know that the heavenly bride, who would become the Mother of heaven, earth, and humankind, was close by. I had come to understand God's will, but I couldn't say anything. To recognize the bride was Father Moon's mission and responsibility.

The heavenly bride

A short time later, Mrs. Oh Yeong-choon, the devout member who had taken in my mother, went to her job in a clothing store on the second floor of the Nakwon Building in central Seoul. She assisted the store owner at making garments. The owner was a longtime member we called "the prayer grandmother." When Mrs. Oh arrived, the owner was sewing together a man's suit. Mrs. Oh sat next to her as she pumped the wheel of the sewing machine, and asked casually, "Oh, who is the suit for?"

"This suit is for Father Moon" was the grandmother's answer. "He is going to wear it at his engagement ceremony." Mrs. Oh perked up immediately, and her eyes widened as she asked the natural question, "Who is to be the bride?"

"Well," replied the grandmother nonchalantly, "the day of the engagement has been decided, but the bride hasn't been chosen yet. However, the ceremony is going to be held soon, and so I am making his suit."

Mrs. Oh's mind was buzzing. "Who is going to be the bride?" She pondered the question but couldn't come up with any possibilities. Mrs. Oh was a person who often heard God's voice in revelations. In fact, she had been offering prayerful devotions for seven years for the sake of the appearance of the True Mother. She right away took her question to God in prayer, and she received a revelation: "Because Eve fell when she was 16 years old, the heavenly bride needs to be younger than 20."

This had never occurred to her before. It was only then that she understood the logic of God's will. She asked God again and again, "Who is the heavenly bride who is younger than 20?" And before long, she thought of me. "I know Hak Ja Han, who is around 16," she said to herself. "She often sits right next to me in church! Why didn't I think of her? Could it really be her?"

At 10:00 that evening, Mrs. Oh was making her way home after finishing her work. She was on the Noryangjin bus as it was crossing the Han River when God spoke to her: "It will be Hak Ja. It will be Hak Ja." God's revelation descended upon Mrs. Oh like a wave of energy in the autumn night sky. She arrived in her neighborhood around 11:00 p.m., but instead of going home, she hurried to see my mother, who lived near her.

"Soon-ae, are you sleeping?"

"Not yet. Come in!"

"How old is your daughter?" My mother gave her a puzzled look. Mrs. Oh had skipped all formalities and asked a point-blank question.

"Why are you visiting me in the middle of the night to ask me how old my daughter is?"

"Don't change the subject; please just tell me."

"She's 16, turning 17 next year."

"When is her birthday?"

"She was born in 1943, on the sixth day of the first lunar month. She has the same birthday as our Master. Why are you suddenly asking me such questions?" Mrs. Oh and my mother were old friends. They were the same age, and they had attended the same church in their hometown in North Korea. In addition, their mothers were very close friends. My mother, in fact, was living in Noryangjin, across the street from Mrs. Oh. Mrs. Oh had found this place for my mother when she had fallen into poor health while doing her church work.

Just as abruptly as she had arrived, Mrs. Oh bid my mother good night and departed, leaving my mother to figure out what was on her mind.

<hr>

The next day, as soon as it became light, Mrs. Oh was on her way back to work at the Nakwon Building. God's revelation about me completely distracted her, and the workday came and went without her realizing what she was doing. When she finished her work, she went directly to see a fortune teller. To this day, Koreans often consult fortune tellers for guidance about marriage, and that's what Mrs. Oh did. She described to the fortune teller the two persons about whom she was consulting, without mentioning their names. Right away the fortune teller's eyes widened.

"There may be a large gap between the ages of these two persons, but it doesn't matter. They are a match made in Heaven. I have rarely seen such a couple whose fortunes are so aligned." Mrs. Oh felt her heart was about to explode. She calmed herself and went directly to the church to meet our Teacher and tell him everything. As soon as she gained a private space with him, she blurted it out: "Hak Ja Han, the daughter of Hong Soon-ae, is the heavenly bride." She waited for a response, but Father Moon didn't say a word.

Father Moon had listened to many members suggest who might be his bride, and none of them had paid much attention to me. I did not worry about that. I kept my mind on Heaven. I knew then, and know now, that a person's destiny is not contingent upon external evidence. God is the judge, and it is predestined that the only begotten Son will marry the only begotten Daughter prepared by God, and that this is in the hands of God. I knew it was Father Moon's mission and duty to recognize the only begotten Daughter. I may have been young in years, but my heart toward God was unwavering. I waited for the time.

One day not long after that, hearing the sound of a magpie sitting on the branch of a tree outside the window of my dormitory room, I had a premonition that I was about to receive good news. I went to the window, opened it, looked up toward the sky, and I heard God's voice. Those were days in which God was giving me revelations not only in my dreams but also like waves coming down from the clear blue sky. I heard the words, "The time is near."

It was the voice of God. I had heard it often since I was a child. I had always felt that I would meet a very precious person one day. As if someone were pushing me, I closed my books and left the dormitory. Something was telling me that my mother was not feeling well.

As I was crossing the Han River on the bus, many thoughts flooded my mind. Does crossing the river mean that I am crossing over to a different world from the one in which I have been living? How many stories are embraced by the river, swirling beneath its confidently flowing surface? Is the heart of God, who is searching for us, like this river?

I got off the bus and started walking up the Noryangjin Hill toward my house. As I climbed the slope, an unusually bright winter sun drew me onward in spite of the wind from the Han River blowing against my forehead. When my mother saw me, she did not seem at all unwell; she looked rather excited and gratified to see me arrive. My confusion as to what drew me home dissipated right away, as she held the door open and quickly put on her coat. "I have received a message from the church," she told me. "We have to go there right now."

To me, it was a given that the news that awaited us at the church, whatever it might be, had been prepared by God. The scene of my first meeting with Father Moon, which was just after I had finished elementary school, passed before me like a panoramic vision. I recalled the dream I had had after that meeting. Father Moon appeared in it with a young and gentle face, and I clearly heard God's revelation: "Prepare, for the time is near."

Recalling this strict command from Heaven, walking toward the church, I surrendered myself completely, with a heart filled with trust in my Heavenly Father. "Until now I have lived according to Your will," I said to Heavenly Parent in prayer, "Whatever be Your will and providence, I am one with it already."

Because I knew God's sorrowful grief, a courage based on my faith in God rose up within me. I felt I could gratefully accept whatever might be asked of me. Then I heard God's voice again. I felt the same presence that I felt in the upper room of the Inside-the-Womb Church, when Grandmother Heo anointed me, and when the monk passing by our house had prophesied about me. Bathed in that presence, I heard the words,

"Mother of the universe. The time has come." It was like the sound of a gong reverberating in the air. The voice spoke again:

"I am the Alpha and the Omega, and I have been waiting for the Mother of the universe since the creation of the world." When I heard those words, I knew what my future was to be, and it settled in my heart and created an ocean of calm. In the Garden of Eden, Adam and Eve talked with God directly and heard God's words with their own ears. I had had such direct conversations with God from a young age.

I continued walking, going to church while holding my mother's hand, as I had done so many times before.

My mother and I arrived at the Cheongpa-dong Church. It was February 26, 1960, a day when winter was withdrawing and spring was signaling its advent. Father Moon met with my mother and me all day in order to come to a conclusion about the heavenly bride. He and I talked about many things over the course of nine hours. At his request, I drew him a picture. I spoke clearly as I answered his questions about my hopes and aspirations. Remembering how Jacob received God's blessing at Bethel, I happily, yet seriously, said to him, "I will bear many heavenly children."

What God told Jacob at Bethel came into my mind: "And thy seed shall be as the dust of the earth, and thou shalt spread abroad to the west, and to the east, and to the north, and to the south: and in thee and in thy seed shall all the families of the earth be blessed." I determined that I would embrace all the people of the earth and bring them new life as God's good children.

When Isaac went up Mount Moriah with Abraham to offer a sacrifice, he asked his father where the offering was. Abraham answered that God had prepared a sacrifice, and said nothing more. With that, Isaac, even at his young age, could understand the situation and realize that he was the sacrifice to be offered to Heaven. Just as Isaac obediently lay upon the altar, I knew that God had prepared me as the heavenly bride and that this was God's predestined providence. I had no questions or doubt in my heart; I had only the desire to keep going on the path. I accepted God's command in a state of complete selflessness.

On our way back home from this extraordinary day, my mother looked at me with warm eyes. "You are usually so meek and calm; I didn't know you could be so bold." I reflected on the fact that the Holy Wedding is not based on how bold a person is. In order to multiply God's lineage, the True Mother has to bear many good children, and therefore she would have to marry in her teens. Such a bride should be of a patriotic family, I realized as well, with a life of faith inherited over three generations.

Three years before that, a number of single women believers had put themselves forward as marriage candidates before Father Moon. Several around the age of 30, in particular, had high hopes, as Father Moon himself was nearing 40. Even in that circumstance, and having publicly announced the date of the Holy Wedding, Father Moon had maintained silence. He was waiting on Heaven to decide who would be his bride. He knew that God is the one to prepare the only begotten Daughter. Only God can confirm the bride for whom the marriage supper of the Lamb is conducted. God alone knows who is to become the Mother of the universe and the Mother of peace.

For the salvation of all of humankind and realization of a world of peace, I determined myself and declared before Father Moon that I would rise to the position of the True Parent. I accepted Father Moon as the only begotten Son for the accomplishment of our Heavenly Parent's will. It was God's call to me to become the heavenly bride and the Mother of the universe. I knew that my path would be unimaginably difficult. Yet I pledged I would live for God and absolutely fulfill my mission to save the world.

I pledged before God and Father Moon, "No matter how difficult the path may be, I will complete God's providence of restoration during my lifetime." And then I pledged one more time, "I will do whatever it takes to fulfill our Heavenly Parent's will." I have defined and lived my life with that commitment.

The course of human events is often unpredictable. Church members were so astonished when the news spread that Father Moon had chosen Hak Ja Han, that 17-year-old nursing student, to be his bride.

Some people thought it was a false rumor. Some were taken aback. Some rejoiced, others were jealous. I remembered Father Moon's words from four years before, "You will need to make sacrifices in the future," and I knew that each day was going to be a learning experience concerning what that meant.

When my maternal grandmother's ancestor Jo Han-jun showed sincere loyalty and devotion to his country, he received the revelation, "I will send to your lineage the princess of God." In return for my ancestor's devotion, his sacrifice with no desire for recognition, God chose our family to exemplify the tradition of loyalty and filial piety. My mother was born to my grandmother, who had deep piety, and I was born to my mother. I trace God's will to send to the world His only begotten Daughter, which has borne fruit through me, back to my ancestor Jo Han-jun.

To fulfill my mission as God's only begotten Daughter, I have a firm belief and unflinching will for the sake of every nation, every religion, every race. Going beyond all fallen world boundaries, I am called to reconcile nations and races with benevolence and love. I am called to be like the ocean that accepts and absorbs the water of all rivers, big and small alike. Embodying our God who is our Heavenly Mother as well as Heavenly Father, I am called to embrace all who are lost and have no one to receive them, with the heart of a parent.

I set these things in my flesh and blood, in my beating heart, and have not for one second forgotten the will that God entrusted to me. Sixty years have passed since our Holy Wedding, and my husband is now not with us physically. More than ever, no matter what my age or physical condition may be, my beating heart drives me forward on the path to become the Mother of the universe and the Mother of peace— one in mind, one in body, one in heart and one in harmony with the One who guides the providence.

Our Holy Wedding Ceremony

Jesus was born to humankind 2,000 years ago. God intended that Jesus find his bride and that they would stand in the position of Adam and Eve, who were lost at the very beginning of human history. Together, Jesus and his bride were to have grown to attain the position of True Parents, providing living examples of a true husband and wife, parents, and family. However, God's hope for Jesus and Israel was not realized. The Lord went a secondary course, dying for us on the cross. We cannot imagine how devastated he must have been! When Jesus returns, his priority is to find the bride, with whom he will create a true family, society, nation and world. Through the True Parents, the sorrows of heaven and earth can be alleviated, and the victorious foundation for God's ideal world can be laid.

In this providence, the prophesied marriage supper of the Lamb, the day of our Holy Wedding, was the turning point, the day when God won His victory and recovered His lost glory. Furthermore, this was a day of joy for humankind, as it inaugurated a new history in which all can live together not only with their True Father but also with their True Mother.

<hr />

At the age of 15, Sun Myung Moon received his mission from Jesus Christ on Mount Myodu. It was a mission that would bring him severe hardship. It led him to study in Japan and to teach God's word in North Korea after Korea's independence, where he would face life-threatening hardships and unspeakable suffering. Communist Party officials and police cruelly tortured him to the brink of death. Tossed out as a lifeless body, he revived and continued his mission, only to be arrested once again and sent to a forced labor camp near the city of Hungnam. It was only the arrival of UN troops that saved him from execution there.

With two of his followers, he headed south to begin his ministry again. Amid the clash of communist soldiers and UN troops, they were among the last to cross the frozen Imjin River into South Korea, and from there they walked hundreds of kilometers to the southern part of the peninsula. After planting his church in Busan he settled in Seoul. Yet his trials continued and once again he was imprisoned, this time by the South Korean government. This course of hardships, during which time he relentlessly focused on teaching many new members about God and the mission of the Messiah, was the course he had to pass through to meet the only begotten Daughter prepared by God, and to hold the marriage supper of the Lamb.

Members of the early Unification Church endured bitter ordeals together with Father Moon. As the year 1960 approached, they were filled with indescribable hope. Father Moon was turning 40, and he had prophesied that this would be the year of the Holy Wedding of God's first Son and Daughter, the only begotten Son and only begotten Daughter. And that promise was fulfilled. At the Cheongpa-dong church, at 4:00 in the morning on March 27, 1960, the first day of the third lunar month, when spring was in full bloom, Father Moon and I held our historic engagement ceremony.

We had invited 40 men and 40 women to witness the ceremony, but members wishing to see us had come in great numbers, and the small church was packed to overflowing. The engagement ceremony, held in two parts, was conducted in a holy atmosphere. It concluded with Father Moon's benediction, reporting the profound meaning of the ceremony to heaven and earth. The 6,000-year history of humankind, he prayed, was the anguished course necessary to receive the True Parents. That Jesus could not become the True Parent was the sorrow of all people, but the day of our engagement ceremony was the blessed day that finally relieved that sorrow.

April 11, 1960: The first part of the Holy Wedding, in western attire

April 11, 1960: The second part of the Holy Wedding,
in traditional Korean attire

Fifteen days after the engagement ceremony, at 10:00 a.m. on April 11, 1960, the 16th day of the third month by the lunar calendar, we conducted the Holy Wedding. Seven hundred or so members chosen from our churches across Korea gathered at Cheongpa-dong Church to attend this splendid event, long awaited by our Heavenly Parent. Because even more members flocked to attend the Holy Wedding than the engagement ceremony, the church was overflowing, and those who could not enter the building filled the alleyway beside it. The atmosphere was nonetheless solemn and reverent.

The small chapel of the church was decorated beautifully and meaningfully for the occasion. The walls and floor were covered with white cloth, and a platform was set up to the left of the door. Dressed in a long, white skirt and top, with a long veil covering my head, I walked down the stairs from the second floor, arm in arm with the bridegroom, as members sang a holy song, "Song of the Banquet." All in attendance warmly welcomed us, and the Holy Wedding ceremony thus commenced. The first ceremony of the Holy Wedding was held in Western-style clothing, and the second ceremony was held in traditional Korean-style clothing, complete with robes and headdresses.

The significance and value of this joyful occasion should have been praised, glorified and honored by all nations and peoples. Yet it was marred by a distressing incident. The day before the ceremony, the Ministry of Home Affairs, responding to a Christian group's accusations, arrested and interrogated Father Moon. He was able to return to his quarters in the church only after being subjected to humiliating questions until 11:00 p.m. Yet under the grace of God and the Holy Spirit, Father Moon and I, and the entire congregation, put aside this painful experience as if it had never happened and conducted the marriage supper of the Lamb with serene hearts.

God's predestined will was that His only begotten Son and Daughter would become one flesh through the marriage supper of the Lamb and that, through them, the dwelling place of God would be with men and women. True men and women are the rightful rulers of creation, the entire universe, heaven and earth. The Holy Wedding finally realized this ideal, which Adam and Eve had failed to achieve. Thus, these ceremonies marked my formal enthronement as the Mother of the universe and Mother of peace.

After the ceremony, Father Moon and I, as husband and wife, ate at the same table for the first time. It goes without saying that newlyweds expect to go on a honeymoon and dream of their cozy life together, but it was not so with us. Our thoughts were fixed only upon God and the church. Nonetheless, I treasured every glance we shared and felt a love infinitely profound, a holy love that we wished to bequeath to all humankind.

We then changed into bright Korean traditional wedding outfits, and my husband and I sang and danced to return glory to God, enjoying a merry time together with the members. When the members called for the bride to sing, I sang a song called "When the Spring Comes."

When the spring comes,
azaleas bloom in the mountains
and meadows.
Where the azaleas bloom,
so does my heart.

Spring signifies freshness and newness. I love spring, as it is the season of hope. Spring brings with it the expectation that, as we leave the cold winter behind, our days will be vibrant with life. It awakens our dreams.

As I sang, I was thinking that the history of the Unification Church should begin anew with this coming of spring. The appearance of the family of the True Parents on earth that day flung open a new door in the history of God's dispensation. The day of the Holy Wedding

Ceremony, conducted after we had lived through perilous years, was the day of God's greatest delight.

In the New Testament's Book of Revelation, it is written that the marriage supper of the Lamb will take place when the Lord comes again at the end of times. That prophecy was fulfilled by the Holy Wedding, by which the only begotten Son and only begotten Daughter, lost at the beginning of human history, were brought together as bridegroom and bride and anointed as the True Parents. As we were joined as husband and wife, I made a firm resolution in front of God:

> *During my lifetime, my beloved husband and I will bring to a conclusion the history of the providence of restoration through indemnity, during which God has laboriously toiled. I know that what hurts God's heart more than anything else are the religious conflicts that take place in His name. Without fail, we will end them.*

A small boat on heavy seas

In the side streets and workplaces of South Korea, people were whispering out of worry, anxious over the fate of their nation. "Doesn't it feel like something is about to happen?" one would say, to which his friend would respond, "I feel the same way. We live in troubled times. If only there were someone who could set this world right."

I was sure such worries would soon dissipate. The year of our Holy Wedding Ceremony, 1960, was a turning point, for great changes were taking place both at home and abroad. In South Korea, the people's longing for democracy burst forth, and they ousted the authoritarian Liberal Party. Overseas, John F. Kennedy was elected president of the United States, and we felt the way opening toward a new era.

But history is never that simple. The rifts of the Cold War grew deeper, and conflict worsened between the communist realm and the

Free World. A flame of popular outcry for democracy flared up in the Soviet Bloc nations of Eastern Europe, but the state crushed its advocates, and the fire grew dim again. It seemed that the time for peace was not yet at hand. People continued praying for a true leader to appear.

Great changes also were taking place for the Unification Church. Virtually the whole of Korea had stood in opposition to our church, with Christianity issuing the most scathing criticisms. But now, on the foundation of embracing a young woman leader, the True Mother, we began ecumenical dialogues and transitioned from Christian denomination to global religious movement. Our members prayed that we could be a beacon, shining forth a new hope of salvation. In particular, women, who so long have been oppressed, perceived that a true women's movement was being set in motion.

Three days after the Holy Wedding Ceremony, my husband and I visited Ju-an Farm in Incheon, not far from the border with North Korea, with several members. We planted grapevines and gingko and zelkova trees. As I planted a young sapling, I offered a prayer: "May you grow well and become a big, strong tree that will bear the fruit of hope for the people of the world." I was not praying only for that particular tree, but for success in the mission given to my husband and me. As a tree provides people with fruit as well as shade, so should we and all people of faith.

From the outset, high waves and strong winds battered the small boat of our newly married life. Fortunately, I was prepared for that. It is said that newlyweds know nothing but happiness, but that was not our main purpose. My husband and I were not in a position to focus very much on our personal contentment.

Our first living space was a small, sparsely decorated room at the back of Cheongpa-dong Church. On one side, it connected to the chapel, and on the other to the tiniest of courtyards. Our kitchen was small and old fashioned, with a rough cement floor. I cooked for my husband in that kitchen, which was always smoke-filled from coal briquettes. From the first day I prepared his meal, I was quite at home in that kitchen, which was similar to many my little family had occupied. I was quite deft with the cutting knife, even though my hands were cold. When people saw me preparing the various dishes without much trouble, they were surprised. Until a few weeks prior they had thought of me as only a teenage nursing student.

The church was always crowded with members, and my husband and I seldom spent time by ourselves. In such a public setting, Father Moon and I would sit across from each other and talk about our plans for the world. Members would show concern and say to us, "Please, you really should eat now." We would look at the clock and often see it was 2:00 or 3:00 in the afternoon, and we hadn't given a thought to lunch. I focused on the many tasks that would be entrusted to me in the future. I realized that not only Korea but also the rest of the world was expecting me to extend my helping hand.

Beginning with our first daughter, Ye-jin, I gave birth to children one after another. The church headquarters that served also as our home was a small and poorly insulated Japanese-style house, and I suffered postpartum ailments as a result of delivering babies there. I was young but, as women have done from time immemorial, I quietly endured the pain of childbirth. Within my heart, Heavenly Parent was present at every moment. No matter how difficult the situation and surroundings, I was filled with joy. Never for a moment did I lack the helping hand of God, working His miracles in the background.

Within a few years, our small quarters were filled to bursting with our many children. Perhaps that is why they grew up loving and caring for one another. I considered them to be miniature expressions of God. I would kiss their cheeks and chat affectionately with them, and I prayed for them ceaselessly. I knew that God comes to dwell in the home where parents and children are harmonious.

Mother Moon as a young wife, standing in front of her home,
the Headquarters Church in Cheongpa-dong, Seoul (1960s)

Even before our wedding, with God's providence at the forefront of my mind, I resolved to have 13 children. Today people look at you askance if you have many children, but I saw that God wanted 12, to signify the perfection of east, west, north, and south. When you add one, corresponding to the central position, you get 13, which opens the way for the continued development of the providence to its ultimate conclusion.

God's dispensation for the salvation of humankind is not something that happens in one generation. To carry it out, God has sought out and established central people throughout history. Two thousand years ago, how did God send Jesus, His only begotten Son without original sin, to this earth through the people of Israel? The Bible records that God had to restore a pure lineage in several stages. There are unresolved issues connected to this lineage that I must set straight during my lifetime, and so I set to recover and rightly establish the lineage of goodness centered on Heaven. In order to give rebirth and resurrection to this complicated lineage and thus transform it into the true lineage whose center is God, I willingly took the risks that come with pregnancy and childbirth, including managing the birthing pains that put a woman's life in God's hands.

I gave birth to 14 children over a period of 20 years. The first four were born in our small private quarters at Cheongpa-dong. It was not until my fifth child that I was able to go to a hospital. Though it taxed my body, I gave birth to children year after year. Our second daughter died a few days after her birth. Our final four were delivered by Cesarean section. It is rare for a woman to go through a C-section more than once. When I said that I would undergo it for the third time, my doctor hesitated, saying it was dangerous, especially for a woman of my age. The doctor did not understand how I could insist so calmly on having another C-section, and he wanted to explain the issues to my husband. I assured him that my husband would agree with me, and I went through it for a third and then a fourth time, thus fulfilling the promise I had made to God.

My husband, being a charismatic spiritual leader, sometimes received unwanted attention from women. There was once a woman who appeared in front of him claiming to be Eve, and another who hid under his bed. As God's true son, and as a true husband and father, he never wavered. He, and I as well, felt only sympathy for such women.

I encountered similar advances. Once, while my husband was away on a world tour, a strange person shouted loudly, "I am Adam," jumped in front of me and tried to assault me. At the time I was seven months pregnant, and I was so shocked that I almost miscarried. I encountered the same forms of hardship that Father Moon did. At times my reality turned into a whirlpool of tests and ordeals, and in my heart I would feel like a little boat floating on rough seas.

Knowing well my mission, I overcame those hardships through prayer. My silent perseverance and constant prayer actually deepened the members' devotional life. I always strove to maintain a generous heart, and my unwavering faith as a young person encouraged those around me. The greater my absolute obedience to and reverence for God, the more hope everyone felt. Sometimes my elders would hold my hand and whisper into my ear, "Thank you so much for the grace you have shown us through your sacrificial love."

Victory through perseverance

"Oh, no, I've lost another pair of shoes." Even before the member would finish his sentence, those around him would know what had happened. Poverty sometimes makes people do bad things. At the end of Sunday services, we often would find that a pair or two of shoes were missing from the shoe rack. So, whenever I had a little extra money, I would buy new shoes for members who had lost them. I also prayed that the person who had taken the shoes would set his or her life straight.

Between 200 and 300 people would attend our services and other events, and there was never enough rice to serve them all. So we made porridge by boiling barley in a large iron pot. As the event progressed inside the church, outside we would make a wood fire and cook the barley porridge. Members would sit down in little clusters and share bowls of the porridge, and they were more grateful for this than anything else. "All of this is a gift from God," they would say.

When I was pregnant I craved tangerines, but we could not afford them; they were so expensive. One member learned about this, however, and bought some tangerines for me. I ate six or seven of them on the spot. I was so grateful, I cried.

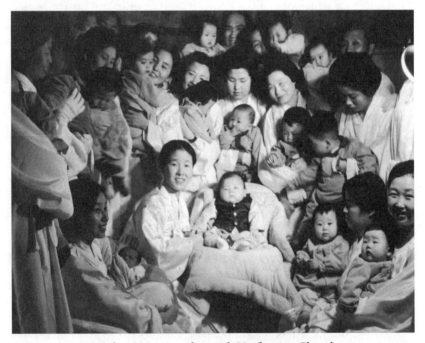

Mother Moon together with Unification Church
wives and their young children

When a church holy day would approach, I felt more anxious than excited or happy. I would have to start making preparations two weeks in advance to organize the deliveries of the offering table towers of fruit and delicacies, banners, flowers and candles, hoping that there would be enough for each member to have an apple or a candy. Once we had made this offering to God, I would feel immense satisfaction.

From my birth until my marriage, my path had not been easy, and after marrying, personal challenges impacted not just me but also our movement. So I never deviated from the path of faith, obedience and love for God. Just as Satan tested Jesus and Father Moon, he tested me. I persevered through those ordeals with ever-deepening devotion because it was at such times that I felt most keenly the grace of God. In the midst of pain, God came very close to me and guided me with pillars of cloud and fire.

My husband and I always conversed intensely on various matters. We could do so out of our infinite trust in each other. We went through so much together that we could understand each other with only a look. The life of Father Moon and the path I have walked bear an uncanny resemblance. Most people assumed that I was so happy and that I wanted for nothing. "You received the seal from God as His only begotten Daughter," they would think, "and you were born as a perfected being. Therefore, you attained your position with no effort." Many people were like this. They believed that as the Mother of the universe I blissfully had met Father Moon, formed a happy family and enjoyed life. That describes my life from one perspective, but I have scaled mountains as treacherous and impassable as any in this world. I was able to surmount them all with my husband's love, which was more than any wife has ever received.

Although I had 14 children, I never once thought that I had too many. Nonetheless, my children had to go through difficult experiences. When they went out to play, local people would glare at them. "Your father is Sun Myung Moon, isn't he?" adults would shout at an innocent five-year-old. "Do you know what your father does? The Unification Church is creating such a disturbance in the world!" While in Korea they were criticized for being the sons and daughters of Sun Myung Moon, and when we moved to the United States, they faced discrimination for being Asian. It pained me to see my children suffer, but I did not lament or blame others. I held them in my arms and set an example for them by offering prayers of gratitude.

My husband and I cared for our children with love and devotion, but because we had so much work to do for the church and the providence, we were unable to spend much time with them. One day, when my husband was on his world tour, Hyo-jin, barely three years old, sat on the bedroom floor and began to draw. Normally he liked to draw cars or bikes, but that day he clumsily drew a face on the white paper. Even though I knew that it was his father, I asked him, "Hyo-jin, who is that?"

Hyo-jin did not answer me, but drew a face on another piece of paper. Though it looked different from the first one, it was still without a doubt his father's face. Hyo-jin was usually very active, but on that day he sat quietly and continued to draw. He did not grow tired of drawing his father's face, even after spending the whole day at it. And he did not stop drawing it the next day or the day after. It was only when his father returned that he stopped drawing. I can still remember quite vividly how brightly he smiled at his father as he was embraced by him. It was as if he had been given the world.

Seven sons and seven daughters

True Father and I offered three generations as a True Family to God, culminating when we with all of our children, their spouses and our adult grandchildren, taught God's word and ministered the Blessing in 180 nations, in what we call the Jubilee Years, 2006-07. I risked my life to bring our children into the world, and now they have their own missions and responsibilities that Heaven wishes them to fulfill, and that I also hope they can accomplish. Although, as their parent, I may be unable to help them enough, I pray for them every day.

If I had experienced only joyful things, I never would have been able to look into people's deepest, innermost hearts. I never would have known the joys of the kingdom of heaven. I have passed through the bottom of hell and experienced every kind of bitterness in life. God wanted me to train myself. What I needed was untiring faith, strong will and perseverance. That is how I reached this point today.

No matter who you are, you will not experience only sweetness and joy on the path to the kingdom of heaven. Going through spiritual struggle is, in fact, a most precious blessing. Through it you can feel the grace of God. Only when you pass those tests can you be born anew as a true human being. The fruit of perseverance will grow and ripen within you, and one day will become the source of your deepest pride.

I grew up in a time of global turbulence, from which my homeland of Korea was not exempt. As our people endured Imperial Japan's colonial rule and the Korean War, a wild rush of confused ideas and values wreaked havoc on our traditions. The people of the world, even the Christian nations, struggled as their societies descended into chaos. Where were we to turn?

When there was no institution to depend on and no shelter to protect my heart, I remembered one thing: "God is my Father." I grew up holding the belief that I would realize the dream and hope of God. Convinced that within my lifetime I would complete the long, sorrowful providential journey to restore God's original ideal for His children, I retained my faith, no matter what happened.

It was with this heart that I decided to receive the Blessing in marriage with Sun Myung Moon and, with him, work to prevent religious conflicts and factions from continuing beyond my generation. Conflicts caused by religious divisions must now stop. I am also determined to resolve racial divisions and the conflicts that have arisen from them.

In 1982 I accomplished one of my promises to Heaven. In the two decades after our Holy Wedding, I bore 14 children, seven sons and seven daughters. When they were just days old, my husband and I offered each child to God and the world. Each has supported us heroically in their own way and each is now pioneering their own course. They have given us more than 40 grandchildren.

Now I am always on the move, traveling the five seas and six continents, working to establish a world without war and conflict, and to release God from His sorrow.

CHAPTER 4

GOD'S LIGHT SHINES UPON A PATH OF THORNS

Rain and cold wind give way to peace

"Already 60 years have passed," said one of my oldest friends from the early days of the church.

"There is a saying that time is like an arrow," I replied, "and it is so true. The path of the last 60 years has flown straight to the target, filled with difficulties and obstacles together with joy and success."

It was April 2014, and she and I were participating in a ceremony commemorating the 60th anniversary of the founding of the Unification Church. I reflected on the church's original name, which is the Holy Spirit Association for the Unification of World Christianity, and its establishment in a tiny rented house in Bukhak-dong, in the

Seongdong district of Seoul on May 1, 1954. Thinking back on days gone by, our early members who had gathered expressed deep gratitude to each other, recalling the decades of hardships we endured, as brothers and sisters in one family.

Despite the dire poverty in which the Unification Church began, the Holy Wedding in 1960 launched a new era. We have grown from a handful of members into a global movement, and we see that the Divine Principle teachings have spread to the ends of the earth. It truly is a miracle.

How did God bring this to pass? The key is the salvation of marriage, the oneness of husband and wife made in the image of God. As God called Father Moon to begin his historical mission as a teenager, God also called Hak Ja Han, a young lady of 17. Nobody could fathom His choosing someone so young. I sensed that I would one day represent all women—God's daughters, the world's mothers. Jesus revealed the heavenly bride as the Holy City coming down from heaven, and I accepted this call with firm resolve and I grew from the position of a heavenly bride to Mother of the universe. By God's hand, this Mother, who prays and longs for God's Blessing for all 7.7 billion people on earth, can now advance peace widely.

<hr />

As we entered the summer of 1960, our members undertook 40 days of evangelism throughout the country. We called it the New Mind, New Village, New Love Movement. In all the districts of the entire country, a flame of faith rose up strongly. Some 600 missionaries and local members visited 413 villages and put the word of God into practice in substantial ways. During those 40 days, they cleaned neighborhood pathways, taught the Korean alphabet in village halls by the light of kerosene lamps, assisted farmers and shopkeepers and shared the Principle. The members survived on a daily bowl of powdered mixed grains and overcame fatigue and fierce rejection from people, some of whom called them heretics. They often were lonely, like poplar trees standing alone at the center of a field.

By the hand of God, the greater the people's condemnation, the faster our good results appeared. Soon, high school students and other youth joined the witnessing program, providing even more energy for the rebirth of life and prosperity in local villages. Even a first-year middle school girl participated—such was the enthusiasm of those days in Korea. As we repeated those seasons of enlightenment, education and service, the Holy Spirit came down. Throughout the cities and towns, families offered their large living rooms to serve as night schools. The alphabet was taught to young people who could not attend school—and to women. From the hidden paths of rural villages, a wave of hope washed through South Korean society, a positive influence for needed social progress.

Then, starting in the mid-1960s, the government also began sponsoring rural enlightenment and literacy programs throughout Korea—the Sae-ma-eul (New Village) Movement. Its officials acted as though we did not exist, but we carried on. In the town of Chungju, members used their bare hands to build classrooms with mud walls for dozens of shoeshine boys. In later days, those actions gathered the momentum for establishing what is now the Sunhak Educational Foundation.

On a nationwide scale, our work sparked young leaders in farming areas to establish agricultural schools that spurred a wave of modernization. Some of these schools were on the cutting edge of a movement to transform our society, combining technical and spiritual advancement. As one might expect, the government's New Village Movement, through its administrative power, appropriated all of this, and since the Unification Church was considered heretical, we were pushed to the side. From both the left and the right, voices continued to condemn us.

As one might imagine, our church leaders and missionaries experienced many difficult days. With no financial support, they felt fortunate to have even one meal a day; three full meals a day was unheard of. Sometimes, out of concern for the missionaries, middle school students secretly left the lunch boxes that their mothers had prepared for them in front of our missionaries' doors. When the missionaries thought of the students sacrificing their lunches, and were faced with the idea of eating a lunch box that a student had given them, they were inexpressibly miserable. However, their responsibility was to convey the new understanding of truth, and they resolved to honor the sacrifices that had been made to help them.

My husband and I did not just send missionaries to their areas; we visited our local churches throughout the country several times a year. We would bring with us food, clothing and supplies we had gathered. There was never enough, as there were many other service projects and activities to support, but we brought all that we could. When we walked into view, hand in hand, the missionaries in the pioneering areas would greet us in tears. We would uplift and encourage our members and talk together, without realizing we had stayed up all night.

Our members who worked on American military bases would sometimes bring chocolate, bananas or cookies to church. I would put these gifts in a wardrobe or on a shelf and would wrap them and give them to the missionaries when we went out. One missionary sister burst into tears when she received the wrapped bundle. A few months later, she returned for a visit, held my hand tightly and said, "I brought that package to my pioneering area and ate it together with our members. Your encouragement gave us power when we conveyed the words of the Principle." Such words always gave me great joy.

The pioneer centers were hardly what one would call churches. They usually consisted of a single room, and our missionaries often were too poor even to put up a sign. Anyone who entered would immediately wonder if it was really a church. On the one hand the impoverished appearance saddened my heart, but on the other hand, I felt proud of our members and comforted them. "Our church's downtrodden circumstances may seem miserable to ordinary people," I would say softly, "but in the future, we will hoist a flag of victory and receive the love of people the world over."

That is why wherever we went, we were not ashamed. No matter who we met, we were confident. We tried to register our church with the government, and we were rejected several times, as a torrent of opposition flowed from established churches, who sent petitions of protest about us to government officials. Finally, in May 1963 the Korean government registered our organization legally as the Holy Spirit Association for the Unification of World Christianity.

As the 1970s approached, it still was a turbulent time for the world. North and South Korean discord threatened to flare up into another war, and the international situation was volatile. Communism was expanding across the globe on many fronts. Knowing the inhumane brutality of communist governments from our personal experience, my husband and I launched a very successful educational initiative called "Victory Over Communism" (VOC). Ours was the only voice in the world to clearly explain the fallacies of its materialistic and atheistic theory while offering a God-centered counterproposal. VOC strengthened the resolve and understanding of South Koreans and it had a huge impact soon after in Japan, turning back its far left-wing factions through peaceful means.

At that critical moment, my husband and I once again urged our members, especially the women, to take action. Our Heavenly Parent knows the power of women. Our movement did not truly begin until our couple's Holy Wedding, because we are a family movement and it takes a husband and wife to create a family. My husband is the world's foremost champion of women as the moral leaders of the family and society.

With this conviction, we called Korean blessed wives to sacrifice their family life for a time and as missionaries go to the streets, to the halls of government, to the churches and temples and from house to house, to provide education, empower the people and multiply the patriotic spirit. The wives responded. Each entrusted their young children and sometimes ill, elderly parents to their husband's care and set out.

The mother is the center of the family, and when she is not home, even for a day or two, the family suffers. Our wives and mothers went out, not for a day or two, but for three years. For every father who had to cradle and feed a child begging for his mother's milk, a mother on mission was squeezing milk out of her swollen breasts and weeping. It was almost like Jesus' three years of public ministry, or my husband's three years in a North Korean labor camp. Wives who were pregnant when going out would return to give birth, and after 100 days, go back to their mission field. After the three years, when the mothers returned, their youngest children didn't recognize them and even resisted them. Such is the incredible sacrifice of heart offered to our Heavenly Parent for the restoration of the world.

When a woman has a baby, she experiences the pain of childbirth. Despite this, the midwife's job is to encourage her to push more. Like midwives giving birth to a new world, my husband and I pushed our Unification family members. Historically, every time danger appeared, the Korean people, farmers and loyal patriots defended their homes and their nation. With that spirit, our members rose and defended their homes and nation against communism. My husband counseled these courageous women, "The people do not understand unification now, but if the 30 million people of Korea join together with the Unification Church, this nation and these people will not perish."

The blessed wives buried their pain in their hearts, for they knew that their mission was for the sake of the nation. In hindsight, their work has borne great fruit and can only be considered the most praiseworthy act of patriotism. Thus far, it has been hidden from view in our nation's history but one day it will be revealed.

As the Unification Church spread to other countries, blessed wives around the world followed the example of the early Korean wives and their families. Thus, this brilliant chapter has been written in the history not just of Korea but of all nations. All blessed wives stand on this foundation and are carrying on this tradition. It is a story of women sacrificing to preserve the nation and world. One of its fruits appeared 20 years later, in our meeting with Mikhail Gorbachev, then president of the Soviet Union. This opened the door to teach the young people of the former Soviet Union our God-centered worldview, the democratic spirit and ethical values, which contributed to the reconciliation of East and West and the downfall of communism. Another fruit was our trip to North Korea in 1991, when we met North Korean leader Kim Il Sung. Our harrowing but thoroughly triumphant visit opened the way for dialogue between North and South Korea and prepared a foothold for our work there.

"My last moment on earth is approaching"

The foundation for our breakthroughs in the Kremlin and North Korea also includes the selfless work of European members. One day in the early 1980s, we received a one-page letter from one of them. It concluded with heartrending words: "My last moment on earth is approaching. This is the last greeting I give you here on earth. I will meet you in the spirit world. Please live a long and healthy life."

This young man was behind the Iron Curtain in a communist prison, and this was his final letter, written just before his execution. The instant I read it, my body stiffened, as if my blood had turned cold and blue. My tears froze. I couldn't say anything. I felt like the fabled woman Mang Bu-seok, who died and turned to stone. I just stood there.

My husband and I had to quietly, secretly, hold such beloved people in our hearts. As the True Parents of all people, our path, with theirs, was perilous and desperate. Unable to talk with anyone about such things, we could only weep inside and proceed with broken hearts.

~~~

For many years in Korea, whenever our members gathered, sooner or later, a lively discussion would take place about our movement's strategy. "We must turn our eyes to the wider world now," someone would say. Another would retort, "Isn't it too early? We don't even have a church building here in Korea!" And a third would join the fray: "Okay, so we build an attractive building, but if it's only for Korea, will God like it?"

Of course, my husband and I were well aware of the issues and knew that both evangelizing internationally and building a strong church in Korea were important. But we steadfastly chose "the world" over "Korea," and as a result, the appearance of our first churches remained shabby. Up until the 1980s, we could not present to the nation even a single decent church building. Our members might have wished to have a place where they could gather with guests and comfortably hold services, but it was not to be. Small A-frame structures with green roofs were all we had.

In the public square, as well, people ridiculed us, asking why we and our members kept talking about restoring the world when we didn't even have a decent church building. From a humanistic perspective, they had a point, but they did not know the Principle. Our church was created for a higher purpose, and we put working for humanity and the world first. The salvation of the world took precedence over our task in Korea.

~~~

In 1958 our first missionary crossed the sea to Japan, and the next year, a few trusted members pioneered missions in the United States. Given the impoverished state of our Korean church, it was almost unthinkable to start foreign missions in Japan and the United States. But our purpose went beyond being solely a Korean group. To bolster these budding foreign missions, Father Moon undertook a 10-month world tour in 1965. The course included a period where he drove with a few followers to every state in the continental United States, to consecrate prayer sites that we call holy grounds in each. He met our missionaries and their young members in the United States, Europe and other countries, and met prominent public figures, including former US President Dwight Eisenhower.

On this momentum, the flow of Unification missionaries into Europe, the Middle East and South America began to rise. Supporting the organization and coordination of all these missions made conditions arduous, both in the mission field and in Korea, and sometimes Korean members would shake their heads and say, "Things are getting worse."

But in the 1970s, the Divine Principle of the Unification Church spread through the world. Many tens of thousands of young people heard the lectures and left their old lives to dedicate themselves to God's providence. It wasn't long before the countries of the world, as though with one accord, gathered their energy to oppose us. But our movement was like a roly-poly toy—the persecution hit us, and we bounced back; it hit us again, and we bounced back again—even stronger.

In 1975 we held mission conferences in Japan and in America, from which we selected young missionaries and dispatched them to some 95 new nations in addition to the more than 30 already with active missions. There were many reasons to delay or slow down our evangelical outreach, but we could feel God's urgency and pressed forward. I recall my husband's words, shared late one evening: "There will always be reasons that we cannot send them. But if we do not send them now, we will never send them. There will never be a moment without difficulties. Let us make a firm decision when things seem the most difficult."

May 2017: At a reunion for the 1975 international missionaries, participants review a display of their original reports and letters, now carefully archived at the East Garden Museum in Irvington, New York.

That 1975 cohort of faithful men and women represented not one nation, but three: Japan, the United States, and Germany or Austria, countries that were enemies during the Second World War. We sent them in groups of three, one Japanese, one American and one German or Austrian. Their unity with each other was the foundation for outreach and service that bore great fruit over the decades.

Unlike many Christian missionaries sent out from the United States and Europe, our international missionaries did not receive any financial support from the sending church. They left with enough money to survive for a few days, a suitcase of clothes and a Divine Principle book. Instead of living in nice buildings or homes, they stayed in tiny rooms or huts. They had to improvise mission plans and work together despite having different cultural backgrounds and speaking different languages. Faced with so many unknowns, those who were leaving and those who were sending both had to maintain a brave face, knowing each missionary was stepping into an unpredictable future.

Our missionaries committed to a five-year tenure, but more than a few who went to Africa and the Middle East remained for 20 years and more. Once or twice a year, if they could, they would attend a world mission conference at our East Garden facility in New York.

One young missionary arriving at one such conference burst into tears upon seeing my husband and me. It was her first time meeting us. Hearts that wanted to weep in joy and sadness … how could there be anything but that? The person who wanted to weep the most was me, but I knew if I did so, the happy occasion would turn into an ocean of tears. Therefore, with the heart of a strong mother, I embraced that young woman instead.

The next day, I took all the missionaries out and bought them blouses and scarves or dress shirts and neckties. "This looks good on you," I would say to each of them, adding, "You have worked very hard."

But together with my sincere consolation, I would ask them to be strong and press harder: "If you sacrifice a little more on the way of the will, a peaceful world will come about in our time."

Near the close of these conferences, the missionaries would pledge their new resolve in front of God's will and depart again to the front line of His dispensation. My heart of loving admiration for our leaders and tribal messiahs who have left their homeland for the sake of humanity remains unchanged to this day.

Whenever we sent missionaries to unfamiliar lands, my husband and I held onto Heaven and prayed earnestly for each one of them. In the 1970s and 1980s, the Unification Movement faced intense opposition the world over. An unknown party even sent a bomb threat to our church's Belvedere Training Center in Tarrytown, New York. But the opposition was particularly intense in communist bloc countries due to our public speeches, rallies and educational programs to defeat Marxism-Leninism. We especially prayed for our missionaries who went into communist countries, as we knew there was the possibility of martyrdom. To our sorrow, that concern became a reality.

In these "Iron Curtain" countries, surveillance, deportation, shadowing and terror were our missionaries' everyday experiences. In 1973 in Czechoslovakia, the police arrested most of the core members. Almost 30 young people received prison sentences of up to nearly five years; others were released but endured ongoing repression. In 1976 in France, unidentified assailants bombed our Villa Aublet Church in Paris, injuring two members. Our French members marched from the Eiffel Tower to the Trocadéro calling for religious liberty and winning the sympathy of many. Finally, when it was revealed that communists were involved in the bombing, prominent leaders, including US congressional members, publicly condemned the attack on religion.

Even worse tragedies occurred. In the flower of her youth, at the age of 24, Marie Živná, one of the most faithful members in Czechoslovakia, died in a cold Bratislava jail cell. In December 1980, in Tanzania, Japanese missionary Masaki Sasamoto was shot and killed, also giving his life as a martyr. Numerous missionaries in the United States and other countries lost their lives while on fund-raising drives or in the course of outreach activities.

Despite such tragedies, the missionaries continued their work. In the 1980s, European missionaries working strategically behind the Iron Curtain called their project, "Mission Butterfly." The Butterfly missionaries cautiously witnessed despite the constant danger of being tracked by the secret police and arrested, forced to leave the country, or worse.

In 1987, my husband and I quietly gathered the Butterfly missionaries at our East Garden residence. We listened to their moving stories late into the night. There was no stopping the flow of tears. The missionaries shared, from deep within their hearts, stories that they had been unable to tell even their parents or brothers and sisters. Hearing their stories, we felt deeply concerned about their harsh circumstances.

Because these missionaries were viewed as enemies of the state, staying in their mission country was filled with risks, but this only intensified their prayers and faith in God. As one missionary said to us, "I don't know when or where I will run into some kind of danger. I only know that my life is being directly supervised through God's revelation. If there is a dangerous situation, God appears in my dream and guides me along the path I should go."

As they departed to their posts, putting our short meeting behind, I hugged them one by one and sent them off, waving until they were out of sight. Thinking that these young, pure-hearted missionaries were acting out of their deepest passion for God and True Parents, bound for lands more brutal than battlefields, without as much as a promise as to when we would meet again, my heart ached and my eyes blurred with tears.

That our missionaries were persecuted for nothing other than faith in the True Parents was truly a sorrowful reality of history, and their determination to advance was truly a glory of history. Chosen members went to every corner of the globe. Despite suffering and danger, they leapt into many kinds of work: organizing service projects, establishing schools, providing vocational training, cultivating the wilderness, building factories, houses and communities—and raising the necessary funds by their own wits and Heaven's assistance.

Each time I saw missionaries off to cross unfamiliar seas and continents, the limitation of what I could give them pained me. I encouraged them by saying that when our dreams are realized, God will give us all the greatest of blessings. Seeing how those words strengthened their resolve, I realized that spiritual encouragement was stronger support than any physical provisions.

In the early stages of the movement, our members were the most pitiful of people: chased and cornered, thrown out of their houses on snowy nights, praying in tears against the outer walls of their own home. Deported from unfamiliar lands, jailed, shot at and even killed while out fundraising, they had to find their way in the desert with nothing but starlight in the night sky to guide them; these faithful souls pushed their way through dark forests alone to share God's word. Holding our sorrows deep inside, we kept our faith and disseminated our beliefs. Today the Family Federation for World Peace and Unification serves in more than 190 nations, and this activism for peace and true family life grew from the seeds of our missionaries' sacrificial love.

A speaking tour stained with tears

"Mom, you're packing your suitcase again?" I didn't answer my third daughter, Un-jin, right away. My eldest daughter, Ye-jin, who was beside me and had been silently helping me pack, asked, "Mother, where are you going this time?"

That is the first thing my children would ask when they saw me take out a suitcase and start packing. Children wish for their mother to always be near them, playing with them, embracing them. However, bound by church activities, meeting with people and taking frequent trips, I was away from my children more than I was with them. Taking out my suitcase to pack my things signaled to my children that I was at the beginning of another mission far from home.

Although traveling can be enjoyable, when it is a mission, challenges set in from the moment you leave. Even if you stay in a palace, your heart is not at ease, as it is not your home. Furthermore, if you are entrusted with a public mission, each step you take is laden with heavy responsibility.

For a decade after the Holy Wedding in 1960, I was rarely at home, so I was rarely comfortable. I went around the entire country, one day visiting a small village near the demarcation line with North Korea, another day journeying to a remote island village, taking part in events and sharing time with members. My heart was not able to relax for even a single day.

In 1969, crossing the ocean to Japan marked the beginning of my life of international tours. I had a demanding schedule, and as I arrived in each new city, I treated each new land as my own and the people in each country as my brothers and sisters. Nonetheless, I would find time to buy postcards, and at the end of the day, though it was often past midnight, I would write letters to my children, who were wishing I were at home. Here is one of them.

Dear Hyo-jin,

I miss you and want to see you. My son, whom I always call to and think of and run to and hug, my good, cute, precious, beloved son, whom I never want to let go of, I miss you.

So, Hyo-jin, though we are separated for a while, you are one of Heaven's happy sons.

Our filial son, Hyo-jin! Our goodhearted and wise Hyo-jin, I love you. I know you will become a filial son of heaven, a filial son of earth and a filial son of the universe; you will become a good example of a filial child.

Both Appa and Omma feel so sad that we are too busy following the will and have such little time to spend with you. Yet we feel so proud and secure because of you. Hyo-jin, you are different from other children. Even though you run around with your friends, you must remember your origin is God, and not damage His dignity.

Appa and Omma are always proud of you. When we see you in the near future, can you surprise your Appa and Omma a lot? Appa and Omma have a great dream for you. Omma is waiting and always praying for that.

Stay healthy. Goodbye.

The fact that I could not spend much quality time with my children due to my various public responsibilities always weighed on my mind. Despite this, my children were very mature for their age and grew up well. Once my eldest son Hyo-jin was interviewed by a newspaper reporter.

"What do you respect most about your mother?"

Hyo-jin answered without hesitation.

"I admire my mother's love and perseverance in embracing my father and making him happy. All mothers in the world are great, but my mother especially absolutely trusts and encourages us. I'm always deeply moved by how she does that. It's really amazing that she gave birth to 14 children even though she's always so busy with global affairs."

December 24, 1972: A card Mother Moon sent to eldest son Hyo-jin, seen here practicing violin

Even on the hottest of summer days, I will not get into a cold swimming pool. It's because, as I mentioned, I gave birth to many children, four of them through cesarean sections. When I was giving birth to our sixth son, Young-jin, I was in danger because his head was so large. My husband was in Germany, and I was told it would be dangerous for both mother and baby if we did not act within 30 minutes, so I had no choice but to undergo a cesarean section. Once you've had a cesarean section it becomes difficult to give birth naturally. That being so, I prayed with a desperate heart. During that prayer, the scene of Jesus' crucifixion came to me. I managed the pain with the resolution that, through the birth of new life, I would overcome the force of death that surrounded Jesus on Calvary.

As it is for all women, my giving birth to a new life was an experience of heaven and hell. I did not find it easy to have four C-sections, yet each time I gave birth I was ready to die for the sake of God and for the sake of a new life.

In the same way that our house grew lively as we filled it with children, our churches kept springing up in cities and villages, filled with new members. From the outset, however, our goal was not to have the biggest church in Korea. Our goal was to bring salvation to the world, as a true church that would wipe away all of humanity's tears. To accomplish that goal, I went on multiple world tours following the first one in 1969. From the early 90s, I was the keynote speaker. I gave more speeches at more rallies, events, gatherings and seminars that I can count. My footprints are found in almost every corner of the globe, ranging from unfamiliar metropolises to small primitive villages, from deserts scorched by the burning sun, to thick jungles and breathtaking highlands. At each place, marginalized peoples, helpless women, children and minority groups were waiting for me. And I anxiously looked forward to seeing them.

I knew I could offer them peace of mind and that every step I took advanced the cause of peace. Knowing this enabled me to return to a room in a different hotel every night, and resume the work at dawn the following day. It was typical for me to enter such a room in an unfamiliar city and sleep in a chair for a few hours, or to close my eyes while leaning back in a waiting room at an airport. Sometimes I came and went from a city without opening my suitcase. My mind was on meeting the people who were waiting for me.

When I spoke in a communist nation for the first time, I sensed the presence of spirit persons outnumbering the living people who received me. While the region was embroiled in war, I went to Croatia. The moment I entered my hotel room, I knew that there were souls that had undergone unjust and miserable deaths, waiting for liberation. To liberate them, I did an all-night prayer vigil.

When I go to Africa, I take antimalarial medication. Once, an incorrect prescription caused me to suffer severe side effects, and I caught malaria, experiencing pain and a high fever. My hectic tour schedule left me no time for treatment. Somehow, along the way, the malaria disappeared.

In the autumn of 1996, I went to Bolivia, where I had an experience I cannot forget. The capital, La Paz, is the highest major city in the world, at an altitude of almost 4,000 meters. Non-natives inevitably suffer from altitude sickness. Scheduled to speak for nearly an hour, I had an oxygen tank beside me at the podium. To make matters worse, the podium started to tip over every time I leaned on it slightly. The only solution was to have a strong young member hold the podium steady while I spoke. People were concerned, but I smiled throughout the speech. I felt nauseous and had a throbbing headache and my legs were trembling but I ignored it all. Under such circumstances, on the verge of collapsing, I kept a stiff upper lip and carried on. The audience was impressed, and people complimented me for my presentation. A local dignitary said, "She really is a person sent by God."

The event was a tremendous success, and at the victory celebration that evening, I warmly held the hands of each participating member individually. Even though I was exhausted, I maintained a high spirit for the sake of the precious guests, VIPs and members who had come from far away to meet me. It turned into a joyous occasion as we encouraged each other. When I returned home, my husband, who listened to all my speeches by phone or, later, through the internet, patted me on the back and expressed his appreciation. "Where else could you get such a blessing," he said, "having such success at a place that is 4,000 meters closer to heaven?"

Besides bringing the word of God, during my tours I conducted ceremonies to liberate the spirits of those whose lives had been sacrificed. The True Parents' victory upon the earth has opened the gates of resurrection in the spirit world. The members in Austria, in the spring of 2018, carried out such a ceremony. If you follow the Danube River west from Vienna for about two hours, you come to the village of Mauthausen. Amid its beautiful scenery is a visitors' center in front of a depressing and sinister-looking building. That building with its towering walls of thick, gray brick brings on tears of bitter grief, for during the Second World War it was a concentration camp. There, the Nazis incarcerated Jews and many others. Many of the almost 200,000 people that passed through Mauthausen met miserable deaths.

What remains are not relics from 70 years ago. The true pain one feels there is that of the spirit persons who are stuck in that prison, trapped in their resentment. They can resurrect only after the True Parents of healing and hope can console them and alleviate their bitter resentment and sadness.

It happened like this: I had traveled to Vienna to hold the 2018 "Peace Starts With Me" Rally in the Wiener Stadthalle. The event was a great success. Dr. Werner Fasslabend, Austria's former defense minister and a great senior statesman, welcomed me to the podium, and more than 10,000 people heard my message of hope for the future and for a Europe that would live for the sake of others. I was especially encouraged by the bright spirits of the young people who pledged themselves for peace. But the next morning at breakfast, some of our European leaders came to me with serious faces to present a special request that I permit a ceremony of liberation at Mauthausen. They had heard about my liberation prayers offered for the victims of slavery on Gorée Island in Senegal, and urgently asked me to extend the same heavenly grace to the victims of Nazi persecution.

I sent special representatives to hold a liberation ceremony in Mauthausen. They presented lilies, which represent eternal love, and offered special prayers, opening the gate to alleviate the suffering of those tormented souls. They prayed that those people, now in the spirit world, could release their sadness and resentment and become absolute good spirits who would find their way to the realm of blessing and joy that God has prepared for us all.

It is important to build memorials and educate people about historical wrongs. Still, the higher priority is to release the bitter anguish and anger harbored by those who came before us and who suffered and died unjustly.

Wherever I go, people who don't know me grasp both my hands tightly, not wanting to let go. Their sorrow upon my departure is deeply engraved in my heart. Many people want to see me, and after we spend time together, they feel an emptiness when I'm gone. This is because we are bound by Heaven. Our original parents broke away from God's embrace 6,000 years ago. The only begotten Son and only begotten Daughter are reconnecting heaven, earth and humankind and guiding people to live a true life. That is why some people are brought to tears when they meet God's only begotten Daughter.

I have traveled hundreds and thousands of kilometers over the decades to convey God's love. Although my journey has often been very difficult, I have always been happy. My words and footprints will never disappear. Each and every day they will multiply, bearing fruit that will nourish this world and beyond.

Daffodils

"What does 'belvedere' mean?" I asked our first missionary to the United States. "In Italian," she answered, "it means 'beautiful scenery, a magnificent view.'" Dr. Young Oon Kim was a former professor, a Korean woman educated in Methodist theology in Canada who had joined our movement by the guidance of Jesus. Having mobilized American members to raise the necessary funds by selling candles, this devoted missionary prepared this training center for our international movement. Called Belvedere, it is a lovely estate on the Hudson River in Tarrytown, New York. I liked the name as it befits a place where people can deeply experience God's love in a serene environment.

Beginning in 1972, amid Belvedere's beautiful trees and expansive lawns, our American members and guests were taught the Principle through workshops ranging from a two-day weekend to 100 days. My husband gave sermons at 6:00 a.m. every Sunday as well. The training center would often be crowded with young people from all over the world who came to meet my husband and me.

In the early years I planted yellow daffodils at Belvedere and our nearby East Garden residence and conference center. Why daffodils? Daffodils are the harbingers of spring. As the first flowers to pierce through the frozen ground after withstanding the cold of winter, they herald the coming of warmth and new life. I am always amazed at this providence displayed by Mother Nature and by the strength of the sprouts that appear where snow still remains. Roses and lilies that bloom in spring or midsummer are beautiful, but I most appreciate the little daffodil, whose humble, unassuming bloom breaks the spell of the cold winter. Called to be the only begotten Daughter and True Mother, my path is to break through the icy grip of human sin and help bring God's blessing to the world. I often identify with this lovely flower.

~

It was a joy to return to Belvedere for a special event in the summer of 2016. It was June 1 and the American members were commemorating the 40th anniversary of the God Bless America rally at Yankee Stadium. That 1976 rally was a monumental event for us. There, my husband proclaimed America's responsibility as the land God prepared to bring the unity of all races, nations and religions through its Christian spirit and foundation.

That God needed to call a Korean movement, the Unification Church of Sun Myung Moon and Hak Ja Han, to remind America of its destiny is somewhat ironic. Following God, we sought with all our might to awaken America, which had fallen into chaos and corruption. At that time, Father Moon and I were known only as the founders of an emerging religious movement from the East. I feel today, a half a century later, as I did then—desperate with the hope of giving birth to God's global peace kingdom.

With this heart, I felt so grateful to the families that gathered on that day at Belvedere to celebrate this 40th anniversary. It was a sea of daffodils. They were in their twenties in 1976, and now here they were, with their children and grandchildren. At one point, we sang, "You Are My Sunshine." It is a simple song but one that I will never forget, for to me, and to all gathered on that day, it has deep significance. I was overcome with emotion, silently meditating, reliving the memories that flooded through me.

~

The Puritan spirit of seeking God and religious liberty at all costs gave birth to the United States of America. Nonetheless, over time, America permitted a selfish and decadent culture to emerge and displace its original concern for God's will. Traditional Christianity lacked spiritual resources to prevent the rise of sexual immorality and materialism. Arriving here in December 1971, my husband and I, with our members, invested all our strength to resurrect the founding spirit of America and awaken Americans to their God-given responsibilities. God's dream is for all people in the world to live with gratitude in the peaceful, happy realm of God's love. To achieve this, we knew we had to stir up a revolutionary culture of heart. This was the impetus for our Yankee Stadium rally on June 1, 1976.

The year 1976 was the bicentennial of the founding of the United States. As Koreans, citizens of a republic that owed its existence in large part to the United States, we love America. Since 1972, my husband had been speaking emphatically throughout America, saying, "God sent me in the role of a doctor and as a firefighter to save America." We believed that America is a chosen nation, and we declared as our theme for the 1976 rally, "God Bless America." We raised our voices to shout that God needs America to overcome communism and restore family-centered morality.

Throughout April and May of 1976, our worldwide membership prayed for success at Yankee Stadium. Volunteers came to New York from across the United States, as well as from Japan and Europe, to invite people to attend. They reached out tirelessly and enthusiastically. We tried in those two months to awaken a sleeping giant, to revive the democratic world by countering the influence of communism and the culture of drugs and free sex that was destroying the moral fiber of America's young people. We considered the bicentennial a crossroads, an event that would signal whether or not we could change America's direction. Through our members' hard work, people from throughout the tri-state area and our supporters from other states and nations gathered.

And on that first day of June, others gathered as well. Just as in Korea, where from the right and left, Christians and communists united to accuse and attack, outside Yankee Stadium the demonstrators were yelling, screaming and heaping all kinds of ridicule upon us. The police couldn't handle it, so we sent many of our core members out of their seats inside to cordon off the crowds of opponents and allow the more than 50,000 people to enter peacefully.

June 1, 1976: The God Bless America Festival, Yankee Stadium, New York

As history records, however, the real drama of Yankee Stadium was not in the protests. The real drama was the weather. Even though the sky was clouding up, thousands of people were in their seats and more thousands were entering the stadium. The banners and signs, sound system and staging were all set up; the band and choir were in place. Suddenly a violent rainstorm swept in from Long Island Sound. Fierce winds blew, rain poured down, our God Bless America banners were torn off the outfield walls and our posters were soaked. The equipment onstage was blown around. The rain soaked the people as well; it was an indescribable mess. And outside the stadium, the crowd of opponents was yelling, screaming and heaping all kinds of ridicule upon us.

Unification Church members lead the crowd in
"You Are My Sunshine," the song that created a miracle

One would have wondered, was God truly with us? Was this all part of God's plan? Then one of our young American leaders jumped onto the top of the home team dugout, raised his arms like a conductor in front of an orchestra, and started singing at the top of his lungs, "You are my sunshine, my only sunshine. You make me happy when skies are gray."

It was like a signal flare. With one heart, everyone began to sing, "You are my sunshine, my only sunshine!" A magnificent chorus spread through the stadium and tears of joy mixed with the drops of rain flowing down everyone's faces. The summer squall, our opponents' criticism, and the scramble to protect the equipment—these had only bolstered our spirit. Even though we were soaked, no one sought shelter. Heaven was the shelter that united the people of all races, nations and religions that filled the stadium.

That singing was the condition of faith and unity that moved God. The skies over the stadium began to brighten. The darkness cast in both heaven and earth was lifted. Rays of sunshine appeared, and the festival, which seemed utterly demolished, was reborn. Our volunteers swept the stage, wiped off the media equipment and cleared the grounds of fallen signage. Now, with the sunshine warming everyone, the program began.

Before he went out to the stage, my husband said a prayer. Then he grabbed my hand and said, "Thanks to your sincere devotion and prayer, I am going on stage today." My husband's smile of gratitude was warmer than the sun that was shining through the clouds. I truly felt that we and our entire global family had pierced the darkness. From the borderline of death, we had resurrected into a bright future for heaven and earth. I brushed the cold raindrops from my face and gave him a hug of encouragement.

We had strong faith in God and in the salvation of the world, and we did not lose courage, because we were fully aware that God was with us. Compared to the hardships and oppression we faced in our homeland before coming to the United States, this was nothing. We transformed shouts of opposition into songs of glory. The pouring rain and gusts of wind blew away our signs but not our love.

As my husband took the stage, the audience greeted him with loud applause. "Who are the true Americans?" he asked. "True Americans are those who have a universal mind. True Americans are those who believe in the one family of humankind, transcendent of color and nationality as willed by God. True Americans are those who are proud of such international families, churches and nations consisting of all peoples." With faith and courage, the rally was a great success.

It was 30 years later, in June of 2006, on our sprawling complex on Cheongpyeong Lake in the Republic of Korea, that our movement opened its global capital, the Cheon Jeong Palace. In its gardens, I did not plant roses or lilies. I planted daffodils. And early each spring, as I see the yellow flowers peeking out from under the melting winter snow, I'm gently reminded of the Yankee Stadium event.

Daffodils, which overcome the wind and snow, are a signal for the advent of new life. Their bright little petals, the color of sunlight, are the first sign that spring has finally come. They will always be here, in a special place in my heart. To me, they symbolize the beauty and peace that is blossoming worldwide in our movement. They are seemingly small, but within them is a surge of new life that leads us to forget that there ever was a winter.

As a summer rain fell upon the lawn

In his 1991 novel, *Mao II*, an American writer, Don DeLillo, described the Unification movement's mass weddings as opening the path forward for humanity. Interestingly, he depicted our 1982 Blessing Ceremony at Madison Square Garden as having taken place at Yankee Stadium. Mr. DeLillo in any case described a oneness and harmony among thousands of young couples devoting their marriage and family to God, and observed, "We all are Moonies, or should be."

Back then, we were known, often not affectionately, as "the Moonies." The name was a creation of the media. We were new and exciting. Regardless of the name, Mr. DeLillo grasped something profound. I'm sure millions of Americans had similar intuitions. Everyone indeed should—and will someday—participate in the Blessing of marriage for world peace.

When my husband and I arrived in the United States in December of 1971, five years before the Yankee Stadium Rally, we saw a world adrift on a chartless ocean with no compass. The threat of communism was growing and Christianity was losing strength. Christian theologians even came up with justifications for communism. Young people wandered about, having no purpose or goals, seduced by sexual temptation and the false freedom advertised by the birth control pill. The United States, founded in the blood and sweat of people of faith who had crossed the Atlantic, risking their lives in pursuit of religious freedom, was breaking its covenant with God.

From the moment of our arrival in America, we rushed forward infused with heavenly energy. Increasing numbers of young people in the United States and the Western world were drawn to our idealistic teachings. We shared our hearts with the members about the challenges the world was facing and the responsibilities that, together with them, we wished to fulfill. "The democratic world is facing an urgent crisis due to the threat of communism," we explained, "We must invest everything in order to overcome this."

Within two months of our arrival, my husband and I conducted a speaking tour of seven cities, mobilizing members in New York, Philadelphia, Baltimore, Washington DC, Los Angeles, San Francisco and Berkeley. It was difficult at first, but by the time we reached California, we had overflow audiences for our three nights of talks. In those cities, some among the young people who attended our speaking events committed themselves to our cause. By early 1973 we had several bus teams covering the country and a house center in most states. From these groups, reinforced by energetic leaders and members from Japan and Europe, including the Korean Folk Ballet, we formed the One World Crusade and a choir, the New Hope Singers International. We loved their fiery passion and desire to enlighten the world.

Through my husband's energy, in 1972, the year after arriving in the United States, we set in motion so many projects. We convened the first meeting of the International Conference on the Unity of the Sciences, at New York City's Waldorf Astoria Hotel. We established the American branch of the Professors World Peace Academy and strengthened the already-existing Freedom Leadership Foundation, dedicated to the victory over communism. At Belvedere, we taught hundreds of young members to live according to God's word, and in the fall of 1973, with our mobile teams and local centers fully functioning, we conducted a second national speaking tour, this time of 21 cities. In each city, we hosted a banquet for social leaders and clergy, where numerous mayors presented us with keys to their city. We then held three nights of public talks on God, America and the future of Christianity.

At that time, a crisis arose in America. In 1972, Richard Nixon had been elected to a second term as president by an overwhelming majority, but one year later, popular sentiment had turned against him. The media and Mr. Nixon's political opponents were demanding that he resign from office over the Watergate affair. His supposed allies had no power to defend him. Even Christian leaders drew back and kept silent.

It was my husband who spoke out. Our movement published "America in Crisis: Answer to Watergate: Forgive, Love, Unite" in 21 leading newspapers. This was not about forgiving President Nixon alone, Father said, but about forgiving, loving and uniting as a nation for the sake of the world.

Mr. Nixon's commitment was to win the Vietnam War and keep communism out of southeast Asia. In opposition, communist affiliates confused the American public, mounting demonstrations against him on college campuses and even on the National Mall. Seeking to awaken reverence for God and ignite a fire among Americans thirsting for righteousness, our members began demonstrating for God and the dignity of the American presidency. We gained media attention and the president himself took notice.

Early in 1974, President Nixon sent us an invitation to meet him in the White House. Mr. Nixon was anxious, aware of the likelihood of impeachment. As members covered the White House in prayer, my husband counseled him to stand strong, confess any wrongdoing and call for national prayer, unity and renewal.

September 18, 1974: The New Future of Christianity rally,
Madison Square Garden, New York

On the heels of our meeting with the president, we went out again, this time to speak in 32 cities, completing our coverage of all 50 states, including Alaska and Hawaii. At first, most Americans were perplexed to hear about a Christian leader from the East. But to know us is to love us, and wherever we went, people were touched and took something valuable from our message. Public interest increased by the day, and with it came controversy.

The final tour of that era, this one of eight cities, began that September 18 at New York City's Madison Square Garden, with a speech entitled, "The New Future of Christianity." It was the first really large venue the Unification Church had sought to fill, and the event had an amazing impact. More than 30,000 people packed the Garden, while another 20,000 had to be turned away.

June 7, 1975: the World Rally for Korean Freedom, Yoido Plaza

Without a moment's rest, we held even more rallies that impacted the world. Our confidence to fill large arenas led to greater gratitude to God, our Heavenly Parent, and to our members who were, and are, devoted to Heaven's principle and providence. In the midst of this, in Korea, we displayed the power of the Victory Over Communism (VOC) movement at a rally of 1.2 million on Yoido Island in Seoul. This led to a nationwide movement aimed at the reunification of North and South Korea in the 1980s. The VOC teaching spread beyond Japan and Asia. Through the Confederation of Associations for the Unity of the Societies of the Americas (CAUSA), leaders in the Western Hemisphere, including national leaders in Latin America and 70,000 members of the clergy, attended the CAUSA workshops.

The Yankee Stadium Festival, on June 1, 1976, was the first half of the God Bless America Festival, held to honor the bicentennial year of the United States' founding. With its success, we decided not to wait, but to hold a rally in Washington, DC, at the Washington Monument, in September, just three months later. Not surprisingly, members of the US government with less-than-noble motives worked with narrow-minded religious leaders and "anti-cult" groups that preyed upon members' parents to launch an all-out attack on us. Always on the lookout for a controversy, the media built its audience by articles and news reports disparaging and criticizing us.

Arrayed against us at the Yankee Stadium and Washington Monument events were more than 30 opposition groups, including the US Communist Party. Nonetheless, without a trace of fear or the remotest consideration about pulling back, my husband and I set aside our personal safety and dedicated our lives to the future of the United States. We invested all we had to wake up the American churches and people to the reality of God, the truth of the Bible and the supreme importance of God-centered marriage and family life, beyond race, nation and religion. Declaring this message on the vast expanse of the National Mall was our goal, and nothing could change that.

September 18, 1976: The God Bless America Festival
at Washington Monument, Washington DC.

After a good deal of back and forth, 40 days before the rally, the government granted the permit to hold our assembly on the National Mall.

Now the die was cast. I felt as if I were entering a waterless desert with an oasis 40 days away. On the emotional level, that 40 days seemed as if it were more than 40 years.

Wherever I went, whatever I did, whoever I was with, I could think only about the rally. I was so absorbed in it that I would confuse breakfast with dinner, dinner with breakfast, and miss lunch altogether. I think that I was not the only one.

The rally was neither being held to promote the Unification Church nor to publicize the names of Sun Myung Moon and Hak Ja Han, quite the opposite. We sacrificed so much internally and externally to bring it about. We were informed that there might be a terrorist attack, but we were not afraid of that.

Finally, September 18, 1976, arrived, and with it our rally to mark the bicentennial of the United States took place in the vast grounds surrounding the Washington Monument. My husband and I arose early that morning, prayed deeply and headed to the National Mall with a heart more serious than that of someone on the way to the gallows, not out of fear for ourselves, but because of the enormous providential significance riding on the outcome.

There, more than 300,000 people gathered by mid-day, peacefully, hopefully, and gratefully. It was indeed a grand and miraculous sight. The American media, the government and certain religious hierarchies had opposed the Unification Church but we had surmounted all challenges.

The people of America's humble neighborhoods in Richmond, Washington DC, Baltimore, Wilmington, Philadelphia, New York, New Haven, Boston and beyond, gathered for God and for America. They were what made the Washington Monument rally a huge success. Our members had mobilized all the buses available on the East Coast, more than a thousand, and had to bite their lips as many hundreds of would-be participants were left behind at the gathering places with no more buses to transport them. It is a testimony to the American people's love of God and country that True Parents triggered. We could feel it: God is alive in America.

~~~

My husband and I had emigrated with our family to this unfamiliar land and we took on a challenging course. We concluded our first campaign with the success of the three rallies: Madison Square Garden in 1974 and the Yankee Stadium and Washington Monument rallies in 1976. Uttered with sincere devotion, our prayer was the light that ended the darkness. Its light was cast beyond the open-hearted people who attended our events, to illuminate all Americans and all people in our global village.

Understandably, the American people did not automatically welcome my husband and me warmly when we arrived "fresh off the boat" from a land in the far-distant East. They were unfamiliar with terms they were hearing for the first time, such as "Divine Principle" and "True Parents." There was only one reason that we were able to receive such a broad and deep response within four years of our arrival. It was not just that our message made sense. More than that, it was that our message re-awakened the religious vision upon which the United States of America was conceived. That is what triggered the significant response. Our prayers and sincere devotion, and our message about the importance of the family, summoning young people to recover their sense of morality and to strive for the perfection of true love in the community—this is what moved the hearts of the American people, for it is the founding vision of that nation.

Many young people came to realize that the Principle is the truth and joined our family movement. For these brothers and sisters, the Principle became the core axis of life. They shared the Principle with everyone from fellow youth carrying backpacks on the West Coast to the elite leaders in the universities and the government. They gained the support of people of all races, occupations, ages and educational backgrounds. My husband and I toured the United States to encourage and inspire not just the public, but our members. We called them to establish schools, create newspapers, get their doctorates, link cultures through programs such as the Little Angels, dance troupes and rock bands, raise funds going shop to shop and door to door, create home churches, fish businesses and restaurants, and organize volunteer service projects. On every path we trod, the blood, sweat and tears of our frontline missionaries, domestic and international, continued to flow. I was constantly in prayer.

2016: The 40th anniversary of the Yankee Stadium Rally,
Belvedere, New York

At Belvedere in the summer of 2016, the celebration of the 40th anniversary of the Yankee Stadium Rally brought to mind this entire history. Returning from those memories, I viewed the hundreds of happy interracial families gathered on the lawn at Belvedere. As I rose to the podium, I set aside the emotions attached to that day of celebration and considered the future. Standing and speaking with a heart of grateful love, I let our members know that there is still much work to do. We cannot allow ourselves to be satisfied with those victories from decades ago. At the end of the day, I lingered at Belvedere. A summer rain fell upon the lawn, and once again, deep in my heart, I felt the call to focus my mind and continue on the path toward a world of hope and happiness as the Mother of peace.

A song of victory rang out from Danbury

My husband and I were well aware of the many who opposed us. The charge of "brainwashing" was a recurring accusation. Such scurrilous criticism always followed my husband and me. But such is the story of God's history, and we understood why. The movement against us in the United States reached its crescendo in the late 1970s. The Washington Monument Rally was the tipping point for those who hoped our movement would fail, and critics and fear-mongers now envisioned the Unification Principle spreading like wildfire throughout America. Donald Fraser, a congressman from Minnesota, took the lead on Capitol Hill, opening a hearing in the House Foreign Affairs Committee. We would be accused of involvement in a political scandal nicknamed "Koreagate" in the press. It had nothing to do with us, except that we were from Korea, but it was gaining publicity for members of Congress.

After Congressman Fraser chaired the hearing that investigated, without result, our movement in March and April of 1978, he failed in his campaign to win a seat in the US Senate. In 1980, however, he became mayor of Minneapolis, and he later signed a proclamation welcoming my husband and me to that fair city.

With a congressional committee coming up empty-handed, those who wanted to convict my husband of something, anything, asked the Internal Revenue Service to investigate us. Beginning in the late 1970s, our church was subjected to a full IRS audit. We opened our books, confident that we had done nothing wrong. For two years, we even provided a private office for an IRS team in our Manhattan headquarters building. "I have lived a life of sacrifice and service for America and the world," Father Moon declared publicly, "I have nothing to be ashamed of. This case is the result of racism and religious prejudice."

Although Father Moon had done nothing wrong, on October 15, 1981, the US district attorney in the Southern District of New York, on the third attempt with a grand jury, finally succeeded in lodging charges of tax evasion against him. Our lawyer knew that the newspapers and television stations' persistent attacks on our movement rendered it impossible to convene an unbiased jury of New York City citizens. Also, it would be hard to seat a jury that could understand the complexities of such a tax case. Father Moon therefore requested a bench trial, but the court did not accept this motion. In pleading their case, the government lawyers confused everyone in the courtroom, no one more than the members of the jury.

On May 18, 1982, the jury handed down their verdict. My husband was found guilty of owing a total of $7,300 in taxes accrued over a three-year period, nearly 10 years prior. It is routine for people who underpay their taxes by far greater amounts to simply pay a fine. But for Father Moon, an evangelist from Korea? The judge pounded his gavel and pronounced his decision: "I sentence you to 18 months in prison and a $25,000 fine." Upon this announcement, my husband immediately stood up, smiled, and walked across the courtroom, with his hand outstretched, to shake the hand of the government's lead prosecutor. The lawyer was startled. He turned his back on my husband, stuffed his papers in his briefcase and walked out of the courtroom.

American churches were paying close attention to our case. Holding church funds under the name of the pastor was common practice for them, and this became the basis of the accusation against my husband. The government was prosecuting someone for what was a general church practice, and if they could send my husband to jail for that, it could send anyone to jail." When Father Moon was pronounced guilty, they rose up. With one voice, the National Council of Churches, United Presbyterian Church in the USA, the American Baptist Churches in the USA, the African Methodist Episcopal Church, the Unitarian Universalist Association, the Southern Christian Leadership Conference, the National Conference of Black Mayors, The Church of Jesus Christ of Latter Day Saints, The Catholic League for Religious and Civil Rights, the National Association of Evangelicals, and many others called the decision "an obvious oppression of religion." With them in our ranks, we founded the Coalition for Religious Freedom and Minority Alliance International, which organized rallies throughout the country to protest the verdict. Conscientious people of all denominations and political views recognized oppression when they saw it, and demonstrated on behalf of liberty.

On the foundation of this bipartisan support, we submitted an appeal to the United States Supreme Court. To our great disappointment, in May 1984, the Supreme Court washed its hands of it, thereby affirming the sentence. My husband's response? "It is the will of God." He was not concerned about going to prison. He had already turned the court's decision into the next step of God's plan to awaken America from spiritual death. He was incarcerated on July 20, 1984, at the Federal Correctional Institution in Danbury, Connecticut.

This whole affair was not about taxes. It was about the world's most powerful nation failing to investigate and understand the nature of our movement and the authentic reasons for our growth and influence. It was a misuse of governmental and media power induced by fear and ignorance. But God always works in mysterious ways. The Christian community united with us as it never had before. Major clerics were outraged that what could be characterized as an administrative mistake, if that, could be punished by 18 months in prison. Thousands of clergy throughout the United States protested. Hundreds spent a week in Washington, DC, in the Common Suffering Fellowship. They studied the Principle and America's tradition of religious freedom, visited their congressional representatives, demonstrated outside the White House and proclaimed that when the government threw Father Moon in prison, it had thrown them in there as well.

Besides supporting this domestic ecumenical activism, Unification Church members around the world prayed unceasingly. Having no experience of the earliest years in Korea, they could not digest the reality that the Lord would be in prison. My husband and I comforted them. "From now, a new world will begin," Father Moon counseled our members, our family and me. "Now, not only America, but all humanity will be with us, and the drumbeat of hope will sound throughout the world."

July 20, 1984, is a day I wish I could erase from history. On that day, my husband left our home and was incarcerated in Danbury prison. As we departed at 10:00 that evening, he gave words of hope and encouragement to our members who had gathered at Belvedere. With several members, we drove to the prison. I was resolved not to reveal my emotions. Father Moon had asked the members to dispel their anger and sadness. "Do not cry for me," he told them, "Pray for America."

A feeling of deep darkness descended as we watched Father Moon enter the prison. We stood for a long time at the entrance, as if my husband might just turn around and come back out. With a sigh, I consoled everyone and we turned and walked away. My husband was embarking upon an unfair prison term in a foreign land, and I knew that I had to forgive the people who had put him there. It was our opportunity to practice our movement's most fundamental ethic, "Love your enemies, and live for their sake."

Sacrificing oneself, even in the face of death, and going even further to forgive and love those who accuse and deceive, is what we came to call "the Danbury spirit." The Danbury spirit is to give and give even after everything has been taken away, to forgive those involved, then to persevere, knowing something greater is bound to occur in accord with the heavenly will.

The road was dark on our nighttime journey home. My experiences during the more than 10 years of living in the United States had been more numerous than the pebbles along a riverbank. There were the speaking tours in which we had traversed the continent; there were the path-breaking conferences that reshaped the world of scientists, professors, theologians and clergy; there was the youth with boundless energy welcoming new life in God's love. That road had been strenuous but incredibly rewarding and, in that light, my husband's imprisonment was a painful pill to swallow, a heavy cross to bear.

As a wife, I also was dealing with personal pain. My husband was nearing 65 years of age, and facing prison life by himself in the United States, barely knowing the English language, would not be easy. It had not been so long since I had given birth to our fourteenth child. I had been with my husband every time he appeared in a courtroom, before a congressional panel, or speaking to our members. And now this. It was very hard on my mind and body. Amid all this, I had to fill the leadership vacuum created by his absence.

My husband knew my thoughts and focused himself, and me, and our movement, on the way forward. The first thing the next morning, there he was, on the phone. "Share these words with the members," he told me, "Ignite the signal fire for Christianity according to the call of God."

I shared his words with our leaders and members. Energized by my husband, I knew what we had to do. "Now God has given us our next opportunity," I told them. "We must achieve what we are called to do, on the foundation of all we have accomplished so far. Through constructive activity and sincere spiritual conditions, God's heart will be moved. Our sincere devotion will bring Satan to surrender. Now is the time. History will record this as the welcoming of a new age."

⁂

There is a saying that "when it rains, it pours," and indeed, on my path forward, almost before I could catch my breath, I ran headlong into another unexpected misfortune. A core leader of our movement, who had pioneered the Principle in America and who had actively defended my husband and me in the United States, suddenly went missing. We soon learned that Dr. Bo Hi Pak had been kidnapped and was locked up in a cellar somewhere in New York City. His captors declared themselves ready to kill him.

We had been exposing communist subversion through *The News World* and *The Washington Times* and demolishing Marxist ideological claims before tens of thousands of American clergy through CAUSA. Communists were enraged that the religious freedom of the United States had allowed our movement such influence. Lacking the police apparatus they would have had in North Korea, one leftist cell's ability to act against us was limited. But now, considering us vulnerable with the absence of Father Moon, they resorted to violent criminality and kidnapped Dr. Pak.

With my husband in prison, I had to solve the problem. The first thing I did was earnestly pray that the saintly man who had been abducted would hear my voice. Then I phoned United States Senator Orrin Hatch. Senator Hatch was a warm-hearted and fair-minded man who had spoken out on our behalf during the congressional hearings.

"This abduction is not based on personal resentment, nor is it for money," I informed him. "It is an attack on a man who is unmasking their wickedness through the media and through education." Senator Hatch responded that he would ask the FBI to investigate immediately. Lawyers and my trusted advisors told me that the FBI opening an investigation would increase the likelihood of violence on the part of the kidnappers and that it would be better to negotiate. I could not agree and I continued my desperate prayer.

As Dr. Pak shared with us later, his circumstances soon worsened. The kidnappers beat him severely and applied electric shocks. He lost consciousness and fell onto a cold basement floor. At that time, he heard a voice: "There is not much time, but they will not harm you further today. You will preserve your life if you escape within 12 hours. You can do it; use whatever means are available."

Dr. Pak heard my prayers in a dream. He regained consciousness and determined to escape. Using wisdom, Dr. Pak got his kidnappers to relax the conditions of his captivity and managed to escape. The next day, he returned home. I met him soon after that, and he gave me a full account of what had happened. "The voice of True Mother, which I heard in the darkness, sounded like the voice and revelation of God. Your words awakened me suddenly and gave me the wisdom and power to outwit my captors."

As such events unfolded, a very difficult time turned into a time in which I was full of vigor. My desire to impart merciful love only deepened. Each day was rich with emotions, including cherished moments in which my husband shared with me his affection. At the start of each day, after he finished praying at 5:00 a.m., he would call me from a prison pay phone, and greet me with "My beloved Mother!"

I was permitted to visit him at the prison every other day. I would be driven there in a convertible, and when weather permitted, I would put the top down as we ascended the final hill on the prison grounds. Rain or shine, my husband always came out and waited for our arrival. With a longing heart, I would smile brightly and wave from the car. Sometimes he would look totally worn out, having just finished mopping a floor or washing dishes. What wife would feel comfortable seeing her husband like that? But I would suppress my sorrow and hug him with a bright smile. I often brought our two-year-old daughter, Jeong-jin, for he would be so happy to receive and embrace her.

When our brief meetings ended, my husband would send us off. As we drove back down the hill, worried tears would start to fall from my eyes. Wishing not to turn my face toward him and expose my weeping, I would just keep my face forward while waving good-bye. I knew that my husband would remain in place, his eyes fixed upon me, a prayer in his heart, waving silently until we were out of sight.

Father and Mother Moon with Hyo-jin in a half-way house following his release from Danbury Federal Correctional Facility. He was imprisoned from July 20, 1984 to August 20, 1985.

For the 13 months of Father Moon's imprisonment, I was coping with feelings of sorrow and injustice, but my responsibility to lead our church and the providence came first. I felt responsible for inspiring our members around the world while maintaining a firm axis with my husband, around which they would revolve, unwavering in their life of faith. With God's intervention, we actually enjoyed a sense of stability. When my husband was imprisoned, media professionals around the world gossiped and cynically predicted that the Unification Church would disappear. Some members of the media seemed to be anxiously waiting for that to happen, hoping to proclaim happily, "We told you so! The Unification Church is an empty shell cracking like an egg with nothing inside; its so-called believers are heading for the hills."

That did not happen. Quite the opposite: the number of our members and allies only increased. People understood that the US government had sent Father Moon to serve an unjust prison sentence for the crime of dedicating his life for the salvation of humanity. In their innermost hearts, all people cherish religious freedom.

September 2, 1984: The 13th ICUS in Washington DC. Mother Moon read the welcoming address on behalf of her husband.

Despite Father Moon's incarceration, our global work for peace continued. The 13th International Conference on the Unity of the Sciences (ICUS) was scheduled to convene within a month of his imprisonment. For more than a decade, this annual meeting had brought scientists from around the world to discuss the unity of the sciences centered on absolute values. Staff and the attendees needed to know whether the conference would be held. Critics of the conference scoffed, saying, "It's all about Father Moon. Without him, they won't do it." Ignoring this, I simply said, "We will certainly hold the conference," and the preparations continued.

On September 2, 1984, our International Cultural Foundation conducted the 13th ICUS in Washington, DC. More than 250 scientists attended from 42 countries. I met and greeted them one by one, and took the podium to read the Founder's Address with confident resolution. Even though its founder was absent, the conference was a success. Scientists expressed gratitude and the staff members were happy. Everyone could see that this movement is of God and does not depend upon one individual.

The progress of our international conferences did not end there. In the summer of 1985, the Professors World Peace Academy (PWPA) was scheduled to convene a global congress in Europe. Once again, I heard about the worries of the planners and participants and I guided them as before, "We will hold it as planned."

Geneva, Switzerland was the conference venue. Dr. Morton Kaplan, a renowned political scientist at the University of Chicago, was the president of PWPA. He sought my husband's advice about the conference and met us at Danbury to receive it. Those days, my husband, even from prison, was acting on Heaven's guidance to halt the advance of communism at America's doorstep, in Nicaragua. His inspiration sparked the American president, Ronald Reagan, to take action. As this was unfolding, my husband and I saw that communism's global expansion camouflaged a serious crisis within its own borders and that its entire house of cards was soon to collapse. In 1970, Father Moon had prophesied that global communism would fall in the late 1980s, 70 years after its founding.

And so, to this University of Chicago political scientist, my husband announced our theme for the conference: "The Fall of the Soviet Union." Dr. Kaplan, looking at the global reality externally, objected. "Sociologists don't discuss something that has not happened." But Father Moon spoke with calmness and strength, "Communism will perish and the Soviet Union will collapse. You need to proclaim this fact at the gathering of scholars and professors from around the world."

Dr. Kaplan again hesitated and asked: "How about if we say 'the possible fall?'" Father Moon replied, "No. It's not just a possibility. Believe me and do as I say."

As he departed with me from the meeting, I could see that Dr. Kaplan's head was spinning. He was a world-renowned scholar, and he could not speak what he considered empty words, much less convene a conference based upon them. He said three times that he wanted to tone down the conference theme. I told Dr. Kaplan not to worry about anything and to follow my husband's advice. He still was looking for a way out. With winsome eyes, he came up with, "Wouldn't it be possible to use a word softer than 'fall'?" I didn't budge. My husband and I knew communism would collapse in the Soviet Union within a few years.

From August 13-17, 1985, the second Professors World Peace Academy international congress took place in Geneva with its title, "The Fall of the Soviet Empire: Prospects for Transition to a Post-Soviet World." Hundreds of university professors discussed the fall of communism from all angles. They heard Father Moon's prophecy that "Communism will collapse within a few years." They pricked up their ears, having never dreamed of such an idea. They were amazed that we had the conviction to go against conventional wisdom and political correctness. Their nerves were a bit on edge for another reason as well. They were aware that the Soviet Embassy stood directly across the street from the conference venue.

Some renowned sociologists and professors criticized our proclamation, even quite harshly. But, as we had predicted, the Soviet Union was dissolved just six years later. Interestingly, when the Soviet Union actually dissolved, some of these same scholars explained it as if they had seen it coming, with very few noting that it was Father and Mother Moon who had first predicted what would happen and even convened a conference with that as the specific title. My husband and I just continued on, working for the sake of the future.

Even during his undeserved prison sentence, my husband greatly impressed other inmates with his exemplary demeanor and diligence. At first, the prisoners mocked him for being the founder of a strange new religion from the East and tried to pick quarrels with him. He handled it all with forbearance, warmth and dignity. As he had told me, he was looking forward to seeing whom God had prepared for him to meet there. Prisoners naturally are struggling with anger, resentment and selfishness, and he committed to make Danbury a place where love could flow.

Prisoners soon learned that Father Moon would spend his weekly stipend in the prison dispensary, and through the week, give everything away to lonely inmates. He held an early morning prayer service, and other prisoners gradually joined him. Some of the inmates came to consider my husband a true teacher; some called him the "saint of the prison." Guards and prison officials were also impressed. *The New York Post* published a cartoon at the time of Father Moon's release, August 20, 1985. It depicted all the prisoners bowing to Father Moon, and one prison official saying to another, "Get him out of here before he calls a mass wedding!" My husband and I chuckled over that.

As his wife and the mother of our children, my husband's imprisonment was my imprisonment. The Danbury course parallels Jesus' trial in front of the Roman Procurator, Pilate, and the punishment of his crucifixion. The forces that wanted Father Moon to disappear were always looking for an opportunity. The American FBI apprehended Red Army operatives in the United States who had been sent by the Soviet KGB and North Korea's Kim Il Sung to assassinate my husband. Among the prison inmates were men who harbored the same irrational hatred as those who had kidnapped Dr. Pak. My husband was living with such men, and no one could guarantee his safety. It was a modern version of Golgotha, as if he were on a cross with thieves to the left and right.

Despite such circumstances, we threw our lives into the salvation of America. As a result, although we were harassed, accused and imprisoned, my husband and I never gave up and we never will, whether on earth or in heaven. One with his bones and flesh, with his thoughts mine and my thoughts his, I give my entire mind and body to practice love for the sake of God's dream. I have walked this exhausting life course silently as the one called to bring the human family together as the Mother of peace, to heal our suffering planet as the Mother of the universe, and to bring joy to our Heavenly Parent as His only begotten Daughter.

My husband once called me a High Priest. He said that in God's dispensation until this era, men were the high priests, but we are entering the age of the wife, and women need to carry out the priestly ministry. It is women whom our Heavenly Parent is calling to serve as the mediators of forgiving, purifying and regenerating grace to all humanity.

I will not leave you as orphans

As the Last Supper approached, Jesus comforted his disciples, saying, "I will not leave you as orphans; I will come to you." This passage condenses into a few words the path I have walked. Even though all human beings have parents, as we have wandered through history without knowing God or the true way of life, we have felt like orphans. I have striven throughout my life to lead humanity to the welcoming, forgiving, rebirthing love of God, who is our Heavenly Parent.

As recently as the 1990s, if a woman headlined an event or speaking tour in a rural area of Korea, people would look in askance and dismiss the whole idea. They could not comprehend the idea that a woman could address audiences of women and for women. At that time, women had no public voice. Society officially declared that men and women have equal value, but in practice, such a declaration was hardly worth the paper it was printed on. No one, man or woman, could as much as find a starting point for an intelligent discussion of the matter.

I had long pondered if and when women would fulfill their role as perfected human beings, as fully co-creative and significant members of society, and especially as daughters of God. My husband and I had deep experiences in prayer during the Danbury imprisonment, and we together concluded that it was time for the liberation of all women, and for me to take a public role to teach and exemplify it. Thus arose a careful creation of the spiritual and physical foundations for what came to be called the Women's Federation for World Peace.

My husband began teaching about my position as a true woman standing at God's left side with him on God's right side; about me being a true woman and co-founder of our movement; about me being a true woman serving, as he does, as an individual embodiment of True Parents; and about me being a true woman having the same authority, inheritance and rights as he. After our meetings with President Mikhail and Mrs. Raisa Gorbachev and with Chairman Kim Il Sung, about which I will share, we decided it was time for the declaration of True Parents to the world. As his wife, I am my husband's first witness. And as my partner in the love of Heavenly Parent, he was the first to advocate that I reach the world with our message of peace.

My husband and I founded the Women's Federation for World Peace. After its inaugural rally at the Olympic Stadium in Seoul in April 1992, about which I will also speak below, I held a series of events to launch Women's Federation chapters in 40 Korean cities. I spoke on the theme, "Women Will Play a Leading Role in the Ideal World." We wondered what would be the turnout for these events and were gratified that every venue was filled to capacity. Although the speech focused on women, many men attended as well. I saw the era of women that my husband and I were advocating taking shape before my eyes.

April 10, 1992: 150,000 attend the inaugural rally of
the Women's Federation for World Peace in Seoul

When the Korean speaking tour was over, we planned a speaking schedule for me to launch the Women's Federation in Japan. "Japanese women need to hear these words, too," I told our logistics team.

"True," they replied, "But you speak Korean, and through the interpreter, the original meaning will not be fully conveyed."

"I agree," I said, with the follow-up: "Then I shall speak in Japanese."

When my husband heard about this, even he wanted to talk it over. "It would be much easier to use an interpreter. The speech is long, and you don't know Japanese well. You have to leave soon. Are you confident that you can speak to them in Japanese?"

As soon as the words were out of his mouth, he knew my answer. I didn't need to say anything. I practiced the speech in Japanese for a few days, my motivation being that the Japanese people should not remain orphans. I was determined to explain to them, in their language, the reality that we all have been orphans, and that today, through True Parents, we can become children of our Heavenly Parent.

On September 24, 1992, a crowd of 50,000 people gathered at the Tokyo Dome. It was my first time speaking publicly in Japanese, and this was a prominent venue in Japan's capital. The audience was aware of this. No one, Korean or Japanese, had high expectations for the outcome. The organizers, being prudent, prepared a young Japanese interpreter to stand just off-stage, in case I faltered. But when I came to the podium and began to speak, the audience was surprised. They cheered and stood up to applaud. For a few minutes they remained anxious, thinking, "Surely she'll make a mistake." But as I continued, and each sentence impressed God's word in their hearts, the audience looked relaxed and happy.

Over the next nine days, I gave that speech in seven cities without losing strength, and then for three more days, I delivered it to Koreans residing in Japan. I uplifted the hearts of all Japanese as well as Korean women.

"I need to speak in America," I then told my staff.

"Won't that be difficult?" they responded. "Please, let's take at least a full day's rest before flying." But my mind was already in the West. "Many people are waiting for me," I uttered without thinking, "I cannot rest."

I crossed the Pacific and stepped onto American soil. Speaking in the eight largest cities of the US, I announced that the era of women was near and what it means for men, women and God. On the first day, the people of Washington, DC, thanked me deeply. They had thought of me only as "the wife of Rev. Sun Myung Moon from Korea," but now their perception changed. I was now, "Hak Ja Han, who represents us, and represents the aspirations and value of all women." I planted in their hearts the seeds of female leadership that is necessary to complete the salvation of the world.

My inaugural speaking tour for the Women's Federation continued through Europe, Russia, Asia and Oceania. I will never forget what happened when I spoke in the Philippines. The day before the event, I flew from Los Angeles to Manila. On the plane, I took a short nap, during which I dreamed I was breastfeeding a baby. As I looked at the beautiful baby, I said to myself, "I'm not of an age to give birth anymore."

When I arrived in Manila, I discovered that it was a Catholic holy day, December 8, the Feast of the Immaculate Conception. A woman walking on the street in downtown Manila happened to see a poster advertising my speech. The poster had me in a yellow Korean dress. Suddenly, the thought, "This is the person who will fulfill Mother Mary's mission," came into her mind. Then and there, she decided to attend my event. She was deeply moved by my speech, during which she arose and loudly exclaimed, "The one who came to the Philippines on this holy day is truly our Mother Mary!" Cheers erupted throughout the convention center.

The final venue on that tour was China's Great Hall of the People in Tiananmen Square. It was an event both very difficult and very rewarding. We expected that, since China's open-door policy was in place, everything would go smoothly, but that was not the case. From the outset, the Communist Party and the military had refused to grant a permit. When we explained that it wasn't a political rally, they said, "We will check the script first. It cannot have anything in it about God." That took them a week. Their conclusion: "We cannot allow this kind of content."

I strongly argued with them. They repeatedly gave their reasons to change my speech, but I didn't yield. I insisted that the message had nothing to do with politics and that its focus was on women. The matter stood at a tipping point. At that time, President Deng Xiaoping's son, Deng Pufang, was the chairman of the China Disabled Persons Federation, an organization consisting of 500,000 people. The day before the event, the young Mr. Deng invited me and other Women's Federation leaders to a reception held by his organization. It was a harmonious meeting, where we encouraged one another despite the differences in our systems and ideologies. Hearing of this pleasant experience, that evening, the All-China Women's Federation welcomed us to their gathering. We didn't know each other well, so it felt awkward at first, but soon all of us ladies became friends and had a good time singing happily together.

Even though social receptions and official public events are two different things, with confidence based on our positive experiences with two national organizations related closely to the president, I stood my ground and gave the original speech. The audience in this communist country was surprised when they heard me say the name of God, not just once, but dozens of times. I was calm, as I knew I should be in that circumstance. It was revolutionary to give such a speech in the Great Hall of the People. It was the revolutionary power of a woman. In such circumstances, I carried out that 1992 speaking tour in 113 locations around the world.

When I departed Korea for this speaking tour, I had several outfits, a collection suitable for the variety of climates I would encounter. When I returned, all I had was the suit I was wearing. I always give away my clothes, and I had been gone for most of the year. When my husband welcomed me, his first words were, "You did a good job." Then, glancing at my hands, out of the blue, he asked, "By the way, where's your wedding ring?"

I looked at my hand. Only then did I remember it was gone. "I don't have the ring," I said, "I must have given it to someone."

"To whom did you give it?" he asked, incredulous.

"Ahhh, yes, I gave it to someone during the tour," I said. "But I don't remember who it was. I gave it to someone either to keep as an heirloom or, if necessary, to sell for her family's well-being."

My husband made the natural comment, "It's fine that you gave it away, but you don't remember who you gave it to?"

We really don't focus so much on personal possessions, and that is how we've always been. As we looked into each other's eyes, my husband's gratitude for that quality in me surfaced. He collected himself, smiled and nodded, and the welcoming celebration proceeded.

My husband and I could not have a honeymoon. I didn't mind, but he had always felt remorseful. When we visited the Netherlands during a speaking tour—it must have been 1969—after much thought, he bought me a small diamond ring with some money he had saved. That was the meaning of that ring, but now I had given it to someone and had even forgotten that I had done so. I do give things away out of sympathetic love, and then I let it go. Those who give what they have, give their heart, and even their life, and do not cling to the memory, are the ones whom God visits. My husband knows I am like that, and he is, too. Just as I had done, he let it go.

That 1992 global speaking tour was by no means a vacation; it covered 113 cities, 24 time zones, venue upon venue, check-in upon check-in, crowd upon crowd, schedule upon schedule, pressure upon pressure. I was speaking on the value and mission of women, the way to peace in the family and world, and the love of Heavenly Parent. This was to open the gates for the world's people who are stranded as lonely orphans, to welcome them into the loving, liberating embrace of True Parents. Only when we receive God's Blessing in marriage can we leave the orphanage and receive our inheritance as the sons and daughters of God who enjoy true happiness.

I am here to give my wedding ring to everyone.

CHAPTER 5

THE EMBLEM OF THE KINGDOM OF HEAVEN

The most beautiful flowers of Korea

The first time people hear the Little Angels sing, they are astonished. They feel swept up in a beautiful wave of love and harmony. I hear comments like these all the time:

"To me, it sounds like the voices of angels." And if one person expresses such admiration, the next will pour out even more praise.

"What I am listening to is not a song! It is a happy chorus that brings rain to a parched soul."

If we were to capture the distinctive feature of the Unification movement in one phrase, it would be "the culture of filial heart." "Filial heart," for which I coined the Korean word, "*hyojeong*," signifies sincere devotion and love toward our Heavenly Parent. "Heart," for which my husband coined the Korean word, "*shimjeong*," is the essence of beauty and original root of love. It is beauty that stimulates love to surge forth eternally. The culture of heart transcends time and space. In the world where God's will has been realized, a pure and immaculate culture of heart will flow forth like a river and waft like a breeze through all forms of artistic creativity.

Founded in 1962, the Little Angels have performed some 7,000 times around the world.

As Jesus said of the little children, the kingdom of heaven belongs to such as these. A child sleeping peacefully is the epitome of peace. A child's innocent smile clearly illustrates what happiness is. A child's voice is gentle, but it opens the door to the heart, reconciles strangers, and expresses happiness and peace. It is the power of the innocent voices of children joined in song that led my husband and I to found The Little Angels of Korea, a children's folk dance and singing troupe.

During the Korean War, I saw many talented artists who were poor and homeless, seeking refuge and unable to display their work. During this time of Korea's post-war poverty, few people believed in the power of music and dance. No one even listened when my husband and I talked about culture and the arts. All they did was shake their heads and say, "It's difficult just finding enough to eat... Don't waste your time thinking about culture." But in my view, culture is not a luxury; it is a life essential.

For 5,000 years, the Korean people refined culture as a part of everyday life. We are a people of the arts. The Korean culture is unique and beautiful, even though some of it was lost during the deprivations of the twentieth century. During my school days, one of my favorite pastimes was drawing. I even thought about becoming an artist. Instead of investing in that dream on a personal level, I helped bring the exceptional beauty of Korean culture onto the world stage.

That is how the Little Angels came to be. Korea was in a state of poverty and political turmoil when, on Children's Day, May 5, 1962, my husband and I founded The Little Angels of Korea Children's Folk Ballet. Within our membership, there were many dissenting voices. Their first argument was that if we lacked the money to build a church, how would we raise money to run a song and dance troupe? Some opined that an adult choir would be better than a children's dance troupe. There were perhaps a dozen objections to the plan, but my husband and I remained steadfast, and eventually, everyone united behind The Little Angels of Korea.

The next hurdle was finding a place for the girls to practice. We managed to get free use of a dilapidated warehouse. It had a leaky roof and broken windows. With some hasty repairs we made it into a practice room. There was no stove there, so the girls blew on their hands to keep warm in the winter. Once the news got out about what we were doing, those opposed to our church laughed and said, "Angels fly in heaven; those girls look like they are splashing around in a swamp!"

But the girls and their instructor had a passion to succeed. They kept the Little Angels' motto in their hearts: "A beautiful heart makes a dance beautiful. A beautiful heart makes a song beautiful. A beautiful heart makes a face beautiful." For three years, they went through intense training, shedding sweat and tears. After that training, they departed on a world tour with the grand slogan, "Let's take the Korean flag to the world!"

~~~

The Little Angels' first performance, in the fall of 1965, was at a concert for former US President Dwight D. Eisenhower in Gettysburg, Pennsylvania, a place made famous by President Lincoln's address honoring those who died at that turning point of the American Civil War. This was the start of the Little Angels' travels to showcase Korea's beautiful culture. After the concert, President Eisenhower reminisced about his 1952 visit to Korea and praised the dance troupe highly. "It's as if heaven's angels have come down to earth," he said with a gentle smile.

It was very bold for this novice group to give its first public performance before a former American president. Even singers and dancers who were well-known in their own countries did not impress audiences in the United States. But I was not worried at all. Children singing is innocence itself, and I knew from experience that innocent children create peace and harmony.

Starting with the performance at Gettysburg, the Little Angels brought joy everywhere they went. They performed in many venues in the United States. When they began Korean songs such as "Springtime in my Hometown" or "Arirang," people's brows at first would wrinkle due to their unfamiliarity. Then they would close their eyes and listen. Finally, they would be moved to tears. When the Little Angels danced "The Little Bride and Groom" in their traditional Korean costumes, people would follow along with the beat and respond with heartfelt applause. When a dancer wearing traditional Korean white socks would raise her feet in the air, representing the elegant and beautiful curves found in Korean art, Westerners were delighted. Even without uttering a single word, The Little Angels conveyed our tradition and beauty. They toured the world as ambassadors of Korea's culture, displaying a youthful energy, purity and happiness for which Western audiences were longing.

Heart touches heart

One day, the Little Angels general director, Dr. Bo Hi Pak, received an invitation. It was from the United Kingdom. In the early 1970s, it was very difficult for a Korean to go to Great Britain but, amazingly, the Little Angels were invited to perform for the British royal family. Such an invitation had never before been extended to a performer from anywhere in the Far East, let alone Korea.

The dancers quickly packed their bags. Reaching London required that they change planes several times. At the Royal Variety Performance at the London Palladium, held for Queen Elizabeth II in 1971, among all the outstanding performers, these beautiful girls from the Republic of Korea were a bright light. Their cute yet dynamic and colorful dances brought several standing ovations. The event was highlighted in the newspapers and on television the next day. In the minds of the British people, Korea was no longer a cultural backwater, but rather a nation with a vibrant artistic tradition.

The lovely voices of the Little Angels of Korea have now been heard in more than 80 nations. They have toured five continents and performed over 7,000 times, including at the Kennedy Center for the Performing Arts in 1971, and the United Nations General Assembly in 1973. They have appeared on television more than 800 times and have met many presidents and prime ministers. They performed for the bicentennial celebration of America's independence and the 10th anniversary of diplomatic relations between China and South Korea. They have toured Japan, the United States, Europe, Asia, Africa and South America. Everywhere they have gone, they have received praise and applause. In the spring of 1990, they performed in Moscow, the

Soviet Union, and melted the hearts of communist leaders. In May 1998, their performance in Pyongyang, North Korea, contributed to efforts for reconciliation between North and South Korea.

───✦───

Among the most meaningful of the Little Angels' tours was when they visited each of the 22 nations that participated in the United Nations' response during the Korean War. In 2010, to mark the 60th anniversary of the outbreak of the Korean War, we sent the Little Angels to perform for the war veterans of the 22 nations that had sent troops or humanitarian and medical aid. It was among the most meaningful of the Little Angels' tours. Over a period of three years, they visited each nation, offering a "performance of gratitude" in honor of the veterans. We in Korea had received extraordinary assistance from these nations in our hour of need, and we declared that it was time to give something back. Those whom we met still remembered Korea vividly, and many said they had never ceased loving our country.

Some Koreans at home criticized the tour because we were a private group and did not officially represent the government. But we represented the heart of the Korean people, as well as God's heart. In every country, war veterans proudly came on stage in our performances wearing their faded uniforms and showcasing their medals. This brings up one uplifting story.

Ethiopia and the Republic of South Africa were the two African nations that sent troops. In the 1980s, when communists took power in Ethiopia, they displaced all the Korean War veterans to a camp on the outskirts of Addis Ababa. In reality, that place was like a concentration camp. The veterans shared painful memories of how the regime had persecuted them, and how they had to sell their medals to provide for their families. When they saw the Little Angels, they were moved to tears as they realized that the poor, ragged, divided nation of Korea was now a developed nation ready to thank them. The happy ending is that the Little Angels' concert brought the veterans' plight to the attention of the present government, which is now making up for past mistreatment.

At the tour's concert in Washington, DC, Korean War veterans in their eighties wept when the Little Angels sang "Arirang" and "God Bless America." In Copenhagen, Denmark, Princess Benedikte joined some 300 veterans of the war effort to watch the performance.

After a warm welcome by Nepalese students and citizens upon the arrival in Kathmandu, the Little Angels performed brilliantly at the inauguration of the International Association of Parliamentarians for Peace, an event that took place in 2016. The Nepalese were deeply moved by the concert held at the presidential palace as well as in other performance halls, and their media gave the Little Angels high praise: "The Little Angels are representatives who are answering God's call; they are guardian angels, spreading peace worldwide."

August 11, 2019: Dedication of the Hyojeong International Cultural Center, HJ Cheonwon, South Korea

A child alone may not make much impact but when a group of children come together and sing with pure hearts, their voices can melt hardened hearts and dispel war and conflict. People often think that politics moves the world, but that is not the case. It is culture and art that move the world. It is affection, not reason, that touches people in their innermost being. When hearts become receptive, ideologies and political regimes can change.

Half a century ago, the Little Angels set out to bring Korean culture to the world. They were a harbinger of the Korean wave, including K-Pop, that is currently sweeping the world. Wherever you go in the world, cheers and applause for Korean culture abound. The beginning point of this phenomenon was the Little Angels' concert at Gettysburg in 1965. The children's innocent performances continue to captivate audiences and remind skeptics of the truth that we can become one.

Artistry that enriches the world

In 1984 several talented graduates from the Little Angels Performing Arts School, now the Sunhwa Arts Middle and High School, had returned from their study at schools such as the Princess Grace Academy in Monaco and the Royal Ballet School in the United Kingdom. Recognizing their great potential, we created a professional ballet company, the Universal Ballet, to provide an opportunity for these talented youth to display their skills, delight the public and impact our nation.

At that time, my husband conveyed the internal value of ballet in these words:

"When a ballerina stands on the tips of her toes with her head raised toward Heaven, her posture represents reverence for God. It is an expression of ardent longing. Ballet dancers use the beautiful body given to them by God to express their love for Him. It is the highest form of art."

A scene from Swan Lake, performed by Universal Ballet in North America and Europe. Universal Ballet was founded in 1984 and has given some 1,800 performances, presenting some 100 ballets in 21 countries.

Adrienne Dellas was the company's artistic director. Moon Hoon-sook, my daughter-in-law, a Little Angels alumna who studied ballet at the Princess Grace Academy and was a principal dancer in the Washington Ballet Company in Washington, DC, was a founding member. In the summer of 1984, the Universal Ballet gave its first performance, "Cinderella," at the Little Angels Performing Arts Center in Seoul.

At that time, the National Ballet Company was the sole ballet company in Korea. It performed only within the country, and this put Korea on the fringe of the ballet world. The Universal Ballet Company brought Korean ballet to the world stage. The troupe has toured 21 nations and presented some 100 different ballets in 1,800 performances, reflecting its motto, "Heavenly Art Creating a World of Beauty." Among its many honors, the company has received the Republic of Korea Culture and Arts Award.

Until the early 2000s, the Universal Ballet featured the Russian classical ballet style. After that, it expanded its repertoire to include

European romantic ballets and modern ballets. It now performs ballets from Korea and other nations and creates its own innovative and original performances. It was the first Korean ballet company, and the second in Asia, to perform John Cranko's masterpiece of dramatic ballet, "Onegin." Furthermore, it was the first Korean company to perform Sir Kenneth MacMillan's "Romeo and Juliet," a masterpiece in the repertoire of the UK Royal Ballet Company.

The company also created unique ballets based on Korean folk tales and traditions. One of its most famous works, "Shim Chung," created in 1986, is a tale of filial love. It has been performed 200 times in 10 countries, touching the hearts of people all over the world. During its world tour in 2012, the company was invited to showcase the beauty of Korean ballet in the global centers of ballet, Moscow and Paris. "Chunhyang," an original ballet based on an ancient story of pure love, and the ballet musical "Shim Chung," recast for children, were both very well received.

Years ago, when Korea had nothing to offer the global culture, the Universal Ballet Company stood like a lonely crane. By overcoming many difficulties and touring every continent, it has shown all people Korea's high artistic standard. It will continue to go forward, guided by the love of God.

Media expressing universal values

The year 1975 was a time when a shadow of gloom hung over the world. The United States pulled out of Vietnam that April, leaving the country in the hands of the communists. People were shocked and horrified as the communists in Vietnam and its neighbor Cambodia slaughtered entire populations. Across the globe, communism was gaining in strength.

I was born in North Korea, and I experienced firsthand the cruelty of communism and the wretchedness of war, so I knew very well that when Vietnam fell, it would lead to bloody massacres and the spread of its harsh ideology to neighboring countries.

In Japan of the 1970s, the Unification movement was growing, but communism was also gaining power. The Korean residents in Japan created separate pro-Seoul and pro-Pyongyang groups and they often engaged in confrontation. My husband and I decided that the most effective way to influence Japan as a free society, and protect it from communism, would be to create a newspaper.

In democratic countries, the media is more often one-sided than balanced. Trying to gain market share, editors pander to forces that persecute those who aren't politically correct or who practice a minority religion. My husband and I imagined a different kind of media, one that is constructive and represents fairness and absolute values. With this in mind, in January 1975 we founded the *Sekai Nippo* newspaper in Tokyo.

Our Japanese members had great expectations for the paper but found that maintaining a newspaper is like climbing a hill carrying a heavy load on a dark night. Left-wing groups opposed us in every conceivable way. At the same time, however, *Sekai Nippo* gained support from law-abiding citizens and anti-communist organizations. It became a newspaper loved by the Japanese people. The power of truth protected Japan from communism. To this day, *Sekai Nippo* fearlessly reports the objective truth.

In early 1981 when my husband and I heard that *The Washington Star*, the conservative voice in Washington, DC, was closing down, we were concerned. There were two well-established newspapers in that city, *The Washington Star* and *The Washington Post*. *The Washington Star*, which had been in operation for over 130 years, had run into financial difficulties. Soon there would be only one newspaper in the most politically powerful city of the United States, and that newspaper, *The Washington Post*, was left-leaning in its editorial stance.

There was a need for a newspaper in Washington that would protect faith, freedom and family values, and no American conservatives were willing to step into the breach. When my husband and I decided to take this on, people trying to be prudent and wise told us again and again that it would be difficult to publish a new newspaper in the capital of the United States. We had never shied away from a task because it was difficult, and we didn't then.

May 17, 1982: The Washington Times, *Washington, DC*

On May 17, 1982, after a great deal of effort to find a building and printing presses and hire competent, dedicated staff, the first issue of *The Washington Times* was published. Opponents said that *The Washington Times* would be a propaganda instrument for the Unification Church but such words reflected prejudice.

It is difficult these days to run a newspaper at a profit, and *The Washington Times* lost money from the outset. Yet its absence would leave no conservative newspaper in the US capital. It would mean the newspaper that championed faith and family would have disappeared. Seeing the financial spreadsheets, people wondered, "How long until they close down?" Nonetheless, the more they doubted us, the greater was my husband's and my faith, and the greater was the commitment of *The Washington Times* staff.

Together with them, we resolutely defended democracy while advocating family values, morality and the role of women. As a result, the newspaper's popularity grew. Every year, the paper did better, and now in the age of the internet, it is one of the most influential newspapers in the United States.

At a banquet to commemorate the 15th anniversary of the newspaper's founding, we received congratulatory messages from well-known leaders worldwide. Former US President Ronald Reagan let people know that we played a key role in defeating communism when he said of the newspaper:

"Like me, you arrived in Washington at the beginning of the most momentous decade of the century. Together, we rolled up our sleeves and got to work. And – oh, yes – we won the Cold War."

Prime Minister Margaret Thatcher of the United Kingdom also expressed her gratitude. She sent greetings, saying:

"In difficult times, even more than in easy ones, the voice of conservatism must make itself heard in the media. It isn't always easy, but of this, we can be sure: While *The Washington Times* is alive and well, conservative views will never be drowned out."

The Washington Times is influential, yet it is not a newspaper appealing only to the elite. It represents all people and inspires citizens to live decent and healthy everyday lives. *The Washington Times* has established itself as a voice of truth for people all over the world.

Justice after tears

In the 1990s, when the Chinese government initiated its Northeast Asia Project to clarify historical facts and protect that area's stability, the *Segye Ilbo* newspaper sent a correspondent to the cities of Dalian and Dandong to do research. The correspondent was eager to visit the site of the Lushun Courthouse in Dalian, formerly a Japanese colonial court in that city, which the Japanese called Ryojun. Yet the courthouse, where a number of Korean patriots had been unjustly tried, was nowhere to be found. The Chinese government had long since sold the building.

My husband and I heard this report with heavy hearts. It pained Koreans to hear how the historical footprints of our heroes and heroines of the Independence Movement, who had risked their lives for Korea's freedom, were gradually disappearing. We decided to buy the building.

To us, the Lushun Courthouse is priceless. It represents the suffering of the Korean people in modern history and the legacy of their patriotic spirit. Our viewpoint, shared by many Koreans, was that such a historic site should not have fallen into indifferent hands.

In the end, after negotiating with the owner, the Segye Ilbo Corporation bought the building and restored the Lushun Courthouse as a museum. They invited experts to visit the site and, after conducting thorough research of old documents, they recreated the original courtroom. The Lushun Courthouse site is now a must-see historic landmark for freedom for young people from China and Korea and others who visit Dalian.

As this was a project benefiting all of Korea, we invited Korean citizens to contribute money. In 1993, through the Segye Ilbo Corporation, we founded the Yeosun Patriotic Martyrs Memorial Foundation Corporation. Besides gathering historical stories about the bravery, determination and sacrifice of those who fought for Korea's independence, the Foundation also works for peace in Northeast Asia.

Historically, relations between neighboring countries in northeast Asia have been complicated. Creating peace is like unraveling a ball of tangled yarn; it is difficult to find where to begin. But nothing will be accomplished by sitting with arms crossed. When the Segye Times Corporation reconstructed the Lushun Courthouse, it did so to capture the anguish of the past age and enable visitors to experience the history of the Korean people overcoming a national crisis. It also points to the importance of creating peace within and among nations.

As well as launching newspapers in Japan and the United States, our movement launched *Tiempos del Mundo* in Latin America and *The Middle East Times* in Istanbul. But it was only in 1989 that the Korean government instituted the freedom of the press that allowed us to launch the *Segye Ilbo* newspaper in Seoul.

February 1, 1989: Founding of Segye Ilbo, *Seoul, Korea*

Since a religious movement founded the newspaper, we naturally faced opposition. As in the United States and Japan, mockery circulated. "Just watch it become a mouthpiece promoting the Unification Church," people said, "It'll be nothing but a religious tract." The haughtiest voices predicted, "It'll stop printing before the year is out."

But our determination to produce a professional news source that could serve Korea by providing fair and unbiased news and opinion was unwavering. On February 1, 1989, the presses started up and 1.2 million copies of the first edition of *Segye Ilbo* came rolling out. We held fast to the creed that the news media must be the voice of conscience and of the truth. This conviction has remained steadfast for more than 30 years.

Our efforts garnered more than just verbal criticism. After *Segye Ilbo* exposed the Korean ruling party's corruption, innocent and unrelated enterprises we had founded were suddenly subjected to overbearing tax investigations that drove some into bankruptcy. The government targeted companies such as Tongil Industries, which produced essential machine parts, and Dongyang Agricultural Machinery, which manufactured specialized farming equipment, and forced them to shut down. Various powerful interests demanded that we fire the newspaper's chief editor.

We did not surrender to threats or enticements; instead, we raised the banner of social justice and virtue. Over time, with steadfast publishing of valuable news and opinion, *Segye Ilbo* has prevailed.

When my husband and I conceived of *Segye Ilbo*, we knew it was being born into the world at a turbulent time. Though it has stood alone as a pine tree in an empty field, *Segye Ilbo* has consistently defended justice while exposing fraud, corruption and other social ills. The newspaper caters to no political ideology or religious group. Its editors and reporters are exemplary professionals investing their blood, sweat and tears for the citizens of Korea and of the world.

Giving creates prosperity

As a little girl, I never had money and hardly knew what it was. When I got a bit older, in the maelstrom of the division of Korea, we had to flee our hometown empty-handed to preserve our lives. We remained penniless for a long time. Moreover, my maternal grandmother and my mother were devoted to God's will and our lives had little to do with money.

After I married, tithes and offerings came in and went out just as fast for public purposes. I did not have any concern about making a fashion statement. Sometimes, when I saw an expensive purse, I wondered, "What might the money in that purse be used for?" More important than how much money is in a wallet is the question of how it is spent. The path of one's money shapes one's fate. According to God's word, our responsibility is to have dominion of love over all things and to share our prosperity. As explained in Genesis, God made Adam and Eve and told them to "be fruitful and multiply, fill the earth and have dominion over all things."

Our movement's economic activities began humbly in Father Moon's mud-walled hut in Beomil-dong, Busan, during the last months of the Korean War. Father Moon and one disciple, Won Pil Kim, would create and sell simple portraits for American soldiers. When the church moved to Seoul, members collected stamps and sold them, and they colored in black-and-white photos and sold them along the roadside. Through these and other small businesses, we supported our missionary activities.

Our first step on the path to a real business venture was in 1960 when we set up Tongil Industries. Korea now exports all kinds of merchandise throughout the world, but in the 1960s, no one would ever have imagined that Korea's machine industry would develop as robustly as it has. We began Tongil Industries with a Japanese lathe that was destined for the trash bin. Our prayer was that God would bless our new company and that it would one day become the world's foremost manufacturer of machine parts. By developing our expertise, Tongil Industries grew from manufacturing the Yehwa Air Rifle to making parts for equipment used in our country's defense. As a leading machinery enterprise in Korea, we not only acquired technologies to help Korea, we went on to share our technology with people around the world.

Next, we established the Ilhwa Company Ltd., which pioneered the export of high-quality ginseng products. Ginseng was unknown in the West at the time but now it is a household item. Ilhwa is recognized both for its excellent products and as a leader in ginseng science.

Research and development of Ilhwa Company Ltd,. ginseng products for health

Inspired by our vision, our members have started many businesses. While this supports the economic development of our country and the world, our purpose goes beyond that. Our goal is for all people in the world to enjoy mutual prosperity. We believe in sharing the tools of technology among all peoples. With true family values and technology in harmony with the natural world, we all can live and work together in a pleasant social environment.

Our philosophy of living for the sake of others is the driving force behind all of this. It is a fundamental truth that we should take care of those who are less fortunate than ourselves. A wealthy person who is grateful to others and helps others will create a wealthy community, nation and world.

The creation is a gift God has given each of us. Every human being should be able to enjoy this gift fully. It is contrary to God's will for one individual to gain possession of everything, or for one country not to share its scientific developments, technologies and resources in times of need, or use such things to dominate other nations. Yes, some person or group in some country develops each new technology. The next step is to enable others to benefit, so that all can enjoy health, well-being and comfort. This is the way of mutual prosperity.

We should not take pride in having crisp bills inside fancy purses. Instead, we should focus on how our assets can benefit others. True pride comes when we spend our money for purposes larger than ourselves.

Science is a stepping-stone

Once in a while, you hear religious people devalue science as having nothing to do with God, and secular people devalue religion as having no practical use. Both sides separate God and science. Both are in error. God wants us to develop science and technology as tools with which we can exercise the dominion of love over all things. And that is God's great blessing. We must love nature with the same heart as God, and cultivate it for the benefit of humanity. This is God-centered science and technology.

In 1972, my husband and I convened the first International Conference on the Unity of the Sciences (ICUS). As with any new project, we endured many obstacles and birth pangs to bring it into the world. And then, after ICUS was launched, many scholars accused us of using scientists to legitimate ourselves. In many cases, the development of ICUS went like this: A scholar would be approached with a personal invitation saying, "Professor, I sincerely invite you to attend this upcoming Science Conference."

He or she would send a response that said, "I have heard that the founders of this forum are Rev. Dr. Sun Myung Moon and his wife, and I am opposed to them."

Several years later, this same scholar would accept our invitation and present his or her work at the conference. This was because he or she had realized the true motivation of ICUS. As the years passed, we received enthusiastic responses from distinguished scholars worldwide who were wary at first, then participated and became loyal supporters. This was because through ICUS they discovered a larger purpose for their work.

<hr />

We always considered ICUS themes with care. The first ICUS, which convened in New York City, was on the topic, "The Moral Orientation of the Sciences." My husband and I, as the founders, wanted to raise the question of what science could do for the sake of humanity.

"The purpose and goal of science are to realize humanity's dreams," my husband said in his opening address. "Scientific civilization, by its very nature, must be shared by humankind as a whole."

We convened the second ICUS in Tokyo in 1973 under the theme, "Contemporary Science and Ethical Values." Thanks to the participation of five Nobel Prize laureates, the conference attracted much attention. While the first conference assembled just 20 scientists from seven nations, the second ICUS drew 60 participants from 18 nations. In just one year, it had become a global forum.

Father Moon gives the founder's address at an early ICUS

By 1981, when we held the 10th ICUS in Seoul with 808 scholars attending from approximately 100 nations, ICUS had become the leading global forum of its kind. During that event, we proposed the free and generous exchange of technology among nations, something that had never been imagined in history. Our view is that because science and technology are revealed and given by God, they are the common wealth of all humanity. We emphasized that no country should monopolize these common assets. My husband and I sponsored the ICUS forums to promote the free exchange of science and technology.

Our intention especially was to see science and technology shared with the developing countries in Africa, Latin America and Asia. Put another way, we wanted developed countries to globalize the cutting-edge standards of science and technology by sharing their tools and methods with developing nations. To set an example, when we saw food shortages in some parts of Africa, we donated machinery for a German missionary to build a sausage factory in Zambia. We arranged for education in advanced methods of crop cultivation and livestock breeding. In South America, we raised cattle. Also, we planted trees and took other measures to keep nature green and pristine.

In Kona, on Hawaii's Big Island, we started a coffee plantation. Harvesting coffee beans is strenuous work and cultivating the plants requires great skill. Initially, we suffered serious losses because we did not spray pesticides, which damage human health. In time, we found a way to repel insects without using harmful chemicals, and now we're producing premium coffee that is pesticide-free.

We purchased automobile assembly lines in Germany and established automobile factories in China and North Korea. When we saw farmers doing the back-breaking work of sowing rice by hand, we acquired an agricultural machinery factory and supplied them with the equipment they lacked. Looking upward into the sky, we established Korea Times Aviation to support state-of-the-art aviation technology and space engineering. These efforts and more naturally go through ups and downs, but our vision is unchanging. We learn as we go and our investment will continue.

February 23, 2018: The 24th ICUS (Seoul); following a hiatus since the year 2000, ICUS was relaunched with the 23rd ICUS in 2017

For years, the ICUS forums led to countless scientific collaborations and new friendships. In 2000, we entered a new phase of the providence and put ICUS on hold. I renewed the annual International Conference on the Unity of the Sciences in 2017. The 24th ICUS, held in 2018, gathered hundreds of participants devoted to pioneering new paradigms for scientific research. In my opening remarks to that conference, I cast the vision:

"To solve the many problems facing our world, whether they are religious or scientific, first you must know correctly about God, who is the origin of the universe, and about True Parents. Then you will be able to find the solutions."

ICUS is gathering scientists, engineers and inventors to harmonize the technologies and tools in our hands with the ecology of the natural world as well as our original human nature created by God, for the purpose of realizing authentic human happiness and lasting peace.

CHAPTER 6

CREATING THE ROAD TO ONE WORLD

❧

One street, one global neighborhood

On the southern Japanese island of Kyushu, there is a small port city named Karatsu. This city on the shores of the Korea Strait is famous for the pottery that bears its name. Karatsu pottery was originally created by Korean potters. During the 1980s, key members visited this city several times on our behalf to develop an international project. Karatsu was the launching site for an initiative that my husband had announced at our International Conference on the Unity of the Sciences in the autumn of 1981—the construction of an international peace highway circumscribing the globe.

The vision is for a high-speed transportation artery linking the entire globe. On the day of its completion, much of our world will become one village linked by one road. The process of constructing the highway itself provides the world's peoples and governments a common purpose. The transnational lines of commerce and recreation that open up will stimulate inter-ethnic exchange of culture and goods and draw us to live in harmony as neighbors.

That highway would pass through a tunnel connecting Korea's Busan with Karatsu, and there, in 1986, we commenced a pilot tunnel construction. I had long been interested in visiting the site. Finally, in 2016, I had the opportunity to go and see it. During my visit, I renewed our movement's commitment to the peace highway. I believe that the world's peoples are ready for this and that the time is ripe for launching the project based upon a global plan. To tell this story to the world, from the streets to the senate buildings, I had already created an affiliated project, "Peace Road." It consists of public activism publicizing the international highway, and it has turned into a global movement for peace. I'll share more about Peace Road later.

November 14, 2016: At the construction site of a test tunnel built for the Korea-Japan Underwater Tunnel, Karatsu, Kyushu, Japan

Regarding construction, the biggest challenges are those of crossing the spans of ocean that separate Alaska from Russia and Korea from Japan. The divides between those territories are both physical and spiritual, and the joint commitment to building a road uniting them will represent important steps toward peace for the human race. Of course, it is not an easy task. Since the dawn of human history, there has been no greater engineering and social challenge. Yet I know that it is possible and that it represents the ultimate task that must be accomplished in our era—the harmonious cooperation of all peoples and governments.

Attitudes that persist based on the tormented history between Korea and Japan are a huge obstacle, and they give rise to opposition to the tunnel. But we have to forgive, forget and set our minds on the positive outcomes. An undersea tunnel connecting Busan in Korea with Karatsu in Japan will boost our respective abilities to contribute to the global economy. The anchor cities of Karatsu and Busan will become hubs for global trade, linking the Eurasian continent to the Pacific region. The tunnel will unite these two nations' cultural assets, both traditional and cutting-edge, for global tourism. Most importantly, its construction will plant the roots of peace in Asia. And cooperation between these two countries will serve as a model for Heaven healing the wounds of conflict and hostility felt in nations and among peoples throughout the world.

The reality is, however, that these two nations pursue their own interests. I encourage their leaders to think about England and France, who waged wars against each other for a century yet joined hands to build the Channel Tunnel that connects them together. If the Korean and Japanese peoples open their hearts and accomplish genuine forgiveness and reconciliation, we will see the Korea-Japan Peace Tunnel built in our time. This tunnel will not just symbolize, but realize, humanity's future based not on fear but on hope.

My husband and I therefore prayed that constructing this tunnel as part of the peace highway would create a low-pressure area on the

Korean Peninsula, into which the high-pressure areas surrounding the peninsula to the east and west would converge to bring unity on the peninsula. Looking at a map with a motherly heart, I feel as if the island and continent long for each other, and the peninsula is where they meet.

The second major challenge for the International Peace Highway is that of crossing the Bering Strait between Russia and the United States. That location will prove to be even more challenging than the Korea Strait. The Bering Strait once represented the ideological divide between the democratic and communist camps as the United States and Russia grappled with each other. Connecting these two nations is a vital step toward global peace and unification.

I want everyone to be able to travel the International Peace Highway by car or even bicycle from Cape Town to Santiago, from London to New York. I want taking a trip with your sweetheart through any country around the world to be as easy as visiting your hometown. One end of the highway will be the Cape of Good Hope at the southern tip of Africa; the other end will be Cape Horn at the southern tip of South America. It will cross the Bering Strait to link the African continent and Eurasia with the Americas. From the perspective of this highway, Korea will be the midpoint. By Heaven's grace, the birthplace of the True Parents, for whom humankind has long awaited, will be at the very center.

Many people question how we can accomplish such a formidable task. Yet history shows that all great achievements have come amid difficulties. If it is the will of God, there must be a way. We already have the engineering prowess to construct a bridge-tunnel complex spanning the Bering Strait. Concerning the cost, we need to put it in perspective. Compared to the money that the world is investing in wars that do nothing but destroy nations and people, the cost of a bridge-tunnel constructed for the sake of peace is insignificant. Nations and movements sacrifice lives and resources following the logic of power—a foolish and ineffective way to resolve perceived injustice or settle disputes. Our Heavenly Parent is showing us the path of true peace. As the Book of Isaiah says, now is the time to beat our swords into plowshares.

I have mentioned the Peace Road project. It consists of events in which people of all ages and nationalities, wearing Peace Road tee shirts and carrying a Peace Road flag, ride bicycles or walk to show their support for our proposed International Peace Highway. Their path ends at local government centers where officials and social and religious leaders speak at rallies, publicly announcing their support for the initiative and stimulating publicity in local media. Leaders and citizens of many countries, including members of the International Association of Parliamentarians for Peace, have welcomed the Peace Road movement. In 2015, people in more than 120 countries participated. All together, the peace riders that year symbolically traversed the world in 93 days.

Bold love breaks an iron curtain

With the coming of the year 1990, people were feeling hopeful that the world might truly change. I would hear one person saying, "The term 'Cold War' will soon no longer be heard," and another responding, "That may be your hope, but the Soviet Union is holding on, and communism is gaining power in many countries. Peace cannot be so easily achieved." They would agree on one point—it won't be easy.

In the late 1980s, with American conservatism on the rise, the Solidarity movement generating success in Poland, and *glasnost* and *perestroika* progressing in Russia, the world was entering an era of reconciliation, at least on a superficial level. But at the same time, Moscow-directed insurgencies were building momentum in Africa, Asia and Central America. Moscow had succeeded in forcing the United

States to pull out of Vietnam, allowing communism to run rampant there and in the killing fields of Cambodia. Marxists were still bent on their ambition to communize the entire world.

At that time, my husband and I sponsored the World Media Association fact-finding tours, taking Western journalists to see firsthand the conditions in the Soviet Union and other communist states. Informing journalists with indisputable facts was an effective step toward ending the Cold War. Besides taking the blinders off these journalists' eyes, the tours generated positive relations with Russian media. In addition, we welcomed the teams from communist countries during the 1988 Seoul Olympics, serving them with Korean food and gifts. On that foundation, my husband and I decided to go to Moscow to meet President Mikhail Gorbachev.

Seventeen years earlier, on July 1, 1973, we had declared that one day we would "march to Moscow." As we fought to overthrow communism, we had envisioned holding a rally in Red Square, and in October that year we announced this to our members. Most were enthusiastic, though the prophecy reminded some of the dream-like visions of Don Quixote. Sunburst, one of our church bands, turned our vision into a song, "Red Square," with the immortal refrain, "Must Go to Moscow!" Although the accomplishment of that goal took longer than we wished, my husband and I never forgot our commitment. We believed that winning the Soviet leadership's heart in Moscow's Kremlin Palace would tip the scale toward liberating God and all of humanity.

Our Victory Over Communism work over the years was ultimately not about a political system, nor was it a public relations strategy to gain support from anti-communists. At its root was, and is, the question of "God or no God." The real purpose of our struggle is to liberate the communist world—and the West as well—from atheistic materialism. During the Cold War, most people in the free world, including the journalists on our fact-finding tours, had no idea what life was like under communism. Others in a position to know chose to turn a blind eye, hesitating to take action out of fear. In the meantime, hundreds of millions in the communist world endured dire circumstances, some not knowing where their next day's food would come from. To save these suffering millions, our Heavenly Parent pushed my husband and me to win over the Soviet Union—and opened the path by which we could do so.

Engaging the leadership of the Soviet Union was certainly no simple task. President Gorbachev had been implementing gradual reform, but he had to deal with an entrenched bureaucracy programmed to maintain a belligerent posture as the leading nation of the communist world. Hidden behind an Iron Curtain, the Soviet Union projected the image of a powerful, iron-fisted empire.

A few days before we departed for Moscow, my husband and I sat down to discuss our plan with senior members of the Unification Church. Some of them tried to dissuade us, arguing that it was too dangerous for us, as notable opponents of communism, to walk into the communist stronghold. No one could derail my husband's and my determination, however. Nonetheless, my husband, recognizing the seriousness of the matter, was considering the future. As he looked into the face of each and every one there, he said something unexpected: "It's time to decide who will lead the movement when I am not here."

All voices were silenced. Again he looked at the church leaders, one by one, and then spoke with care and gravity. "Even if I am not here, it is fine as long as Mother is present."

His statement conferred on me the serious position of co-founder of the Unification Church. Everyone was surprised at what Father Moon was saying, but I just listened quietly. Having accepted the mission of God's only begotten Daughter and Mother of peace, for 30 years

I had done my utmost to help my husband at the forefront of God's providence to save and guide the world. Now he had made it clear that Heaven's authority is equally with father and mother, husband and wife. It seemed he was making the announcement at that moment in case anything unfortunate happened in Moscow.

Later, Father Moon decided to share the same message with thousands of New York area members who had gathered to honor the 1990 Parents' Day with us. In his keynote address, he set into the public record that which he had stated to our leadership. There in the New Yorker Hotel, he declared, "Even when I am alone, I represent True Parents. And the same goes for Mother. When she is alone, she represents True Parents. Now there is nothing to worry about. Fundamentally I am the first founder of the church and Mother is the second founder. Until today, women have followed men, but from now on, they are on a horizontally even footing."

This was not a one-time statement from my husband. At a meeting on June 15, 1991, True Father proclaimed his *gomyeong* at Clearstone Deer Park Lodge in Canada, in the presence of representative Japanese women leaders. The *gomyeong* is a final decree a king leaves for his subjects before passing away. In this proclamation, my husband declared that after his ascension, I would continue our God-given mission and that the Japanese woman leaders should take responsibility to support me.

On November 27, 1994, at Belvedere Training Center in New York, Father Moon again announced my public mission as the movement's second founder. At that time, the educational program for 160,000 Japanese women and significant events in certain nations had concluded, so my role was expanding. On that day, I resolved in front of members, "Let's all pledge to become the family that will unite and establish the traditions of the True Parents."

April 9, 1990: The 11th World Media Conference, Moscow

In April 1990, a few days after that Parents' Day celebration, my husband and I, with our eldest son Hyo-jin, arrived in Moscow. The venue was the 11th World Media Conference and the 1st Summit Council for World Peace, sponsored by the World Media Association and the Association for the Unity of Latin America (AULA). During the conference, President Mikhail Gorbachev invited the participating world leaders to the Kremlin Palace. I was the only woman included on the invitation list and was treated very graciously. My husband and I awarded President Gorbachev the Grand Cross Medal for Freedom and Unification, which was presented by Ambassador Jose Maria Chaves, Chairman of AULA. We held President Gorbachev's hand and offered a simple benediction: "God bless you, Mr. President."

Of course, it was absolutely unacceptable under the communist regime to pray for God's blessing in the office of the president of the Soviet Union, the epicenter of the ideology-driven atheist state. Nonetheless, President Gorbachev was warm with us and struck a friendly tone in our chat after the prayer. "Mrs. Hak Ja Han Moon," he remarked, "I do like your traditional Korean dress. It looks beautiful on you."

April 11, 1990: Father and Mother Moon
with President Mikhail Gorbachev

I answered with a smile, "The First Lady Raisa always looks beautiful, too! Women all over the world respect her. I'm looking forward to the pleasure of meeting Mrs. Gorbachev tomorrow at the Little Angels' performance. My husband told me you are a handsome man, and I can see it's true." Through our conversation the atmosphere became friendly. President Gorbachev's smile was truly warm and bright; I had the impression that we all were flying on the clouds. I thought, "This is the power of prayer and the hand of God."

As the meeting went on, my husband did not hesitate to advise President Gorbachev. "The success of the Soviet Union depends on whether you put God at the center or not," he said, and he was emphatic: "Atheism will lead to nothing but self-destruction and disaster." Father Moon told President Gorbachev that the only way for the Soviet Union to survive was for Russia to continue his economic and political reforms and to allow freedom of religion. President Gorbachev's face showed he was well aware of the enormity of Father Moon's advice, yet he could not help but receive what we said. Never before had anyone said anything like that in the Kremlin. Looking back, I feel confident to say that the words we exchanged at that moment changed the history of the world. I truly felt that heaven and earth were listening to every word with bated breath.

April 11, 1990: Media conference participants meet with President Gorbachev at the Kremlin

Our meeting in the Kremlin and the overall conference created heavenly energy, and our movement's fortunes in the Soviet Union began to advance. President Gorbachev's confidence in my husband and me, and the Unification Church, increased by the day. It is amazing that, after that, the Soviet government would allow more than 3,000 Russian students and professors to travel to the United States for Divine Principle education. It was revolutionary.

The next year, a coup d'état took place in Moscow and instability ensued for a short time. President Gorbachev's efforts for political reform and openness had stirred up a reaction among the communist elite. The president was placed under arrest at his residence on the Crimean Peninsula. The insurrection lasted for three days and failed. Inspired by the road to democracy that President Gorbachev had pioneered, the people, especially the young, arose in Moscow in his defense, with Russian President Boris Yeltsin taking the lead in organizing the resistance. Those protestors, surely among whom were many we had educated in America, were the driving force in bringing Gorbachev and Yeltsin together, dissolving the Soviet Union and ending the Cold War. President Gorbachev's open-hearted reception of the prayer, "God bless you, Mr. President," that my husband and I offered in his office surely brought him a stroke of heavenly fortune.

I must add that all this would never have happened were it not for the work of the "butterfly missionaries" of our movement from Europe. Called to this mission, they had departed from their own countries and entered the Soviet Union and Eastern Europe as underground representatives of True Parents. The fall of the Soviet Union was the climax of God's invisible plan for which these faithful people had set conditions at the risk of their lives. Through a complex interweaving of events, each of them played a role in bringing about the dissolution of the Soviet Union and the shift toward democracy. Even today, they continue to pray and work for religious freedom and social progress in Russia on its path forward.

The year after our meeting with President Gorbachev, the Soviet Communist Party was disbanded and what I thought of as a frozen kingdom melted into the mists of history. During the 70 years since the 1917 Bolshevik Revolution, as communist governments took control of a third of the world's population, the blood of hundreds of millions of people had been shed. At long last, the Soviet Union lowered its red flag, its atheistic worldview discredited. When the Soviet dictatorship declared its own demise, the communist assertion that progress takes place through class conflict, struggle and hatred, was revealed as totally false.

History will show that my husband and I were skating on very thin ice when we entered the Soviet Union to meet President Gorbachev, and that this meeting took place at exactly the right time. In declaring that the world's only hope is a God-centered worldview, we played a decisive spiritual role, and the world's political landscape was forever changed.

An enemy becomes a friend

In 1946, the year after the restoration of Korean independence, Father Moon was arrested while evangelizing in North Korea. The police accused him of being a spy for South Korean President Syngman Rhee and locked him in the Daedong Detention Center in Pyongyang. His captors severely tortured him and threw what they thought was his dead body out onto the snow. His followers found him and in grief began preparing his funeral. Of course, Father Moon did not die. He clung onto life and, with the help of their prayers and herbal medicines, astonishingly, he revived.

A year later, Father Moon was arrested again and incarcerated in Hungnam special labor camp under a regime of forced labor at the nearby Hungnam Nitrogen Fertilizer Factory. For two years and eight months, he suffered indescribable hardships. It was an environment in which most prisoners died of malnutrition and physical exhaustion within six months.

As this was taking place, my mother and maternal grandmother also were imprisoned by the communist police for our religious beliefs and practices. They were released after much hardship. I have already recounted our separation from the rest of our family, our escape in 1948 with the help of my uncle, and our arduous journey to the South.

Over the subsequent decades, the North Korea government continued to treat us as its enemies. My husband and I had been carrying out Victory Over Communism activities throughout the world, and we received information that North Korean leader Kim Il Sung wanted to assassinate us. Our members' seven-day public fast and prayer across the street from the United Nations in 1974 publicized the plight of Japanese women held captive in North Korea. In June 1975 , shortly after the fall of Saigon, we held the World Rally for Korean Freedom, which brought over 1.2 million people to Yoido Plaza in Seoul to stand strong against communism.

With neither fear nor anger, my husband and I prayed ceaselessly for reconciliation between North and South Korea. We were not responsible for the division of the Korean Peninsula, but we took responsibility for its peaceful reunification. We have always felt that ending the conflict on the Korean Peninsula would turn the world toward peace. Hence, after returning from our meeting with Soviet President Mikhail Gorbachev, we decided that we would have to meet Chairman Kim Il Sung of North Korea. We set a goal: by the end of 1991.

For more than 40 years, my husband and I had been unable to return to our hometowns. Through the 1980s, we taught our principles in every corner of the world, but we couldn't go to North Korea, which is only an hour's flight from Seoul. It was the same for all displaced Koreans who had ended up in the south after the Korean War. Nothing can alleviate the longing and anguish that results from the inability to visit one's hometown, especially when it is so near. Nonetheless, the reason my husband and I wanted to go to North Korea was not to visit our hometowns and relatives, even though we missed them dearly. In fact, the experiences we had been through in the North would lead most people never to want to set foot there.

The determination we made to go to North Korea seemed an impossible dream. North Korea would not even allow groups of journalists from the West to enter. But we continued our sincere prayers of forgiveness and reconciliation, and had our members reach out to North Korea in any way possible, believing that God could make a way out of no way. In answer to our prayers, in mid-November 1991, while in the United States, a courier brought us a sealed invitation. We opened it in private. Addressed to us personally, it stated that Chairman Kim Il Sung was inviting us to visit North Korea.

Without informing our staff of our ultimate destination, we packed our clothes and departed for our church workshop center in Hawaii. Our family and personal staff were curious. "It's warm in Hawaii," they said. "But you are packing winter clothes!"

Arriving in Hawaii, my husband and I lived at the workshop site and concentrated our minds in prayer. Before setting foot in North Korea, we had to resolve any painful feelings knotted up in our hearts. We had to forgive Kim Il Sung, whose regime had hurt the nation and world, not to mention our extended family and ourselves. If we had thought of him only as our enemy, we could not have forgiven him. Only in the position of his parents, only with the heart of his mother, could I forgive. To save her son sentenced to death, a mother will even seek to change the laws of her country. That is what the maternal heart is like. With that heart, I pledged to forgive my enemy. I did not pray for our safe return from North Korea.

Those were serious hours in which we offered endless prayers. Just as Joshua circled Jericho seven times, we went around the Big Island of Hawaii again and again, offering our sincerest commitment to Heaven. Only after we had dissolved all the buried pain did my husband and I inform those who needed to know that we were on our way to North Korea.

Those around us expressed the natural reactions. "You are going to the place that is controlled by your enemy. It's extremely dangerous, completely different from going to Moscow. There is no Western or South Korean embassy there; no protection whatsoever. Whatever the letter said, there's no way Kim Il Sung will allow you to enter, unless he's planning to keep you there forever."

Though spoken out of concern for our well-being, such words tempted us to dwell on our private feelings and fears. Yet we knew that we had to truly forgive North Korean leader Kim Il Sung and embrace him with unconditional love, no matter the risk. We identified with Jacob offering everything he had, going at the risk of his life to meet with his brother Esau, who intended to kill him. After enduring 21 years of indescribable hardships while maintaining sincere devotion to his brother who hated him, Jacob gained the heavenly wisdom necessary to win Esau's heart. To change an enemy into a friend is truly impossible without the heart of a sincere parent.

A few days later, with our minds clear and hearts resolved in unity, my husband and I, with a small staff, flew to Beijing. As we were sitting in the airport waiting room in Beijing, a North Korean representative appeared and handed us an official invitation. The document carried Pyongyang's official seal. On November 30, our group headed to North Korea on Choson Airline's special aircraft, JS215, sent by Chairman Kim. For our benefit, it flew over my husband's hometown, Chongju, before landing in Pyongyang.

As the plane passed over Pyong-an Province, where both my husband and I were born, we looked down on the Cheongcheon River, in which we both had played as children. I felt as if I could reach down and touch its blue ripples. Had that river been flowing peacefully during the sorrowful four-plus decades since our territory was recklessly torn apart?

The chill of the cold winter wind we felt as we disembarked at Pyongyang Sunan Airport dissipated as we received the embraces of my husband's relatives. Of course, they all were grandmothers and grand-fathers. They grabbed hold of our hands and wept. A waterfall of tears surged in my heart, and I'm sure my husband's as well, but I bit my lip and held them back. We had committed ourselves to this venture for the sake of Heavenly Parent and the world, not for the personal happiness of our relatives or ourselves. There would be another trip for that, we assured each other, casting our bread on the waters.

We settled in at the Peony Guest Hall, and the next day, in accord with our lifelong tradition, we arose early in the morning and prayed. If there were surveillance cameras in our room, all those prayers crying out for the unification of the Korean Peninsula were recorded. That day and the next, we were given a tour of Pyongyang.

Our meeting with a group of major North Korean government leaders at the Mansudae Assembly Hall on the third day of our stay has become a legend in North Korea. My husband and I knew that to speak for God and against the government's "Juche" ideology in North Korea could be grounds for execution, but we were resolved to risk death for the sake of peace and unification. Let it go on record: Standing in the heart of North Korea, Father Moon denounced Juche thought and the Juche kingdom. He said loudly and clearly, "The unification of North and South Korea cannot come based on Chairman Kim Il Sung's Juche thought. North and South Korea can be unified peacefully, and Korea can become the nation that can lead the whole world, only through the God-centered ideology and 'head-wing' thought of Unificationism." Furthermore, he refuted their propagandist posture that the Korean War started with the South invading the North. By the end of his speech, Father Moon admonished them, "How can you call yourselves leaders? You cannot even control your own sex organs!"

The North Koreans were taken entirely by surprise. Their security personnel were anticipating the signal to rush in with guns drawn. Even though they to some degree knew what Father Moon was planning to say, our members accompanying us broke out in a cold sweat.

I had toured the whole world with my husband, and we had met the leaders of many nations, but nowhere did we have to maintain courageous determination and serious resolve comparable to that day in Pyongyang.

⸻

Father Moon's speech went far past the schedule for lunch and everyone ate at separate tables in dead silence. Many thought that the chances of meeting Chairman Kim had just evaporated. My husband said it didn't matter; he had said what he came to say.

On the sixth day, Chairman Kim sent two helicopters to transport us to Chongju, Father Moon's hometown. As Chairman Kim had instructed, highway crews had newly paved the little road to my husband's boyhood home, set up dignified tombstones and planted turf at the graves of his parents. They even had painted and decorated the house where Father Moon was born and spread sand on the earthen floor and yard. We visited his parents' tombs and offered flowers.

I gazed at the sky in the direction of Anju, my hometown, 18 miles away. Is the old house that embraced me so snugly still standing there? Is corn growing in the backyard field these days? Where is my maternal grandfather's grave? I was curious about everything, but I held it inside. We had come to meet with Chairman Kim Il Sung on behalf of our Heavenly Parent, and to shape the future of our homeland. We had come for the sake of the nation and world. I could not entertain my personal feelings in light of that historic summons. I was there so that the day would come when all Koreans and all peoples will be free to visit their hometowns.

It was on the seventh day that we finally met Chairman Kim. As we entered the Chairman's white-stone official residence in Majeon, Hamgyongnam Province, he was waiting for us. Without regard to protocol, my husband greeted Chairman Kim as if they were old friends, and Chairman Kim reciprocated, and we all took a deep breath as the two joyfully embraced each other. Chairman Kim, seeing me in a traditional Korean dress, politely gave his welcome.

December 6, 1991: Meeting with North Korean leader Kim Il Sung;
Father and Mother Moon were in North Korea for eight days.

The first order of business was lunch, and while we ate, we began our conversation by unreservedly sharing small talk about such things as hunting and fishing. Gradually, Father Moon and I introduced our current activities, including the World Culture and Sports Festival planned for the coming August. Hearing that it would include a Blessing Ceremony for 30,000 couples from around the world, Chairman Kim offered the Myeongsasimni Beach in North Korea's beautiful Wonsan district, where the sweetbriar is beautiful, as its venue. He also promised to open the port of Wonsan to transport all the couples to that site. Then all of a sudden, there were so many things to talk about. The conversation took on an energy of its own and continued far beyond its scheduled closure. My husband embraced his enemy, whom he had been preparing for decades to meet, with deep and intense love.

Chairman Kim was impressed by our sincerity and accepted our proposals in a bright manner throughout the meeting.

At that time, visitors from the free world visited North Korea at the risk of their lives. Communists hate religion, and my husband and I were co-founders of a religion. In addition to that, we were leaders of a global movement to end communism. Our trip to North Korea was not for the sake of joint economic ventures. We didn't go with a duplicitous motive, feigning interest in North Korea's benefit while actually being there for our own benefit. Such is typical of the political world, but that was not on our minds. For the sake of genuinely following the providential will, we went only with the heart of God, to enlighten and lovingly embrace the communist leaders and open the way for genuine unification. We entered that land relying only on God and advised its supreme leader to receive Heaven's decree.

While in North Korea, even though we were honored as state guests, we could not sleep comfortably, knowing that there were thousands upon thousands of families separated and longing for each other because Korea was not yet unified. We stayed awake every night, seeking to connect heavenly fortune to that place through our heartfelt prayer. We spent those nights submitting ourselves to God, for the sake of the unification of the Korean Peninsula. Political negotiation and economic exchange will come only on the foundation of the true love of God. By making this our focus, our talks with Chairman Kim opened a new chapter for the unification of North and South Korea.

Looking back, I reflect that it was at the moment communism reached its zenith that my husband and I risked our lives to go to Moscow and Pyongyang. With joyful hearts, as representatives of the free world, we embraced enemies who had severely persecuted us. By our doing so, they were moved, and we could reconcile. Thus, we laid the foundation for unification and peace. We went to North Korea not to get something but to give genuine true love. For the sake of God, my husband and I forgave the unforgivable; for the sake of humanity, we loved the unlovable.

August 5, 2007: Opening of the World Peace Center in Pyongyang, built by the Unification movement.

Soon after the completion of our eight-day mission, North Korea's Prime Minister Yon Hyong-muk led a delegation to Seoul and signed a "Joint Declaration on the Denuclearization of the Korean Peninsula" with the South Korean government. Over the coming months, our movement set up an industrial enterprise, the Pyonghwa Motors factory, as well as the Botong River Hotel and the World Peace Center, all in Pyongyang, as the cornerstone for unification. Afterwards, the seeds planted by my husband and I at that time bore fruit with the visit of the South Korean president to North Korea to discuss the path toward unification. On that foundation, the shoots of peace and unification are growing. When those shoots blossom into full bloom, the earnest prayers my husband and I have offered for Korean unification will be remembered forever.

After our meetings with President Gorbachev and Chairman Kim, my husband and I mapped out our next steps. We envisioned God-centered organizations that would fill the vacuum about to be created by communism's demise and undergird effective peace-building. With the tangible menace of militant communism now fading, the reformation of religious faith and family-based morality was the next mountain to climb.

It had taken more than 50 years to sweep international communism into the dustbin of history, but the decline of religion and family life is a subtler and, therefore, more pernicious threat. Religious leaders are tasked by God to guide people to live responsibly, but the influence of religion in modern times has been declining. Our challenge now became the restoration of religious faith as society's compass.

Thus we intensified our investment in bringing religious leaders to see beyond their denominational horizons, end interreligious conflict, and work together based upon universally shared, God-centered values. These are the same absolute values around which we called scientists, media professionals and political leaders to work. Healthy societies of all races, nations and religions arise on the foundation of morality and ethics, which in turn arise on the foundation of the love of God between husband and wife, parents and children. This love of God in the family is the source of absolute values, values that are universally shared and taught by all religions. We inspired faith leaders to work together and teach these universally shared values. We actually have invested more of our movement's resources on this than on the growth of our church.

Our vision brought together religious leaders and government leaders, centered around a common purpose of peace and true freedom. Renowned people from all walks of life who empathized with our objectives became "ambassadors for peace" through the work of the Federation for World Peace and the Interreligious Federation for World Peace. Starting in 2001, in Korea, the activities of these peace ambassadors quickly spread throughout the world. Inspired by this vision, peace ambassadors in 160 countries are putting down roots of true peace through project work in a broad range of fields. Where there are disputes, where poverty hinders education, where there is religious intolerance, where people lack sufficient medical care, peace ambassadors alleviate their pain and help them improve their lives.

Then, at New York City's Lincoln Center on September 12, 2005, we inaugurated an umbrella organization, the Universal Peace Federation (UPF). Following that event, my husband and I embarked upon a tour of 120 nations to meet ambassadors for peace and establish UPF national chapters. UPF brings together people and organizations across the world through programs supporting the realization of a world of genuine peace.

The Universal Peace Federation is now an NGO in General Consultative Status with the United Nations Economic and Social Council (ECOSOC), where its representatives work with like-minded, peace-loving global citizens.

A United Nations peace garden

"I did not learn to yield. I did not learn to kneel." These bold declarations are spoken in the epic Korean film, *The Great Battle*, by one of Korea's famous military heroes, Yang Man-chun, Lord of Ansi Fortress. The 2018 film, seen by millions of people, depicted the true story of how Yang Man-chun and the soldiers and people of the Ansi fortress-city held off the Tang Dynasty's army of 500,000 men for 88 days in AD 645.

The Ansi fortress was the final bulwark of the failing Goguryeo Dynasty against the powerful and fearsome Chinese invaders. Yang Man-chun was not fully allied with Goguryeo General Yeon Gaesomun, but as Ansi fortress commander, he invested everything to unite his people despite suffering, hunger and death. They ultimately forced the Chinese to retreat and saved the fortress.

This is just one of many stories about the brutal foreign invasions the Korean people have endured. We have been able to protect our beautiful mountains and rivers for millennia because of our patriotism and willingness to sacrifice. As True Parents, Father Moon and I uphold the Korean Peninsula as the land where all civilizations will blossom and bear fruit.

Nonetheless, the unfortunate 70-year history of division in Korea continues because the ideological barrier between democracy and communism still takes precedence over the love of family and clan. Parents, children and siblings both north and south have had to live for decades without knowing whether their family members are alive or dead— even in the era of the internet. The line of lamentation that divides the Korean Peninsula and separates blood relatives is a geographical line, but that is superficial. The real division is over worldviews and values. It is the fierce confrontation between atheism and theism, over the question of whether or not God exists.

Father Moon and I have invested sincere devotion and great effort to end the Cold War and unify North and South Korea. Beginning in 1968, we spread the Victory Over Communism (VOC) lectures throughout Korea and around the world to reveal the falsehoods of communism. In the 1980s, our members developed VOC materials into the CAUSA Manual and gave CAUSA lectures on campuses, in conferences, to students of all ages, pastors of all faiths and social leaders in all fields. The newspapers we established globally, such as *The Washington Times,* provided accurate information about the tensions on the Korean Peninsula and the reality of life under communist governments.

As I just described, in 1990 we provided the spiritual energy for President Gorbachev to continue on his path of reform, which led to the abandonment of communism as a structured global power. And our meeting with Chairman Kim Il Sung opened the gates of exchange for the sake of unification between North and South Korea. Since then, the UPF has expanded to more than 190 countries, serving as another foundation upon which the international community can cooperate in and benefit from the reunification of the Korean Peninsula.

And yet it seems to me that the new generation of South Koreans do not understand how the Korean War arose and why the unification of our people is necessary. Therefore, today, I am working even harder for this cause. This is one purpose of the Peace Road activism. As a culmination of the Peace Road events in 2015, riders in Korea cycled to the Imjingak Pavilion, located north of Seoul at the Imjin River, which divides the Koreas. From that site, they could see the demilitarized zone (DMZ) and North Korea. The participants created a dramatic moment by singing in Korean the song, "Our Cherished Hopes Are for Unity."

All Koreans feel a deep gratitude to the United Nations. Were it not for the United Nations, the Republic of Korea would not exist. When the North Korean People's Army, with Soviet backing, invaded South Korea on the morning of June 25, 1950, their ambition was to communize South Korea. They might have succeeded, as Korea was a small, poor country whose name was hardly known to the wider world. But the United Nations swiftly called on its member nations to defend democracy on the Korean Peninsula, and 16 countries sent troops while others sent medical support. The UN forces fought hard, risking their lives in an unfamiliar land to protect freedom and peace.

At that time, as I mentioned above, my husband was confined in a death camp, sentenced to hard labor at the Hungnam Nitrogen Fertilizer Factory. He was freed soon after the UN forces landed at the port of Incheon in September 1950. They pushed their way up into the northern part of the peninsula as far as the city of Hungnam. The prison camp guards were killing all the prisoners, but the night prior to my husband's scheduled execution, the guards learned about the approaching UN forces and fled. Heaven surely was behind the UN Security Council's decision to send a multinational force to turn back the communist invasion. The ultimate reason for the UN peace-keeping action was a hidden one, to save the only begotten Son and protect the only begotten Daughter. In accordance with God's will, our lives were preserved.

Why would God have protected our nation, the Korean people, in that historically difficult and troublesome crisis? The world was just recovering from World War II, and now it plunged into another tortuous battle on a global scale. The fact that our national anthem includes the words, "May God protect and preserve our nation," points to the answer: It can be explained best in terms of God's providence.

To complete the providence, in 1943 God sent His only begotten Daughter, the first woman who could receive God's first love since the Fall of Adam and Eve, to Korea. As do all people, this only begotten Daughter had to grow to maturity. She needed time until she could recognize, understand and accept her responsibility for the salvation of humankind. A child cannot simply go out and lead the providence. That is why God protected His only begotten Daughter until she grew to the age when she could know Heavenly Parent's mind, feel Heavenly Parent's heart, and determine with her own will to own Heavenly Parent's mission.

God preserved the environment of religious freedom for the sake of the fulfillment of Jesus' final words in the Bible, "Surely, I am coming soon." Jesus and the Holy Spirit called and led the only begotten Son and only begotten Daughter to complete the mission of the Messiah as the True Parents of humankind. To protect this mission, Heaven guided the UN forces to enter the war to defend freedom.

The United Nations established its headquarters in New York City at the end of World War II. Seventy years have since passed. There are three other major UN offices, in Geneva, Vienna and Nairobi. But even though the world has entered the Asia-Pacific era, there is no major UN office in Asia.

I have recommended that the UN open its fifth international office in Korea, specifically, in the demilitarized zone (DMZ) on the 38th parallel. I am supporting various groups, including the Universal Peace Federation and the Citizens Federation for the Unification of North and South Korea, in their efforts to turn the DMZ into a global peace park. This will bring the issue of Korean reunification to the attention of the world's people as no other action can.

All the nations of Asia would be pleased to serve as the site of a new, global UN headquarters, but I believe that Korea has unique qualifications. It houses the international headquarters of the Universal Peace Federation and of the International Association of Parliamentarians for Peace. Spiritually speaking, as the nation in which True Parents were born, Korea has something very deep within its culture that can serve the world.

Some 70 years ago, the UN forces shed blood and sweat for the sake of peace in Korea. By ending the division on the peninsula, the UN would complete the mission of those soldiers who gave their lives, and inspire peace in the world. In his speech given at the United Nations Headquarters in New York in 2000, my husband announced our vision of a peace park in the Demilitarized Zone. Fifteen years later, in May of 2015, at the UN Office in Vienna, Austria, I proposed that a fifth UN office be built there. The president of the Republic of Korea himself proposed to North Korea at the UN that a peace park be built in the DMZ. If North and South Korea invite the UN to build its fifth office in the DMZ, it will, by that very act alone, turn a theater of war—where so many on both sides of the conflict shed their blood—into a Mecca of peace.

Putting peace into practice

In our peace messages, Father Moon and I advocated that all humanity participate in the cross-cultural marriage Blessing. The cross-cultural marriage Blessing is by far the best way to restore humanity to become the children of God. Grandparents from enemy nations or religions will unite through the beautiful grandchildren they share in common.

That is the ideal, and like all ideals, it takes work to realize. In Korea, one hears, "There are more and more multicultural families, but their lives do not appear to be getting easier." The person next to him agrees, saying, "Many children are ridiculed by schoolmates because their mother is from another country." "Not only that," another person will chime in, "It is not uncommon for brides from overseas to give up and return to their native countries."

Today the number of multicultural families is increasing in the Korean countryside as well as in the cities. Looking closer, we can see that these multicultural families generally comprise a Korean husband and a wife from a developing country and their children. It is not easy for women from other countries to settle in a land where the people have a different language and lifestyle. Added to that, more than a few locals look down on multicultural families and even reject them.

I understand such problems very well. When my husband and I went to the United States in the early 1970s to carry out our mission, I experienced rejection and a sense of isolation that comes from being part of a minority. If this was the case for me in America, a nation with a heterogeneous population, it must be even worse in Korea, a homo-geneous nation. Hence, I hope and desire to support these families who have come to establish happy lives in Korea.

Since the late 1960s, my husband and I have created multicultural families through the marriage Blessing Ceremony, introducing part-ners to each other beyond nation, race and religious background. An upsurge in multicultural families in Korea was especially seen after our

International Blessing Ceremony for 6,500 Korean-Japanese couples in 1988, the year the Summer Olympics was held in Seoul.

October 30, 1988: The 6,500-couple International Blessing Ceremony brought thousands of multicultural families to Korea.

At that time, there were not many Korean women willing to marry men in farming villages, and this was becoming a social problem. For our Blessing Ceremony, women from Japan and other countries agreed to marry Korean men. Everyone knew this would pose many challenges. The Korean people's sentiment was still strongly anti-Japanese and many opposed the idea of a Japanese wife or daughter-in-law in Korea. Similarly, in Japan, parents were unhappy with the idea of their daughters—or sons—marrying someone from Korea, which was less developed economically.

However, Japanese Unificationist women, understanding faith in God, the concept of filial devotion and the idea of "living for the sake of others," agreed to marry Korean men and devoted themselves to their families. Brides from countries such as the Philippines, Vietnam and Thailand similarly came to Korea and established international blessed families.

There were many beautiful outcomes. The women attended their Korean parents-in-law with sincere devotion and created prosperous families. Even if living conditions were difficult, they faithfully took care of their husbands' parents when they were sick and elderly. Some even received government awards for serving their parents-in-law with filial devotion. Some became leaders of women's associations or parents' groups in their villages. Many of these wives and their husbands are now indispensable members of their village communities.

My husband and I realized there were ways to assist not only our church members, but all women in multicultural families in Korea, and we established a Multicultural Welfare Center in 2010. The center helps people from foreign countries learn the Korean language and otherwise feel at home in Korean society. Furthermore, we are assisting disabled people and single-parent families. We set up the True Love Peace School in Korea for the children of bicultural families, to help them with their studies and language skills.

We sometimes hear about Korean celebrities or high-ranking officials whose sons evade the requirement to join the military. That is not the case with multicultural families; in fact, some predict that by 2025, South Korea will have a "multicultural army." Children of international and multicultural families often have dual citizenships, and they can opt out of Korean military service by choosing their alternative nationality. Notably, more than 4,000 sons of couples who received an international marriage Blessing have fulfilled their national military service in Korea with honor. This is something they can be proud of.

Melting Korean prejudice against multicultural families will take time, so we must work hard to see the day that the term "multicultural family" disappears. Discrimination is implicit in that term. A family is a family; no modifier is needed to describe it. "Multicultural" should not be used to label a married couple in which the man and woman are of different nationalities. This is not in line with a universal understanding of humankind nor with God's will.

For more than 30 years, Father Moon and I have been promoting harmony between nationalities, races and religions through the marriage Blessing. Through Korean-Japanese marriage Blessings, we have broken down the barriers between these two nations and their peoples. We have done the same between Germany and France, and many other people of former enemy nations. The brides and grooms who have received the marriage Blessing are living based on the word of God and creating beautiful families all over the world. We do not call them multicultural families; they are simply blessed families.

It seems ironic, but the ultimate goal of religion is to create a world where there is no religion, in the sense of religion being a repair shop. When all human beings become good people, there will naturally no longer be a need to repair our relationship with God. In the same way, when we become "one family under God" and a world of true equality and peace appears, the term "multicultural family" will disappear. The very foundations of that peaceful world are true families and true love.

As we have seen, the road to one world has many dimensions. It is a literal road bonding nations together; it is an embrace of enemies who become brothers; it is turning a war zone into a peace garden, and it is the uniting of men and women of diverse races into literal marriages that recreate the world as one family under our Heavenly Parent. As the Mother of peace, I am calling the world's near eight billion people to travel this road together with me.

CHAPTER 7

TODAY'S GROWING PAINS BRING TOMORROW'S SUNSHINE

⚬✦⚬

Dedicate your youth to exciting goals

Each new generation endures heartache. Sometimes, young people compare themselves to others and lament their status. A desire to give up may pop into their heads and, rather than looking within, they may feel like blaming others or the world they live in. The more difficult our situation, however, the more we have to remember our original dream.

Especially in our younger years, we face countless temptations, endless concerns and unbounded desires. The only way to manage these is to have a strong will, and this means having clearly defined objectives.

The years of our youth are the best time to dedicate ourselves to exciting goals that make our hearts beat faster. Since our youth is brief, it is important to do this without delay. We don't want to be left in regret. We need to set good goals and know who to partner with to achieve them. If we do not live vigorously and create our own path, we will end up sinking into despair and envy.

Some young people complain that adults tell them to work harder, without giving them credit for the effort they are already making. Some become pessimistic, feeling that no matter how hard they try, they can't get ahead—and that society is at fault. But they need to take an honest look at how much effort they have actually made. Complaint and distrust will not get us far. Young people need to follow a virtuous path of sacrifice, service and love. "Youth," by Samuel Ullman, is one of my favorite poems. I like the passage, "Youth is not a time of life; it is a state of mind." With a purpose-driven heart, anyone, regardless of age, can live a fresh life with youthful passion.

In August 1987, Hyo-jin Moon, our eldest son, was president of the World Collegiate Association for the Research of Principles (W-CARP). In existence since 1966, CARP is a campus organization that promotes principles and raises leaders. In that time of ideological confusion on college campuses, Hyo-jin convened the Fourth World CARP assembly in West Berlin, Germany, in the midst of thousands of pro-communist agitators who were holding demonstrations near the Wall. These agitators knew that CARP was opposed to communism, and that 3,000 young people were attending its annual convention in the city. Groups of them protested and created disturbances outside the convention venue.

On the last day of the assembly, Hyo-jin spoke to the audience and then declared, "Let us now march to the Berlin Wall!" After a two-hour march, braving threats and disturbances along the route, they arrived at the Wall and encountered a large group of communist sympathizers. There, our members claimed the area that was reserved for their rally, pushing these counter-demonstrators away. After an energetic rally, Hyo-jin took the stage, spoke with great passion, and then wept as he led the group in prayer at the Wall. They finished by singing the Korean song, "Our Cherished Hopes Are for Unity." I feel that our members' praying and singing together with Hyo-jin that day were the seeds of change: Two years later, the Berlin Wall came down.

The passion of youth transcends borders and breaks down walls. Young people of true passion have the spirit to challenge themselves and the world around them. Many young people today, however, seem to be losing this spirit. Successful cultures train their youth to strengthen and purify their minds and bodies through everything from meditation to martial arts. We should not allow these traditions of training our youth to become relics of the past. We should revive them to create schools in which young men and women can strengthen mind and body and discover their true purpose.

Turn passion into purpose, purpose into principles

As my husband and I traveled throughout Korea and the world, we were deeply saddened to see young people buried in a bleak reality, giving up on their dreams and wandering aimlessly without goals. We saw others who were setting lofty goals but could not accomplish them by themselves. Out of concern for this, in 1993, I went on a speaking tour to guide Korean students at more than 40 Korean universities. It was a long and challenging tour that took me to virtually all the universities in Korea. In several instances, students of differing religious or ideological persuasions opposed my coming and sought to turn me away at the gate. But I persevered and, in the end, I spoke at all the universities.

On this foundation, my husband and I created the Youth Federation for World Peace (YFWP) in Washington, DC, in July 1994, with representatives from 163 countries. People young and old, idealistic and full of energy, gathered with the heart of "Love for God, Love for People, and Love for One's Nation." Everyone felt strong resolve to realize true families and manifest good values in their lives.

After the inauguration, we headed out into the world with the ambition to set up branches in 160 nations within less than a year. The eager responses we got illustrated the burning aspirations of youth. One of YFWP's signature achievements was to bring together youth from North and South Korea in conferences on the principles of peace as first steps toward the unification of the Korean Peninsula.

YFWP's core messages and activities are now blossoming through organizations such as the recently founded International Association of Youth and Students for Peace (IAYSP), Young Clergy Leadership Conference (YCLC) and Youth and Young Adult Ministry (YAYAM). The Generation Peace Academy (GPA) reaches youth in their gap year between high school and college, as does the Special Task Force (STF). These are service and education programs taking place in the United States, Europe and Oceania. These streams flow into CARP, which is ever more active connecting students and professors on college campuses. The goals for all of these programs are to raise up exemplary, loving individuals and families that emphasize purity in love and service to others as an expression of their relationship with God.

Keeping one's mind and body healthy, strong and pure is a lifelong task, and its importance is greatest during our youth. When we are young, we stand at a crossroads. We have to decide whether to take the road that satisfies selfish desires or the road toward a great dream. As we begin the stage of life following childhood, we should be beautiful young men and women ready to launch ourselves into the world with the courage that comes from having great dreams.

The best training is on the ocean

A small stream ran behind my hometown, the village of Anju. Except in the middle of winter, when everything was frozen solid, the trickling sound of running water could always be heard. I became friends with that water and learned many truths from it. Water always flows from above to below. Water embraces everything; it changes its shape to fit whatever contours it meets. In addition, water has duality. It can be peaceful and romantic when still, but if it becomes angry, it can swallow everything in an instant.

That's why the sea can be frightening. I dearly love the sea, as God's deep will can be found within it. My husband also loved the water. Even during our busy schedules, we would find ways to visit a river or the sea. We didn't go solely to admire the scenic beauty or enjoy a leisurely fishing trip. We rode rough waves to tell the people of the world that humanity's future is found in the sea.

In the United States, the waters off the coast of Gloucester, Massachusetts, are famous for tuna fishing. In the 1980s, for weeks on end, my husband and I would board the New Hope before dawn, go out into seas that even experienced sailors feared, and wrestle with tuna so huge they dwarfed the adults onboard. To catch a 1,000-pound tuna, I went far into the ocean, sometimes suffering all day long from the massive waves. Entrusting one's body to the deep blue ocean and riding its waves is self-mortification like no other.

My husband and I took great pains to offer sincere devotions at such times. Having found the road to the salvation of humankind and world peace, we have endured a severe lifestyle. During those times of difficulty, the sea would reward me with a clarity of purpose and the heart to embrace others. It gave me the energy I needed to continue on.

We often took young members with us to fish on the high seas in small Good-Go boats that my husband had a part in designing. We wanted to raise them to become leaders who could work anywhere. When we stayed in Kodiak, Alaska, young people from around the world came to receive our teaching. I did not lecture or preach to them. I only offered the advice, "Go out to sea. On the sea, you will discover what God wants to teach you."

A typical fishing day began with young people rising in the small hours of the morning, donning knee-high rubber boots and sailing with us into the distant sea amid an icy wind. When we reached a point in the vast ocean with nothing but water in sight, we would begin the struggle to catch salmon or halibut. Halibut, a flatfish, live on their bellies deep on the ocean floor. I once hooked a halibut off Kodiak that weighed over 90 kilograms (200 pounds). Seeing such a large fish flapping wildly on the deck is unforgettable. It makes such a noise! The fish was so gigantic that if you held it upright, you could hide three women behind it.

When we got back to shore late that night, completely exhausted and as withered as green onion kimchi, I was still full of joy. On days like that, and even on days when I did not catch a single fish, I learned about perseverance, the laws of nature and overcoming the challenge of rough seas. I call this the Spirit of Alaska.

If young people want to think big, they should go out to sea. It's easy to follow a set path on land, but not at sea. In just a few hours, a sea that had been like a calm lake can turn into a roller-coaster ride on ferocious waves. Young people who train themselves on top of these waves can achieve great dreams.

Besides Gloucester and Kodiak, we chose the Amazon and Paraguay Rivers of Latin America, Hawaii and Norfolk in the United States and Yeosu in Korea as the centers for the ocean providence. In addition to training young people, we invested in projects tied to the rivers and the oceans. One project in Uruguay was to create a high-protein powder from the abundant krill shrimp. When mixed with other nutritious foods, it can introduce valuable nutrients into people's diets in times of food shortage.

At the beginning of the year 2000, we wanted to create something beautiful in Yeosu, a small city on the southern coast of the Korean Peninsula known for its clear waters. In Soho-dong outside the main city, we built the Ocean Resort Hotel, where people from around the world can experience the beauty of land and ocean. We envision Yeosu advancing Korea's marine leisure industry. It can anchor an economic pipeline that connects to the continent. This in turn can support the development of a unified Korean Peninsula.

———————

There is a Western saying: "If you give a man a fish, you feed him for a day. But if you teach him to fish, you feed him for a lifetime." If you can fish, you will never go hungry. Africa has many rivers, lakes and oceans. Therefore, we need to teach its people how to fish and create fish farms. My husband and I have long been involved in projects like this.

The ocean is brilliant and pure. Our youth are also brilliant and pure. When the two meet, our future will change. Just as I have done, our youth should roll up their sleeves and bravely take on the ocean. The ocean is not only where one can cultivate a strong mind and body, but where we can create the future of humankind. It covers 70 percent of Earth's surface. Buried in its depths lie undiscovered treasures. Whoever pioneers the ocean will lead the world.

Love for God, Love for People, and Love for One's Nation

Born during the final years of the Japanese occupation of Korea, I grew up in an oppressed environment. After our country gained independence, oppression continued at the hands of the communist regime. And yet, my family steadfastly attended God, and at the risk of our lives, we traveled south into South Korea in search of freedom. When the Korean War broke out, I moved as a refugee from school to school, from Seoul to Daegu, Jeju, Chuncheon and back to Seoul. This imprinted upon me a great appreciation of education.

Despite the postwar chaos, I graduated from Seongjeong Girls' Middle School in Seoul. I cannot forget that school, my alma mater and cradle of my life. The school you attend during your teenage years can be a significant influence on your future. When I visited the school 30 years after graduating, its name had changed to Sunjung, but some of my teachers were still there. They remembered me and, of course, I had not forgotten them. We were overjoyed to see one another and talked for a long time about those difficult days in the past.

Kyung Bok Elementary School (Seoul)

Sunjung Middle and High School, and
International Tourism High School (Seoul)

This school is now affiliated with our Sunhak Educational Foundation. Applying our philosophy, it has become an exemplary educational institution. Our foundation includes three other specialized schools. Kyong Bok Elementary School, which opened in 1965, has a proud history and tradition. Sunjung Middle and High School produces competent young people by offering character education based on heart, in addition to excellent academics. These schools have international student bodies living and studying together with the aim of becoming global leaders. Another school, Sunjung International Tourism High School, prepares leaders for the hospitality industry. At that school, every year on National Teachers' Day, we invite teachers who have defected from North Korea to attend our Teachers' Day Event, in preparation for the day when the two Koreas will be reunited.

The first school we established independently was the Little Angels Arts School in 1974. As I have recounted, my husband and I went through many difficulties to form and finance the Little Angels of Korea in 1962, which we created to present Korea's beautiful traditional culture to the world. Their training site in an abandoned warehouse evolved into the Little Angels Arts School in 1974 and is now the

Sunhwa Arts Middle and High School. These schools have produced internationally renowned vocalists and ballerinas. When you leave the school through the main gate, you see a sign engraved with the words, "Gateway to the World."

Sunhwa Arts Middle and High School (Seoul)

Cheongshim International Middle and High School (Gapyeong-gun, Korea)

CheongShim International Academy, overlooking Cheongpyeong Lake, is another international middle and high school. We invested a great deal of time and effort into building this world-class preparatory school for global leaders. Starting with its first graduating class in 2009, graduates have entered leading universities, including top-ranking universities in Korea, the Ivy League in the United States and prestigious universities in Japan. The day is approaching when CheongShim graduates will play active roles on the world stage. When that day arrives, Korea will shine as a leader in the field of education.

Our network also includes other schools, from kindergartens to the postgraduate level, in Korea and on all six continents. In the United States, there are middle schools in Maryland, Connecticut and California, a high school in Connecticut, a theological seminary in New York, and a university that teaches Oriental medicine in Las Vegas, Nevada. In Asia and Africa, including Nepal, Myanmar, Mozambique and Rwanda, we have established schools according to the needs of the communities, including technical vocational schools. All our schools inspire their students to devote themselves to the world according to the founding philosophy of "Love for God, Love for People, and Love for One's Nation."

We must improve the results of education. Fully mature individuals do not emerge on their own, nor are they produced by obsessing over grades. We must guide young people to acquire knowledge and wisdom on the foundation of physical fitness and good character. We need to understand that God is the original substance of love and truth and the original form of character, and we need to live by following His will. To this end, beginning with the work of our International Education Foundation in Russia, I have overseen the development and dissemination of character education textbooks that will help cultivate morally sound teenagers and young adults throughout the world. To love people is to practice "living for the sake of others" and foster a spirit of harmony and public service. To love your nation means to cultivate your God-given talents, love your homeland and build God's kingdom. We all are responsible to raise the next generation of truly good and talented men and women.

A university changing the world

November 3, 1989, is an unforgettable day for me. I had traveled with my family to attend the long-awaited accreditation ceremony at Sunghwa University in Cheonan, about an hour south of Seoul. During the ceremony, I received a call from Seoul. "Your mother is in critical condition. She will return to God's bosom soon."

As soon as the ceremony ended, I rushed back to Seoul to be with my family at my mother's bedside. My mother Hong Soon-ae was gradually losing consciousness. Everyone was singing holy songs.

My mother had been extremely happy when the degree programs at Sunghwa University gained government accreditation, and she had remained conscious until the day of the accreditation ceremony. As I put my arms around her, she opened her eyes for a brief moment, stared at me quietly and then gently closed them. That was our last farewell in this life.

To honor my mother's ascension, one distant relative who came to pay respects was a former president of Korea University, Dr. Hong Il-sik. Since the 1970s, he had wanted to create a Chinese-Korean dictionary, but no one in the government sector or at any university would provide the needed support. When my husband and I learned of his vision, we were inspired and offered support. It was only later, as the relationship between Korea and China developed, that Korea recognized the value of his work. I was pleased when, at a later date, Dr. Hong accepted my invitation to chair the Sunhak Peace Prize Committee.

Sunghwa University's roots go back to 1972. We set its foundation when we opened the Unification Theological Seminary at the Guri Joongang Training Center in Gyeonggi-do. It was more than 20 years later, in 1994, that Sunghwa University went international, with a new name, Sun Moon University. Its motto, "Sun Moon is recreating heaven and earth," reflects the university's belief that, through God-centered education, people can impact the world.

My husband and I always supported the advancement of learning as an intrinsic good. There were times when we faced difficulties due to misconceptions that the Unification Church had objectives that would compromise the school's academic integrity. But our goal simply was to provide the highest quality education possible. We frequently invited celebrated scholars in all fields to deliver lectures. Sometimes we would spend tens of thousands of dollars for just an hour of expert training for our students. Father Moon respected the professors, although he really disliked it if they neglected the personal teacher-student dynamic in their classes. He emphasized that a professor's students, not his or her academic colleagues or the school's administration, are the proper ones to evaluate a professor's performance.

Sun Moon University has gradually built an outstanding student body that, in terms of nationality, is the most diverse of all Korean universities. Recently, it received the highest ratings in several evaluations, and has been awarded several government-sponsored research projects. It is a tradition-oriented institution of higher learning with significant influence.

Just as a tree with deep roots grows well, universities develop best when they stand on solid principles and academic research. Sun Moon University sets high standards for its professors, and the lights in their offices are often on deep into the night as they interact with fellow scholars around the world. It is not uncommon for online conferences to continue until dawn.

Sun Moon University (Asan City, Korea)

Sun Moon University is an outward-looking institution with carefully designed and wide-ranging curricula. Its purpose is not for Korea alone; it is for the world. Our aim is to instill people with a global perspective, enabling them to meet the ever-evolving needs of businesses and society. I would like to develop Sun Moon University into the world's foremost institution of higher education, so that young graduates can tell the world with confidence, "I graduated from Sun Moon University." These young people will serve as global leaders.

Its theology department, in particular, will cultivate its students to become teachers who can in turn train leaders around the world. Studying God's word is as important as graduating from a good university, finding a good job and supporting one's family and community. We need to understand there is an eternal world in heaven. Diamonds sparkle wherever they are. The new generation are like diamonds that will shine brilliantly wherever they may go.

Today our movement has schools around the world, from kindergartens to graduate schools. One is the Unification Theological Seminary, established in 1975 with an interreligious faculty—Catholic, Protestant, Greek Orthodox, Jewish and Confucian, as well as Unificationist. Under the leadership of Dr. David S. C. Kim and Dr. Young Oon Kim, its Barrytown campus served as the base for the New Ecumenical Research Association (New ERA), and gave rise to the Interdenominational Conferences for Clergy, the Youth Seminar on World Religions, and the Assembly of the World's Religions. Today UTS is going strong at its mid-Manhattan campus.

The purpose of all these schools is to ensure that increasing numbers of talented young people who know God's heart have access to education to support their commitment to creating a peaceful world. Parents should be passionate and work hard so that our blessed children can grow up pure and beautiful under God's will. Our true hope is to raise our children not just as sons and daughters of our own families but as the proud sons and daughters of God.

A helicopter plants seeds of love

The movie, *The Shawshank Redemption*, made a deep impression on me. The main character is a man who is unjustly imprisoned, endures prison life for many years and finally escapes in search of freedom. Father Moon was unjustly imprisoned six times, and that similarity with the main character made this film move my heart. At the very end of the movie, the liberated prisoner writes in a letter: "Hope is a good thing, maybe the best of things, and no good thing ever dies."

Hope, love, friendship and beauty are unchanging, no matter how much time passes, and their value is eternal. Love awakens hope and courage in the most hopeless of circumstances. Today many people have lost their moral direction, and we lament the dominance of materialism. The only way to heal this pain is by living lives of true love for the sake of others, not thinking about oneself.

I open my eyes at daybreak and begin each day with prayer and meditation. I think very carefully about what I will do for whom, and then I act on that. Religious teachings and political and social reforms are important, but we cannot create a happy world through these alone. True love is giving a pair of socks with your whole heart to your neighbor who is shivering from the cold. Sometimes it is sacrificing completely for an utter stranger whom you may never see again. True love is giving and forgetting that you gave.

Today the Unification Church is recognized as a worldwide religion, but into the 1970s, we didn't even have a decent church building. My husband and I used all the money that church members donated for the sake of society and the world. When missionaries went overseas, they left with just a suitcase. They had to find work on their own and use the money they made to run their own centers. They dedicated the donations that came in to establish schools and medical clinics, and to fund voluntary service. We have practiced this ethic of sacrificial service for the past 60 years.

In Korean, *aewon* means "a garden of love." In 1994, Father Moon and I established a service organization, the Aewon Bank, to enable all people to share love in Korea. It is not a literal bank; it brings people together to offer voluntary services, everything from the provision of free meals, to concerts for charity, to international aid.

In order to expand this further, I established the Wonmo Pyeongae Scholarship Foundation. This actually was the first major action I took after my husband passed away. Monetary offerings of condolence flooded in from all over the world, and I saved all of it as seed money for this purpose. I also sold the helicopter we had used for our mission work and added that money to those funds. It all went into an endowment, out of which we have been able to give $10 million in scholarships to help educate talented people for the future. Excellent students from all over the world, including Korea, Japan, Southeast Asia, Africa, Europe and America, are benefiting from this scholarship.

Of course, I heard some people buzzing about that. "I heard that Mother Moon is selling the helicopter she and Father Moon used together!" one would say, and another would respond, "It's such a historic artifact; shouldn't it be in a museum?" While I respect expressions of regret over the sale of the helicopter, and completely understand the sentiments, I made the decision. It is for the sake of our future leadership. While it is important to honor the past, it is more important to teach God's word and raise future generations of faithful leaders.

The truth that education shapes young people, and that young people shape the future, will never change. To ensure a bright future, it is absolutely necessary to raise up youth of talent, wisdom and virtue. *Wonmo* is made up of the Chinese characters *won* (圓) meaning "round" and *mo* (母) meaning "mother." In the family, it is the mother who embraces each family member with love, despite their different personalities, and guides the family towards harmony. *Pyeongae* (平愛) means to take care of the less fortunate so all can stand on an equal plane in a cosmos of true love. I set the foundation for such education to endure beyond the generations. When children play with a spinning top, it is hard for them at first, but once it starts spinning, they can keep it spinning with minimal effort. A scholarship endowment is the same. It is difficult to establish, but once it is up and running, it is not too difficult to keep going. Education takes time. We need to erect a wall to block the wind and watch our offspring 24 hours a day so they can grow into beautiful and moral adults. It takes nine months in a mother's womb to create a life. Even after such a period of preparation, a baby cannot walk overnight. Children need to go through a period of growth.

I forget myself when doing this kind of work. When I put others first, I feel I am living a life of true goodness. If we devote ourselves to the people around us with the heart that nothing we give for God's purposes will go to waste, we will find true happiness. When we are not fixated on our personal happiness, God will come to us.

The future Joshuas and Calebs

To raise future leaders, in 2015 I founded Global Top Gun Youth (GTGY), which teaches enthusiastic young people from all over the world how to contribute to world peace and the salvation of humankind by living for the sake of others. Among biblical figures, I point GTGY students to Joshua and Caleb, who attended Moses in the wilderness. Throughout their lives, Joshua and Caleb remained loyal to Heaven, and they led the chosen people into Canaan. Caleb completely united with Joshua, and devoted himself to the cause of the nation and its people. I am raising outstanding young men and women through Global Top Gun Youth to be like Joshua and Caleb and lead the world into the Promised Land.

Almost 1,500 years ago in Korea, the Silla Dynasty raised their young leaders through a training program called *Hwarang-do*, which means, "flowering youth." These young leaders were known for their allegiance to the kingdom and determination to overcome obstacles. Hwarang-do took youth from the elite of society and trained them in martial arts, meditation in nature, and methods of resolving conflict between social classes. They were known for never retreating in war and for choosing an honorable death over being taken prisoner.

Young people who are to lead in the future must focus their minds, do well in their studies, and lead lives of sincere faith. Armed with wisdom and practical experience, they can build upon and surpass their parents' filial heart for Heaven. This is why I am intentionally guiding future leaders for the establishment of God's kingdom of Cheon Il Guk under the name *Hyojeong-rang* (youth of filial heart)—it is my hope that they will surpass the Hwarang of old in their devotion to Heaven.

In February 2017, at an assembly at the HJ International Cultural Foundation in Gapyeong county, east of Seoul, we inaugurated YFWP's successor, the International Association of Youth and Students for Peace (IAYSP). I asked the thousand or more participants to be "the special forces that build God's kingdom of Cheon Il Guk." And they put my words into action immediately.

In June of that year, 12,000 young people took part in the IAYSP Youth for Peace Rally in Bangkok, Thailand, where I implored them to "become the leading figures of the culture of filial heart and the light of the world."

Then in September of 2019, at the Africa Summit and Blessing Ceremony in São Tomé and Príncipe, 40,000 young people gathered at the Festival for Youth and Students. The capital city's wide plaza, with its view of the beautiful sea, was packed with young people. That evening, the Hyojeong Cultural Foundation hosted the IAYSP Youth Sounds of Peace, with various performances upholding universal values. The First Lady of São Tomé and Príncipe, Nana Travoada, and the leaders of each cabinet ministry participated in celebrating the revitalization of their nation's youth. It was the largest Youth and Student Festival to date.

I spared no effort to give the young people hope and encouragement, with the words: "You are the hope of São Tomé. Because of you, the pure water, São Tomé can achieve the kingdom of heaven on earth that our Heavenly Parent desires."

For hundreds of years, the French royal family employed elite young soldiers from Switzerland. The Swiss Guard is world-renowned for their dignity, loyalty and selfless service. Today, it is the Vatican that receives the protection of the Swiss Guard.

We are creating the future of God's kingdom of Cheon Il Guk to fulfill God's dream. Like Joshua and Caleb, like the Swiss Guard, the IAYSP must serve the highest heavenly purpose in this time, with an indomitable spirit, never yielding to any difficulty. IAYSP members are the loyal citizens and filial sons and daughters of God's kingdom. They are True Parents' pride and the protectors of Heaven's will. No matter what difficulties emerge in their time, such young people will meet those challenges and emerge victorious. They are the ones who own the future.

When young people dedicate themselves to Heaven with body and soul, no matter their position, they can become filial sons and daughters and patriots remembered by our Heavenly Parent and all generations. They will know that the growing pains they endured for a short time have an eternal value.

CHAPTER 8

THE MOTHER BUILDS THE FAMILY, THE FAMILY BUILDS THE WORLD

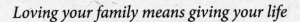

Loving your family means giving your life

"I love you." These are the sweetest words. They are the first words, because through love all life begins. But human beings can speak these words either responsibly or irresponsibly. God also gave animals the power to multiply through love. Animals search for a partner with whom to bear and raise offspring. But they differ from us in that for them, love is instinctual and they are not responsible to make moral decisions related to love. For human beings, in contrast to animals, love is accompanied by responsibility. Love practiced with moral responsibility is what we call "true love."

A husband and wife who believe in the sanctity of love and fulfill their responsibility accordingly are practicing true love. Through their love, God creates a nest of happiness. True love makes us true husbands and wives who, after giving birth to sons and daughters, grow to become true parents. The saying, "When one's home is harmonious, all goes well," is a truth of the highest value; it was true in the past, it is true today and it will be true in the future. True love is the most important factor in creating a happy family. My husband and I bless the marriages of couples of all races, nations and religions and provide True Family Values education for the sake of creating families of true love.

With true love, you can gladly give your life for your family. Sacrificing your life for your family is at once heroic and tragic. I am reminded of a very sad event that took place in Belize, Central America in early 2019. A Japanese couple, Takayuki and Junko Yanai, who participated in the 1988 Blessing Ceremony of 6,500 couples, have been doing mission work in Belize since 1996. One night an armed burglar broke into their family home. He shot at Mr. Yanai, but at that instant their third son, 19-year-old Masaki, jumped in front of the bullet, giving his life to save his father.

When I received the report of this event, I closed my eyes, unable to speak for some time. Of course, no family lives a perfectly tranquil life, but it is truly heartbreaking to see a family meet with such a terrible tragedy.

I also know the pain of losing a family member, of saying goodbye to a child while remaining in this world myself. Four of my children have already departed this life. Is not every father and mother committed to give their life to save their child, as Masaki did for his father? Love between parents and children most resembles God's love. Love within the family is the model of the love that God desires us to practice in all spheres of life.

There are stories like that of the Yanai family, where misfortune suddenly comes from the outside, but there are also stories where families bring misfortune upon themselves. Discord between husbands and wives is one of the main reasons our world cannot be at peace. There are 7.7 billion people on earth today, but the creation of peace really depends upon two people—one man and one woman, that is, a husband and wife. People enter into various types of relationships and encounter different kinds of problems, but the root of all these problems is the same—the flawed relationship between man and woman. Peace will come when two people, a man and a woman, trust and love each other. If men and women can fulfill their mutual responsibility to trust and love each other, the world will become the happy place we all wish it to be.

I'm saying that each person's happiness depends on his or her ability to achieve peace in their marriage and family. When true parents, true spouses and true children form a peaceful family, happiness follows naturally. Harmony is created when parents, children and grandchildren unite in heart. No matter what difficulties come, the parents' heart of love for their sons and daughters and the grandparents' heart of love for their grandchildren should never change. Grandchildren, also, need to respect and love their grandparents. The greatest happiness is generated within the family where three generations live together in love.

Children of true filial piety are those who sacrifice for their parents just as their parents have sacrificed for them. Before striving to be a loyal patriot, each person must first become a filial child before his or her parents and a sibling who sacrifices for his or her brothers and sisters. A man or woman becomes a truly filial son or daughter when he or she is married. Truly filial sons and daughters are those who present children to their parents, thereby becoming true parents themselves.

The family is the world's most important institution, and Heavenly Parent created it to be the environment of the greatest happiness and goodness. The goodness is because your mother and father are there, and the happiness is because your brothers and sisters are there. All people without exception miss their hometown. When we live in a foreign land, our hearts ache for our hometown. We miss our nation because our hometown is there, and we miss our hometown because our family is there.

A flower called sacrifice

It was 1961, and our church was filled with brides and bridegrooms standing solemnly side by side, each bride holding a bouquet. Outside the gate, however, angry parents gathered. Through the windows came the clamor of raised voices: "I'm absolutely against this wedding! Stop it at once! How on earth can you think this is a real marriage?" They energized each other with their outrage. "That Mr. Moon took my daughter to marry her off like this! I will never give my consent—let her out of there!" One of them even threw coal ashes over the gate, dirtying the wedding gown of a beautiful bride.

When the Unification Church conducted its first large wedding ceremony, many throughout Korea stood in vehement opposition. Parents opposed to the wedding turned the neighborhood around our church, where the newlyweds should have been congratulated, into a place of pandemonium. There are no words to describe how severely we were attacked and maligned at that time. Yet we overcame the hurt and embraced the opposition. We have conducted what we call the Blessing Ceremony for over half a century, blessing in marriage hundreds of thousands of couples of all races, nations and religions throughout the world. This is a testimony to the fact that the Blessing Ceremony is a manifestation of God's love and truth.

The marriage Blessing Ceremony conducted by the True Parents is a sacrament rooted in single-minded devotion. It is a ceremony of true love, and true love embodies sacrifice. A poet once said, "Love is the pain of giving up myself." We cannot achieve true love without offering ourselves. Man is born for woman and woman for man. Naturally and joyfully we should sacrifice ourselves for our beloved. This is nowhere more evident than in our cross-cultural marriages.

⁓

"You have graduated from a prominent university, and you have a good job. Think about it—the person who is to be your spouse is of a different race, and her family lives halfway around the world. Are you going to go through with this?" When asked such a question, most people will waver. Our members, on the other hand, immediately answer, "Yes, I will. I am thankful to do this, because it is for a great purpose."

The Unification movement teaches that intercultural, interracial families are the key to world peace. During my husband's life, most of our members requested that he and I arrange their marriage, for the purpose of their making a complete offering of their lives to God. In many cases, if not most, they knew that this meant they would be dedicating their life to someone who is quite different from them, who might not speak their language or know their culture. They wanted their marriage to be grounded in nothing but God, True Parents and the principles of peace. Our brides and bridegrooms requested this path with gratitude, but their parents sometimes desperately opposed it. It was the parents of the thousands of Korean-Japanese couples that faced the greatest difficulty.

One Korean father represented many when he wrote to my husband, "When I think about what we suffered under Japanese colonial rule, my blood still boils. To think that my son will marry the daughter of our enemy nation! I will never accept a Japanese daughter-in-law into our family. Never!" Many parents of the Japanese brides felt the same from their side of the divide.

Jesus said, "Love your enemy." Most people admit that a peaceful world will come only when we love our enemies. Nonetheless, it is not easy for most of us to translate Jesus' words into action. Some brides and grooms bit their lips as they took part in these joint wedding ceremonies. Their course was by no means smooth as they prepared for their marriage and spent the first years of their lives together. But their commitment to live for a purpose beyond themselves, centered on God, gave them the strength necessary to liquidate the underlying terrible history of their two nations that had been enemies. They were able to dissolve this bitter root through coming to understand each other and healing each other's pain.

In the autumn of 2018, we held a Rally of Hope at the Cheongshim Peace World Center, an arena with a capacity of 20,000 located in our HJ Cheonwon complex, east of Seoul. During a members' testimony session, Keiko Kobayashi, a Japanese wife living in Korea's South Jeolla Province with a Korean husband, came to the podium to share her heart.

In 1998, she said, while living a comfortable life as a public official in Japan, she applied for the matching and was matched and then blessed in marriage to a Korean man. She moved to Korea, expecting that they would live happily as newlyweds. However, her hopes for happiness were dashed because her husband suffered from epilepsy. Although he was usually calm, when under stress he was prone to epileptic fits. He grew lethargic and became indifferent about life in general. Nothing could inspire him.

Keiko thought seriously about ending the marriage and returning to Japan. But first she decided to put her mind at ease by traveling to our Cheongpyeong Training Center to offer a week of prayer and devotions before making her final decision. She had already had many good experiences at this Center, participating in workshops with hundreds of members from Korea, Japan and around the world. For several days, she clung to God, prayed to Him, and turned her ears toward Heaven. God heard her prayer, and spoke to her: "My beloved daughter! Just as I love you as my daughter, I love your husband as my son. Can you not take care of him on My behalf, as my poor son whose body is weak and who is living in loneliness?"

Hearing this, she said, she broke down in tears of repentance and sincerely asked God for forgiveness. She returned home, opened her heart to her husband and learned to love him. Soon thereafter, God rewarded her by giving them a lovely son and changes began taking place in her husband. His health improved, he was able to get a job, and the family stabilized. Now they are living happily together, raising five sons and daughters. This is what Keiko shared with the audience.

A few days after that rally, I convened a meeting at Cheongpyeong with more than 4,000 Japanese wives of Korean husbands; they had gathered from all parts of Korea. I gave small presents to those among them who, as luck would have it, had their birthday on that day. I asked them if they had ever received a birthday gift from their husbands. Most of them answered that they did not celebrate birthdays at all because they were too busy with the strenuous task of making a living in rural areas. Yet not one of them was discontented. They testified that their lives were dedicated to God's will and that when they face difficulties their bond with True Parents strengthens them.

I treasure these women all the more because they endured and sacrificed themselves as representatives of their nation. They gathered in Seoul in 2019 to pay respects to the spirit of Ryu Gwan-sun, a girl of 18 who, in 1920, gave her life as a martyr in protest of the Japanese occupation of Korea. Our Japanese sisters gathered in their kimonos to pray for this young woman martyr for independence and to ask for forgiveness on behalf of Japan.

Happiness does not come to us when we have everything. It comes mysteriously, when we have seemingly lost everything yet still feel gratitude. When a woman marries a man with a disability or who is of a different religious background or racial minority, that is where God can work miracles. True love transcends historical divisions that resulted from sin and allows happiness and heavenly fortune to find a home. The blessed marriage tradition places true love above considerations of appearance and social status. A person who develops true character and a warm heart will make a good spouse. When you meet such a person and give him or her all your love, yours becomes a worthy life indeed.

The marriage Blessing Ceremony of the Unification Church movement is the most sacred and precious event in human history. Why? It is because the Blessing imparts Heavenly Parent's spiritual reality and allows a man and a woman to embody it as one flesh. It is the veritable marriage supper of the Lamb of which the Bible speaks. Our larger Blessing Ceremonies gather tens of thousands of couples, but there have been some with just three or four, and once in a while my husband and I have blessed just one couple. Thousands of our representative blessed central families in Korea and throughout the world have also officiated Blessing Ceremonies.

Millions of couples have received the marriage Blessing. You will find these blessed families in every country. Couples composed of a Korean groom and Japanese bride, an American groom and German bride, a Senegalese groom and Filipino bride, all live in happiness. They overcome differences in language and lifestyle. The foundation for this is in the vows that blessed couples make during the Blessing Ceremony, that the husband and the wife will share true love and live in accordance with God's will.

A vision of true womanhood

There is an old saying in the West, "Behind every great man is a great woman." It is true. The wife is necessary for the completion and perfection of the husband. Without his wife, a husband cannot be whole. A society in which womanhood does not complete and perfect manhood cannot give rise to a peaceful and just world.

Women need to fulfill the mission of the wife as well as the mission of the mother. Both are essential to create a peaceful and just world. The mother gives birth to children and is called to raise them through their formative years. That is a right and responsibility given primarily to women.

September 13, 1995: Mother Moon with George and Barbara Bush
at the third anniversary celebration of the founding of
the Women's Federation for World Peace, Tokyo

I have always been saddened by the reality of this world in which so often husbands fail to honor their wives, and children fail to honor their mothers. In every age, righteous women have carried out their missions as wives and mothers in the face of hardships. Following the path of women saints of all religious traditions, the women of our Unification movement, in response to the heart of True Parents, have attended God while shedding their sweat and tears throughout our global village. True Parents revealed the truth of the human Fall, and liberated women to fulfill their responsibilities as true daughters, true wives and true mothers. In this age, by God's providence, what was previously impossible has been made possible.

Women are independent beings who represent God's feminine aspect and thus make men whole. It is time for women to rise above the popular trend of trying to improve their status by imitating men. This only casts the relationship between men and women as one of competition in a culture that ignores their God-given and God-incarnating uniqueness. God designed men and women for a relationship in which each gives their divine and unique gifts to the other, and each receives the other's divine and unique gifts with true awareness and love. Women are not just men's assistants any more than men are women's assistants. Women and men need each other's protection. Through the true man-woman relationship, each perfects the other and becomes one with the other. Each is a part of the other in the creation of a greater whole, embodied as a child, as a family, as a nation, and as the world.

At this time, women need to follow Heaven's way, attend True Parents, and become central figures who together with men bring forth a new world based on the culture of heart. We need to rid ourselves of fallen traits and realize the original culture, bringing to fruition the nation and world of goodness and love long sought by humanity. This begins at the center of the world—the home—where each woman embraces her husband as the embodiment of true love, and raises their sons and daughters with the heart of a true parent.

Based upon God's providence, my husband and I have called women to take the lead in the creation of families that embody God's original plan—families in which the wife lives for her husband, the husband for his wife, the parents for their children and children for their parents. Such a family will overflow with love and God's blessings will come to stay. Women need to walk the path of a true mother and, at the same time, the path of a true wife and the path of a true daughter. Women have the magical power to create harmony and to soften hearts. Brides build bridges. The world of the future can be a world of reconciliation and peace, but only if it is based on the maternal love and affection of women. This is the true power of womanhood. The time has come for the power of true womanhood to save the world.

September 18, 1991: Mother Moon at a speaking event in Japan, with her eldest son Hyo-jin

The new age centers on womanhood

At the end of May in 2016, the United Nations hosted its "Education for Global Citizenship" conference in Gyeongju, South Korea. The UN Secretary General and more than 4,000 representatives of non-governmental organizations (NGOs) from 100 nations came together and held discussions on how to create a brighter world. At that conference, the UN selected the Women's Federation for World Peace to be a part of the discussions as one of the small number of NGOs with consultative status, in recognition of its genuine and wide-ranging activities for peace over the years. It seemed as if just a few days had passed since the Women's Federation was taking its first steps to establish itself in the world. In that moment, WFWP's spirit of peace and service, which we had practiced with devotion throughout the world, shone brightly.

The inception of the Women's Federation traces back to 1991. In September of that year, some 7,000 women, including the wife of the Japanese prime minister, came together in Tokyo, Japan, to inaugurate the Women's Federation for Peace in Asia. As the founder, I gave a speech entitled "The True Love Movement Bringing Salvation to Asia and the World." The next year I gave a speech to 50,000 people in the Tokyo Dome, a crowd that had gathered with only 15 days' notice. I spoke with passion burning deep within, and many hearts were moved.

The following April, 160,000 women from 70 countries gathered in Seoul. Four thousand buses created a traffic jam downtown as they conveyed these crowds to the main Olympic Stadium. This tremendous number of women leaders had come to participate in the proclamation of the era of women. The Women's Federation for World Peace was born on that day. This was not to be just one more women's organization but a mirror reflecting this new age. My speech that day provided a compass to guide humankind out of the world of war, violence and conflict and into the ideal world of one human family led by men and women in harmony, overflowing with love and peace.

Mother Moon studying her speech as she travels between countries

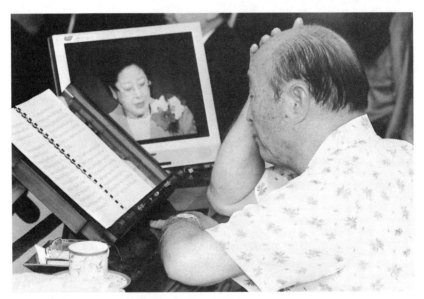

Father Moon attends Mother Moon's speech via the internet

Over the months following that event, I traveled the world to encourage women leaders and launch a true women's movement that could win the hearts of both men and women. I joyfully met with leaders from all walks of life and we held women's conferences successfully all over the world.

⁓

Until now, neither men nor women have known the true value of womanhood. As a result, men have not approached women with authentic appreciation. To break that mold, women in modern times have campaigned to advance their rights and achieve liberation from past restrictions. They have, for the most part, taken a position of complaint against men and channeled their energy into political movements to change laws. With a different perspective, I launched the Women's Federation for World Peace as a movement to awaken women to their true value and help them embrace men and develop themselves in partnership with men.

To be a clear mirror that reflects this age, each woman first needs to be clear and pure within herself. Each needs to find the indomitable power within that is necessary to overcome self-centeredness. She needs to become a true daughter who attends her parents with filial piety, and a true wife who completes her husband with fidelity and devotion. Moreover, she needs to become a true mother who raises her sons and daughters with love and dedication. She needs to form a family of true love that attends God. God will raise up such true women as leaders on the path to world peace.

A mother's hand soothes a stomach ache

"Mommy, my stomach hurts."

When a child complains of stomach ache, his mother lays him on her lap and rubs his tummy without a single word. Her hands may be gnarled and rough, but in a few moments the child feels better. This may be a simple approach, but it is a practice based on love. We all dimly remember our mother's warm touch. This is the very touch with which I long to embrace all of humankind as Mother of the universe and Mother of peace. As we know from our own experience, a mother hears her child's cry very clearly and she has no thought but to quickly run to her child. This is because a mother's love and attention are directed solely towards her children. A mother will walk through a fiery pit without hesitation to save her child.

Koreans often pray for *cheongbok,* which means living in happy contentment even without possessions or power. Health is most important for our happiness. We have a saying, "If you lose your possessions, you have lost little. If you lose your reputation, you have lost a lot. But if you lose your health, you have lost everything." Taking these words very seriously, I have long pondered over the secret of good health. It is not easy for anyone to live their entire life without ever getting sick.

During my early life, I saw many people suffering from malnutrition or whose lives were broken by injury or disease. At age 16, when I entered St. Joseph's Nursing School, I felt joy and pride, knowing I had found exactly what I needed to do. However, in taking on the mission of the Mother of peace, I had no choice but to put that vocation aside. While traveling around the world, I saw many children who could have become healthy if they had better care. Some lost their sight; some had limbs amputated because they could not be treated in time.

This pain remains as a deep knot in my heart. I want to be the mother who can embrace all people who are ill, physically and spiritually. When we injure a toe, we feel the pain throughout our entire body. As the Mother of one family under God, I feel the pain of each person as my own pain. Having fallen ill myself in countries not my own, I know what it means to be a foreigner in need of medical care.

HJ Magnolia International Medical Center, HJ Cheonwon, South Korea

Thus it was with great joy and satisfaction that Father Moon and I decided to realize the dream I had when I attended nursing school. We established an international hospital in Korea where all people can receive expert spiritual and physical care and feel a mother's touch.

When we get sick, from the depth of our hearts, we yearn for our mother's warm touch. However, our mother is not always near us. To provide a mother's touch, after receiving permission to build in 1999, we opened the Cheongshim International Medical Center, now called the HJ Magnolia International Medical Center, in 2003. It overlooks Cheongpyeong Lake, where the waters are clear and the mountains are beautiful. The Medical Center is not a typical hospital. Beyond providing excellent standard treatments, we focus on the true meaning of health. Health does not simply mean having a sturdy body. An original human being has mind and body united in harmony.

Thus, Unification medical science is based on the principles of truth and the spirit of love. The HJ Magnolia International Medical Center is the first facility to develop and implement this new model. Doctors and nurses from various nations take care of patients with a motherly heart in the midst of beautiful natural surroundings, which are Heaven's gifts. They are answering a question that has been neglected until now: "Does faith in God truly enhance our health?" The answer to this question is not difficult. For good health, the harmony of our mind and body is an important agent of healing, and faith is what allows us to realize that harmony. The HJ Magnolia International Medical Center not only uses state-of-the-art medical techniques, but it is also the first full-scale hospital to integrate spiritual healing in the prevention and treatment of disease. Behind this are my prayers for the physical and spiritual salvation of all people so that none may be orphans.

We must take care of our health when we are healthy. Most of the time we tend to ignore that simple fact. In our busy lives, we can easily forget to take care of our mind and body. God gave us the blessing to "be fruitful." That means to have spiritual, psychological and physical health. The mission of HJ Magnolia International Medical Center is to enable people to achieve that joy.

<hr />

Every year a team from the HJ Magnolia International Medical Center, together with volunteers from various walks of life, offers medical services in Southeast Asia and Africa. In these countries many people despair for lack of medical treatment. Lack of medication sometimes leads to amputation, blindness or even the loss of life.

My husband and I established the HJ Magnolia Global Medical Foundation in the hope of relieving some of this suffering. Its purpose is to serve as a foundation for humankind to achieve total health, to provide everything from voluntary medical services in impoverished areas to enlightenment as to the cause of disease and the path of true health.

Women unite religions in the Middle East

In 1969, on our first world tour together, my husband and I visited Israel. The day we arrived was extremely hot. Israel is a small country, one-fifth the size of South Korea. It did not take us so long to visit all the sites mentioned in the Bible. As we toured, we reflected on why the history of this area, which seemed to us so peaceful, has always been rife with disputes, conflicts and terrorism.

The Middle East includes the holy land, where Jesus was born 2,000 years ago. It has been the home of eminent peoples whose flourishing civilizations led global culture. Today, however, it is marred by the bitterness of religious conflict, with terrorist attacks sometimes taking the lives of innocent people.

Trusting God for our safety, our Women's Federation for World Peace dove into the heart of the Middle East to build peace through reconciliation and love. From the late 1960s, Unification men and women missionaries from Europe went out to countries in the Middle East, including Turkey, Jordan, Iran and Lebanon. Some were arrested and some were deported, but others found ways to stay. Even so, those who entered Islamic countries that strictly forbade other faiths to proselytize risked incarceration, beatings or worse from the authorities. Despite this, through the dedication, teaching and service of our members, the local people came to understand them and gradually opened the doors to their hearts.

By the mid-1980s, these missionaries brought eminent Muslim clergy to our Assembly of the World's Religions and Council for the World's Religions conferences, and these clergy in turn brought Muslim citizens from the Middle East and North Africa, sometimes hundreds at a time, to attend 40-day Divine Principle workshops in New York in the early 1990s. Beginning in 1992, Islamic couples who were moved by the teachings of the Principle gratefully received the marriage Blessing.

Upon this foundation, in November of 1993, I traveled to Turkey to speak on "True Parents and the Completed Testament Age." People tried to deter me from visiting the Middle East, saying it would be extremely dangerous and that audiences would walk out if I delivered a speech that did not suit them. That did not deter me in the least, for I had gone through worse situations many times. Even if there is only one person waiting to receive me, I consider it my mission as God's mediator, the only begotten Daughter, to go to the ends of the earth to meet that person and open for him or her the gate of salvation.

As I was forewarned, half the audience in Istanbul got up and left during my speech because I did not mention either Islam or the Prophet Muhammad. I realized that the road ahead in the Middle East would not be a smooth one. On the heels of that event, my next engagement was in Jerusalem. My family and movement leaders again voiced concern. They pointed out that it was an epicenter of war and tried to persuade me to wait until a calmer time.

Nonetheless, I went to Jerusalem and, after my arrival, encountered a different problem. Opposition from Jewish leaders had led to the venue abruptly canceling our reservation. We found another hall, but there, as in Istanbul, many people left during my speech because what I said was not in accord with their beliefs. As in Istanbul, neither daunted nor discouraged, I finished my speech. I knew that God had suffered over the Middle East for thousands of years, and I was experiencing a small taste of that pain. I knew that even those who left early had received something of value that would grow in their hearts.

As the world ushered in the new millennium, the American Clergy Leadership Conference took our ministry for peace in the Middle East to a new level, with an initiative to bring reconciliation between Jews and Christians. Based on the call for Christians to embrace the Jewish people, it was discovered that the cross is a barrier to that unity. Therefore Christians called for the "end of the era of the cross," taking down their crosses and focusing instead on the resurrection and victory of Jesus in love. In May 2003, members of the Christian clergy from the United States and Europe as well as Israel marched through the streets of Jerusalem carrying a cross. In a prayer of repentance and forgiveness, they buried that cross in the Field of Blood, which is said to have been bought by Judas Iscariot with the 30 pieces of silver he received for betraying Jesus. A Jewish woman present at that event said she felt as if 4,000 years of sorrow on the part of her people had finally dissipated.

2003: ACLC clergy and participants march to the Field of Blood, Jerusalem

Within the same year we conducted the Jerusalem Declaration for the reconciliation of the three Abrahamic faiths and held a ceremony in Jerusalem's main park. On that stage, Jewish, Christian, Muslim and Druze clergy crowned Jesus as the King of Israel. Our message was clear: Jesus came to humanity as our King of kings, but he was rejected and crucified, and so could not realize the literal kingdom of God that he declared to be near. The purpose of the coronation ceremony was for people of all the Abrahamic faiths to declare Jesus the true King, thus liberating him—and God—from sorrow. On that day, and others like it, we created the environment in which religious leaders from around the world, together with Jewish and Palestinian Israelis, embraced in tears.

The work carried out for peace in the Middle East was the fruit of many laborers in God's vineyard, including our women missionaries and Women's Federation members, in particular from Japan, who were inspired by True Parents' vision. They left their families to work devotedly for a decade or more in the desert, a land of sandstorms and extreme natural phenomena.

Half a century has passed since my husband and I first visited the Middle East. I still vividly remember the excitement, mixed with concern, that I felt when I took my first steps into the desert with the warm wind in my face. At that time, as we visited three Middle Eastern nations, we earnestly prayed for the entire region to unite in one heart and realize peace.

For me, seeking peace is comparable to searching for a needle in the middle of a sandstorm. Success is accomplished only by the intervention of God, our Heavenly Parent. Thus it was with absolute faith, love and obedience in 1960 that my husband and I resolved never to turn back until we had established a peaceful world. I am so sad that acts of terrorism still continue. When all people realize the significance of the only begotten Daughter, and that she is with them, representing the ideal of womanhood for which all religions have striven, the cycle of tragedy upon tragedy will come to an end—both in the Middle East and throughout the world.

CHAPTER 9

GOD'S KINGDOM
IN OUR MIDST

❧

The most important teaching

We are taught many things in the course of our lives. Our parents teach us even at mealtimes and our teachers teach us most diligently. We learn about science, which explains the order and logic of things, and practical skills that help us escape poverty. Our elders teach us attitudes to adopt in the workplace. All these teachings are important and make us brighter and wiser. Knowledge and wisdom are precious, and we need to pursue them continuously. Nonetheless, of all teachings, what are the most important?

The teachings of religion are the most important. In Korean, the word religion is *jong-gyo*, which is made up of the Chinese characters *jong* (宗), meaning fundamental, and *gyo* (教), meaning teaching. The doctrines of the religious founders, including Confucius, the Buddha, Jesus and the Prophet Muhammad, have served as driving forces shaping civilizations and safeguarding the human conscience throughout the ages. Religion is necessary for the eradication of the world of sin and the creation of the ideal world desired by God and humanity. Accordingly, religion should be our lifelong companion.

October 28, 2018: Rally of Hope for a Heavenly Unified Korea, Peace World Center, HJ Cheonwon, South Korea

Selfishness has become commonplace in our world. We enjoy improvements in living standards based on technology, but with each passing day, we are increasingly isolated. We take little personal responsibility for our country, our society and even our family. The rising divorce rate proves that husbands and wives no longer take responsibility for each other. Parents do not care for their sons and daughters, and sons and daughters abandon their parents to pursue self-centered desires. Can you imagine the pain God feels seeing humanity, whom He created as His children, living this way?

Our world houses many religions. What should those religions teach? Religion must first teach the truth about God. I do not mean simply that God exists; I mean teaching about our *relationship* with God. True religion teaches the nature of God, the reality of God's love, and how to live in that love.

I do everything I possibly can to convey God's truth, traveling hundreds and thousands of miles, crisscrossing the five oceans and six continents. Wherever I go, I meet righteous people prepared by God. No matter how difficult the circumstances, God searches for righteous people. In the Bible, Sodom and Gomorrah were cities of lewdness and immorality. God said that He would not destroy them if 50 righteous people could be found in them. Abraham negotiated the number down to 10. In the end, he could not find even one, and the flames of a volcanic eruption consumed those cities. That is why I tell our church members to look for righteous people prepared by Heaven. In every place I visit throughout the world, I find that God has prepared righteous people. From among all races and nationalities, I find righteous people waiting for me.

In 2018 I visited South Africa, which has experienced heartbreaking agony due to racial conflict. In the past, it was not easy for me to enter the country, but this time the nation welcomed me with open arms. I hosted the Africa Summit and a marriage Blessing Ceremony. More than 1,000 representatives from some 60 nations attended the Summit and adopted my proposal for the settlement of peace and improvement of living standards. The Summit's purpose was to commemorate the centenary of the birth of Nelson Mandela and honor his legacy. The participants cheered the speech of Mr. Mandela's eldest grandson, Zwelivelile "Mandla" Mandela, a member of South Africa's Parliament, in which he sincerely testified to me. "Just like my grandfather," he said, "Dr. Hak Ja Han Moon is an icon of peace in this age. Africa should carry on the work left by President Mandela together with Dr. Hak Ja Han Moon, who has presented a new hope and vision to us through the Heavenly Africa Project."

That day, through the only begotten Daughter who is the True Mother, more than 3,000 couples from some 20 nations received Heavenly Parent's grace in the marriage Blessing Ceremony, the salvation of our age. Jesus said that "the last will be first." South Africa, Zimbabwe and Senegal, as well as Nepal and other many countries, have suffered through painful histories of poverty and political turbulence, yet now they are shining brightly through their faith in the only begotten Daughter. Humanity is seeking the love that comes from True Parents. We long to be true sons and daughters who inherit true love, life and lineage. I open the gates for all to attain true happiness and eternal life.

The great Indian poet, Rabindranath Tagore, wrote a beautiful poem in praise of Korea. At the time, Korea was hidden from the world, suffering under Japanese colonial rule. And yet Tagore prophesied: "In the golden age of Asia, Korea was one of its lamp-bearers, and that lamp is waiting to be lighted once again for the illumination of the East." The lamp of which he spoke is a new expression of the truth. He prophesied that it would appear in Korea and illuminate the world. I am now traveling the world to teach the Divine Principle, the new expression of the truth. The soil is plowed; all that remains is for us to sow the seeds and let them take deep root. This is a task we all must strive to accomplish.

Saving a prison guard

My husband used to say that I am a selfless person. He pointed out, more than once, that I give away my extra clothes to others until my closet is empty. It is true that I dislike holding on to possessions. I want to give all I have as gifts to those who are working hard day and night for the providence. Just as I did at the Cheongpa-dong Church and the Hannam-dong residence in Seoul, here in Cheongpyeong I open up our closet and give away clothes and shoes when missionaries and guests visit. My husband's shirts and pants, belts and neckties, along with my clothes and accessories, find new owners. When I see the hard-working members, I feel at ease only after giving them something, even if it is small.

November 18, 1995: Visiting a social welfare center in Accra, Ghana

I sometimes visit orphanages and impoverished areas when I am in Africa or South America. Turning this impulse to help others into a reality, in the 1980s I founded the International Relief Friendship Foundation. As I have mentioned, I more recently set up the Women's Federation's 1% Love Share project and other non-profit service organizations, and, as I mentioned before, I established the Wonmo Pyeongae Scholarship Fund to award scholarships to promising college students with high ideals. When I see people in need, I cannot pass them by. That is the nature of true love that originates in the deepest heart of Heaven.

"What comes first, life or love?" When asked this question, most people answer that life comes first. "After all," they say, "only when there is life can there be love." In my view, it is love that comes first. Thinking externally, we define our birth as our starting point, but love came before our birth. Our body and mind came from our parents. If not for the love of our father and mother, we would not be in this world. We should never give up love, even if it means having to give up our life. We were born through love, so we should walk the path of love and we should die for love.

I am talking about eternal and unconditional love—true love—not temporary, conditional love. To find true happiness, we need to practice true love. True love means living for the sake of others, serving others, not being served. True love means to forgive endlessly. Jesus told us to "forgive seventy times seven" times. Even when he was nailed to the cross and soldiers were piercing his body with spears, Jesus entreated God, "Father, forgive them, for they know not what they do."

My husband once saved the life of a Japanese prison guard who had severely tortured him. The torture took place at the police station in Gyeonggi Province of Korea during the Japanese colonial rule. When Korea was liberated in 1945, this policeman could not find a way to return to Japan. He went into hiding, but some Koreans found him and were intent on killing him. The policeman, Kumada Hara, was only hours away from death when my husband heard of the plot. He took it upon himself to free Mr. Hara and get him on a small boat heading out of the country in the middle of the night.

The capacity to forgive your enemy and save his or her life does not appear overnight. It requires that we eliminate the resentment and anger in our hearts and see the countenance of God in the face of our enemy. Father Moon could do so because he did not think of Mr. Hara as his enemy. Even while being tortured, he prayed for him and forgave him. This is only possible when you lead a selfless life.

Evil is acting for selfish gain, whereas goodness is to serve others and let go of the memory of having done so. When we give and forget, true love flourishes. We do not run out of love by giving it away. Quite the opposite: True love is a spring that flows in ever greater abundance. When walking the path of love, even when you give something precious, you feel that you did not give enough. Living with true love does not make one prideful; if anything, one feels sorry for not being able to give something even better.

True love moves on a circular path. Where it starts or ends, no one knows. Love within limits is not true love. True love is always new, yet is unchanging. Circumstances and environments change, but true love remains. It does not grow old or stale; it is ever fresh, in spring, in summer, in autumn and winter, in your youth, your adulthood and your old age.

True love is the power that unites a man and a woman eternally. When you love each other completely, your beloved lives within you and you live within your beloved. True love is the only thing people really are seeking. It transforms every sadness and pain into joy. The fallen world programs us to think that when we give something away, it is gone. In true love, however, the more we give, the more we receive. When our mindset changes from wishing to receive love, to wishing to give love, the world of peace will be at hand.

Becoming the light of the world through a filial heart for Heaven

From time to time, I ascend Mount Balwang in Pyeongchang, Gangwondo. At the foot of that nearly 1,500-meter mountain is the well-known Yongpyeong Resort, a property that our members have developed. It is one of the locations where the popular Korean drama *Winter Sonata* was filmed. At the top of that mountain is a rare tree. I named it "the mother and child tree."

It is actually two trees of different species that have grown together and become one. A Chinese crabapple tree that is hundreds of years old is the mother, and a rowan tree that has grown up within it is the child. This "mother and child" tree has flourished like that; they depend on each other and thrive together.

Perhaps when the crabapple tree became old and hollow, a bird dropped a rowan tree seed inside it and a new tree grew there. The crabapple tree embraced and nurtured the rowan tree as if it were its child. Over time, the rowan tree's roots grew deep, until it could support the crabapple tree as if it was taking care of its mother. In the same space, the two trees each blossom and bear fruit.

They are only trees, but they are an example of filial piety. They exhibit what I call *hyojeong*, the beautiful love, care and deep heart of parent and child.

Most Koreans, when they first encounter the term *hyojeong*, tilt their head in puzzlement. It might seem like a familiar concept, but it is not easy to define. They wonder, does it refer to a feeling in one's heart, or does it refer to actual practice? The Korean word *hyo* also means to be effective, so some even think that is the meaning.

The term *hyojeong*, which I created, includes giving one's whole heart, and so "being effective" is not entirely wrong. However, the term *hyojeong* that I have been using has a much deeper and wider meaning. *Hyo* is a term that once was prevalent in the Far East. If we had to translate it into English, we might render it "filial duty." However, the word, "duty" is not enough. *Hyo* means duty motivated by love, duty that is not compulsory but is happily voluntary, and that provides one's life its deepest meaning. Of course, that includes sincerely honoring and truly loving your parents. *Hyo* is a beautiful Korean tradition and also is the foundation of life. It is sad to see that the concept of *hyo* is slowly disappearing in society.

———

When I hear the word *hyojeong*, I think of my oldest son Hyo-jin and my second son Heung-jin, who hold special places in my heart. Both have passed into the spirit world; Heung-jin passed on first. Despite being a teenager, he courageously stood on the front line to protect his father. Heung-jin would always declare, "I will protect Father."

At the end of 1983, at the peak of the Cold War, my husband and I were speaking at large Victory Over Communism rallies in South Korea. We knew that communist sympathizers were determined to stop us. The final rally was in Gwangju, the heart of the leftist movement in South Korea. When my husband was about to go on stage to give his speech, I noticed that his tie pin had disappeared. "What happened to it?" I thought, feeling puzzled. "Where did it go?"

A few moments later, while my husband was onstage giving his speech, on the other side of the Pacific Ocean, in upstate New York, Heung-jin was involved in a car accident. Heung-jin was driving on a two-lane road when a tractor-trailer coming the other way hit black ice and slid into his lane. He veered the car to the right but could not avoid a head-on collision. He swerved in such a way that he took the direct hit on the driver's side, saving the life of his friend sitting in the front passenger seat.

We found out later that there had been agents trying to kill my husband in Korea that day. They had entered the auditorium in Gwangju and tried to reach the stage, but they could not get through the packed crowd and so could not carry out their plan. Satan was targeting the father, but when that evil plan was thwarted, Satan took the son as a sacrificial offering. By sacrificing himself in his father's stead, Heung-jin kept the promise he had made: "I will protect Father."

When Heung-jin was born, he didn't open his eyes for three days, and I felt so worried about him. At the end of his short life, he passed away as a son of the greatest filial devotion to his parents. This deep filial piety is engraved in the hearts of our members.

Our eldest son Hyo-jin loved music. It is not an overstatement to say that Hyo-jin's influence is a major reason that many young people in the Unification movement today are pursuing music. Being the older brother he was, he would always say, "I am the filial son." His heart often seemed sad when he looked at me, because I didn't have as easy a life as some of his friends' mothers had. He used to comfort me by saying in a loud voice, "Mom! When I grow up, I will do everything for you!"

In the early 1970s, after moving our family to America, we saw that many Americans did not respect Asian people. During that time, my husband and I ignored that attitude, but it truly hurt Hyo-jin's heart. There were people who laughed at us as well as people who sympathized with us. Hyo-jin saw all of this. He knew that communists threatened his father, and even though he was only 12 years old, he would take off his jacket and say, "I will fight those people to protect my father."

He gradually came to realize that it takes a lot of time before nations accept new teachings. He would think over and over again, "Isn't there a way to gather everyone, as if in a whirlwind, and convey the message to them all at once?" Then one day, he slapped his knee emphatically and cried, "This is it!" He had found his answer: rock music. He decided to move young people's hearts and guide them to the Divine Principle through music.

Along with leading our collegiate activities opposing communism, he created a youth music culture in our church, including a professional recording studio at New York's Manhattan Center. At one point, he made a religious commitment to compose and record 10,000 songs in three years. No one can write and record, with a band, 10 songs in one day, but he did so, every day, for three years. Hyo-jin forgot about himself and focused on composing songs, day and night. He believed that this expressed the heart of filial piety that made his parents happy, and he believed it was his mission to do this for the sake of the world. Among his many songs, people love *Let It Blow* the most, with its lyrics, "I must find the person that God wants me to be. My heart is beating like the sound of a train, running for your sake."

More and more people were moved by Hyo-jin's songs and the number of members grew. Satan was seething. Hyo-jin immersed himself day and night in writing songs, guiding his musicians, recording and performing, as well as speaking to the members at Belvedere at 6:00 in the morning each Sunday. He held a concert in 2007 at the Seoul Olympic Stadium and then did a concert tour in Japan. These were his last performances. In 2008 he passed away suddenly, due to severe fatigue accumulated through performances and endless songwriting.

Hyo-jin's music was explosive; through it, he expressed his passionate filial devotion—yes, his hyojeong—for his mother and father. To inherit Hyo-jin's spirit, every autumn, in conjunction with the Cosmic Seonghwa Festival to commemorate Father Moon, we hold a Hyojeong Festival to pay tribute to Hyo-jin. Our members are always grateful for his heart to guide people to God through music and media.

A filial son considers what he can do for his parents and courageously follows through. A filial child has the spirit of serving and is welcomed everywhere. Such a child always fulfills God's hopes. That is why the spirit of hyojeong is great; it seeks to serve others and not oneself.

I planted seeds of hyojeong in the world on the fourth anniversary of Father Moon's ascension, which took place in August 2016. After three years of mourning, I transformed the character of Father Moon's memorial service from a sorrowful gathering into a festival that celebrates new hope and peace. I entitled it, "Becoming the Light of the World through a Filial Heart for Heaven." Our Cheongpyeong complex became a garden of joy upon which the sunlight of love poured down.

On the one hand, we retraced the footsteps of True Parents, while on the other, we enjoyed diverse cultural performances. On one day, with the motto, "Food Is Love," we held a "Festival of Sharing True Parents' Favorite Dishes." We filled a gigantic bowl the size of a large dining room table with rice and other delicious ingredients, used spatulas the size of oars to mix it all, and made *bibimbap* to feed 20,000 people in the Peace World Center. It was like a celebration meal bringing all the world's peoples as one family around one table.

This memorial event included other programs as well: lectures, seminars, leaders' meetings, ancestor liberation and Blessing, and so forth, in Korea and abroad, lasting over a month. Our global family together built a spiritual foundation for our future direction.

<hr />

I vividly recall the pledge I made on the day that my husband passed away: "I will revive the church with the spirit and truth we had in the early days." I have kept that promise. The filial devotion of our sons, Hyo-jin and Heung-jin, lives on in my heart, along with the spirit of my beloved husband. When we convey filial devotion to all people, and everyone lives for the sake of others and looks after each other, that will be the kingdom of heaven.

Filial devotion is a pre-eminent practical virtue as well as an eternal pillar of life. We must practice filial devotion while our parents are alive. After they are gone, no matter how much we want to sacrifice for them, it will be too late. We must know how precious this moment is and be proud of it.

Across the table, around the world

An image shimmers faintly in my memory, like a gleam of sunlight reflected by the dew on the grass. I was sitting across the table from my husband, right after our Holy Wedding. He gazed at me with the overwhelming heart of God. It seemed as if a waterfall of tears was about to burst forth from his eyes.

That experience, the two of us sitting together at a small table to eat, treading the path of hyojeong in front of God, recurred many times on our path as True Parents. We communed without a worry, sitting across the table from each other, during the three years we ate only boiled barley, and when we barely had time to catch our breath while on speaking tours, visiting two or more countries in a day. We were grateful for everything, and everything was a source of happiness.

For me, the annual Festival of Sharing True Parents' Favorite Dishes is like sitting across the table from all blessed families. The blessed families are true children of Heaven's lineage, to whom my husband and I have given birth through our tearful embrace. They are called by Heaven, so I call them chosen blessed families. True Father and I will sit across the table from these chosen blessed families forever. We will not forget for even a moment our countless children's intense tears and streaming sweat as they endured lonely struggles for the sake of God's will. My one regret over the Festival of Sharing True Parents' Favorite Dishes is that I cannot in person place a delicious meal before each of my beloved children around the world, and sit across the table from them.

In December of 2019, I had that feeling, sitting across the table from Prophet Samuel Radebe. I had just arrived in Johannesburg to conduct the Blessing Ceremony of 200,000 people. Our airplane landed amid pouring rain. When I walked into the airport lounge, I was so happy to meet Prophet Radebe, who is like a son to me. As soon as he saw me, he said, "Mother! I so wished to see you. Welcome to your home in South Africa!" Dressed in traditional South African clothing, Prophet Radebe welcomed me with a bow, expressing his heart of respect and humility, and presented a bouquet of red flowers he had prepared with care.

Accompanying him was a large group of youths and students of the Revelation Church of God, who greeted me enthusiastically right there in the airport lounge. They gave a special *a cappella* performance of a wonderful song with lyrics that meant, "True Mother came today to bless South Africa and all of Africa." When I said, "It is raining today. I've heard that rain is considered a great blessing in Africa," my words were greeted by loud cheers and shouts from Prophet Radebe, his youth leaders and students.

When it was time for lunch, Prophet Radebe sat across the table from me. The truth is that he normally would not have taken lunch on that day. It was December 5, a very important day for him spiritually. He told me that on that day each year, he goes to a special mountain and offers devotions. December 5, 2013, was the day that Nelson Mandela, one of the most respected figures in the Republic of South Africa and throughout the world, passed away. Prophet Radebe had publicly prophesied that December 5 would be the day of the president's passing. Many were amazed when his prophecy was realized. Moreover, on that day, a boy, filled with the Holy Spirit, testified in a heavenly language that Prophet Radebe is the leader who will liberate South Africa, and then coughed up a lion's tooth and presented it to the prophet. This story is legendary throughout South Africa. That is why on this day each year, Prophet Radebe has gone up to the mountain to offer gratitude for the heavenly mission given to him and to renew his determination to accomplish it.

He felt that it was a most auspicious day for the True Mother to arrive. Despite his commitment to his prayers, he had come down from the mountain to welcome me. Food is love, and to show my appreciation, I served him a bowl of warm Korean noodles. Sitting across from each other, I expressed the love between a mother and son whom Heaven had brought together. He went back up the mountain after lunch to continue his devotions with a life-or-death resolution for the success of our December 7 event.

When Prophet Radebe came to Korea in 2019 to attend the seventh anniversary of True Father's Holy Ascension, he offered special devotions on the top of Balwang Mountain. At that time, our Secretary-General Dr. Yun Young-ho, with whom Prophet Radebe had become sworn brothers through me, taught him how to use chopsticks. So now he did quite well using them to eat the noodles. Prophet Radebe's appreciation of Korean culture was another expression of his love and respect for me, his True Mother.

The path of mutual prosperity

There is a narrow path deep in a forest, barely wide enough for one person to walk along. The one who creates that path sweats profusely, with hands getting scratched while cutting away branches. Thanks to that person, those who come after can walk along the path in comfort. We need to be deeply grateful for the hard work of that first person, and endeavor to make the path wider and more even.

A path through people is harder to create than a path through a forest. Unlike trees that give way to the hatchet, people have their own will. And when something goes against their will, people close their hearts. I shed sweat and tears, trying to open hearts and connect people as one family. I pioneered a path no woman has ever walked, and embraced the world's peoples in the most precipitous places. I quietly practiced true love for human salvation and world peace in situations from which anyone else would have run away. My forgiveness and embrace have moved enemies to tears.

Now we have ushered in the springtime of the providence. Spring is the busiest time for farmers. They must do their utmost to ensure an abundant harvest in the fall. In this providential spring, we need to construct the original world that God planned to realize from the beginning. We can receive the marriage Blessing and share it with our family and tribe. Then we can work together as veritable messiahs to transform our nation. Such is Heaven's decree.

No matter how difficult our work, we need to complete the providence and reveal the truth. When we fulfill our responsibility, following God as sunflowers follow the sun, we will surely realize Heavenly Parent's dream and humanity's hope. The question is whether we will be able to achieve that while I am on earth. If we do, we will stand proud and tall in front of our descendants and all generations to come. There has never been such an opportunity. No matter how young or old you are, you are living in the same era as the only begotten Daughter. This is your golden age. Be grateful and do not miss this time.

We cannot let the world be ignorant of the coming of True Parents and the blessings and grace of God. We must guide all people to attend Heaven. Those who live in the kingdom of heaven on earth can go to the kingdom of heaven in heaven. We have one goal and one path, the path by which we can become God's proud sons and daughters. We need to lead lives such that God can embrace us and say, "Well done, my daughter! Well done, my son!" We need to realize in our hearts that this is the golden age.

True Parents' guiding life philosophy is "live for the sake of others." Wherever I may go, I practice living for the sake of others. I always try to love people more than their own parents or siblings do. People tend to keep the best things for themselves and give things of lesser value to others, even in the relationship with their own parents. If you pursue only personal gain, chains of addiction and greed will tie you down. If you constantly put others first and live for their sake, you are on the path to eternal freedom and blessing.

When I see people in need, I give them whatever I have. A world where everyone gives their best things to others is a world of joy. This is my life philosophy. People who live only for themselves will soon hit a wall. You need to live your life with love and generosity.

Many people suppose that Father and Mother Moon are wealthy. The truth is, we have never owned a house, a car, anything. I am sure no one has been as thrifty as my husband and I. How can we possibly eat good food and sleep in comfort while knowing that missionaries are working through the night at home and abroad? We direct that all donations from church members be used for the poor through building schools and other projects.

We have established businesses around the world—fisheries, machine tool plants, pharmaceutical companies, newspapers, hotels, and more. Just in Africa, our members built schools in Senegal, Mozambique and Zambia; a school for the handicapped in Lagos, Nigeria; an orphanage in Natitingou, Northern Benin Republic; clinics in Cotonou, Benin and Nigeria Cross River State; a sausage factory in Lusaka, Zambia; a hamburger franchise in Côte d'Ivoire; an agricultural school and a food processing factory in the Democratic Republic of the Congo; and a farm in Lusaka, Zambia. We never focused on making a profit; our movement's investment was to benefit the host nations, create jobs and improve society. We endured hunger because we knew there were people who were hungrier. We should not be indebted to Heaven. People who follow the providential path while coveting material things violate heavenly law and bring sorrow to their parents.

Life is like running a marathon without knowing when it will end. A truly successful life is not powered by money, position or authority; it is powered by true love. True love is a mother breastfeeding when she is going hungry. That is the greatest love of all. Love is why we are here, how we should live, and where we are going. No matter the difficulties we face, the answer is to practice absolute faith, absolute love and absolute obedience.

If you reflect on God's heart, you will recognize that the hardships and suffering that you may be going through are nothing compared to His. We have to repent before God. You did not bring yourself into the world. Your life is a gift from God. His will for us is that we make our lives beautiful and worthwhile. When we believe in our hearts that we are here for our children and family, for our spouse, as well as for all humanity and the entire world, we will find happiness.

In all of this, your heart is your closest teacher. In the face of difficulty or confusion, ask your heart. Your Heavenly Parent who loves you resides deep in your heart. You are designed to hear God's true voice. We all need to hone our ability to hear hear the true voice of Heavenly Father and Heavenly Mother in our hearts. Your heart is your eternal guardian. Heartfelt prayer is the only passageway to God. Through such true prayer, you will receive the grace of God and True Parents in even the most destitute and difficult place. The helping hand of that grace leads us on the free and happy path to the kingdom of heaven.

The way of rebirth and resurrection

Don't you miss the sea? In the course of your daily life, don't you sometimes get the urge to rush to the beach and jump into the blue ocean? The sea is the symbol of the mother and the icon of motherhood. The deep sea is like a mother's bosom. That's where we want to be.

When people stand in front of Niagara Falls in North America or the Iguazú Falls in South America, they cannot hide their amazement and awe. Some turn speechless, overwhelmed by the majestic vista. How did these magnificent waterfalls come to be? They are the unification of innumerable streams, large and small. By the law of nature, small streams flow into greater ones. Streams and rivers start at different places but have the same destination, one great ocean.

A stream that refuses to flow simply dies. In the same way, religions that only cling to their own doctrines and refuse to unite with others die spiritually and eventually dry up. A religious teaching that explains God's original nature must now emerge.

When God created us, His fundamental purpose was to enjoy a parent-child relationship of love with us. We are the children of parents, ultimately of our Heavenly Parent. Nonetheless, the original sin separated us from our Heavenly Parent, God. We need to pray about and study what happened. God raised up the people of Israel over the long course of 4,000 biblical years. On that foundation, not just of 400 years but of 4,000 years, He sent His first Son, Jesus, of whom He could say, "This is my only begotten Son." Nonetheless, Jesus' family and the people of Israel could not fulfill their responsibility. Not only his family but even his disciples turned their backs; no one was ready to give their life for him. Only a thief on the cross to his right, as he faced death, testified to Jesus. No one on this earth, not even Christian believers, understood the pathos of Jesus' history.

Jesus is God's mediator, sent as our True Parent, to give rebirth and resurrection and guide us to become God's true children. History records 2,000 years of human suffering since the cross, and it came because those to whom Jesus was sent did not attend him. But who suffered the most? Our Heavenly Parent feels everything we are going through a thousand times more intensely than we do. When children suffer, parents suffer more.

Jesus promised the marriage of the Lamb at his second coming. Marriage brings two, a man and a woman, into one. The time has arrived. The Christian cultural sphere that is waiting for the only begotten Son also needs to receive the only begotten Daughter. As Jesus taught in a parable, God let out His vineyard to new tenants. Those new tenants are to render to the owner the fruits in their seasons. They are the Christians. To those new tenants, God sent the only begotten Daughter.

For this purpose, from before Jesus' time, God chose the Koreans, who originated from the Dong-yi people. They were an agricultural people who revered Heaven and loved peace. In 1603, a Korean diplomat brought Catholic theological writings from China to the Korean Peninsula. Later on, Koreans who adopted Catholic faith endured severe persecution. Then, in the late 19th century, the Korean king and queen accepted Christianity, and it flourished in their realm. In 1920, my husband, the only begotten Son, was born and in 1943, I, the only begotten Daughter, was born.

God's providence is amazing. In 1945, Korea was liberated from Japanese rule, but it was immediately divided into North and South, with North Korea adopting communism. At the time, I was in North Korea, but again, Heaven protected me. Knowing that I could not grow up in safety under the communist regime, God guided me to flee to South Korea with my mother and grandmother.

When the Korean War broke out in 1950, South Korea was completely unprepared to defend itself against North Korea's attack. But Heaven protected me. Sixteen UN member nations joined the war, which was nothing short of a miracle. At the time, the Soviet Union was a member of the UN Security Council. If the Soviet Union had vetoed the resolution, the 16 nations would not have been able to participate in the war. In a dramatic twist of fate, however, the Soviet Union representative was absent from the UN Security Council meeting when the vote was taken. This ensured the participation of UN troops in the war.

God anointed my husband and me as the True Parents in 1960. Since then, we have cultivated blessed families of all races, nations and religions. Now religious leaders in all parts of the world are one with True Parents and are multiplying the Blessing Ceremony. In early 2018, at the Africa Summit in Senegal, a Muslim country, I asked that Africa work together with me to uphold Heaven's will. Heads of state, tribal chiefs and religious leaders of all faiths expressed their wholehearted support. In Europe, Buddhist as well as Christian religious leaders are bringing their congregations to receive the Blessing. Muslims have aligned themselves with the only begotten Daughter. The same is true of Christians in the United States.

We now approach the final task, which cannot be delayed. I must open the age of Cheon Il Guk. Cheon Il Guk is a Korean term signifying God's peace kingdom, in which two become one through love. It is a new age and we need to put on new clothes. As citizens of Cheon Il Guk, we need the clothing of filial piety in our family, patriotism in our nation, saints in the world, and divine sons and daughters in heaven and on earth.

I am on earth to speak the historical truth, and I am neither hesitant nor reserved about it. At the August 2018 Latin America World Summit held in Brazil, I compared today's Christianity to an unfertilized egg that will not yield life. I told this to a large number of denominational and religious leaders, including a Catholic cardinal. I said clearly that present-day religions can bring forth life only by accepting True Parents and receiving and sharing the marriage Blessing. No one objected to my words. Receiving the True Parents is the essential purpose of every religion. To fulfill my mission as the only begotten Daughter, the True Mother and the Mother of the universe, I must give rebirth to the nearly 8 billion people on earth as God's true children.

The Bible says, "Whoever speaks a word against the Son of Man will be forgiven, but anyone who speaks against the Holy Spirit will not be forgiven." As a child is born of the father's seed in the mother's womb, we are born from God's seed in the Mother of the universe. The people who deny their mother will neither prosper here nor do well in the next world. I am the True Mother who brings new life. My heart is always open, and I forgive not just seven times, but 70 times seven.

The true compass in life

In 1960, a few days after our Holy Wedding Ceremony, I had a dream. I was walking down a dark rugged path along a precipitous cliff, with a bundle on my head, carrying children on my back and holding other children by the hand. I could have fallen off the cliff into a bottomless abyss, but I found the light and made my way to a wide, level road.

My path has been one of raising up every valley and making every mountain and hill low. From the day of our Holy Wedding, my husband and I traveled the world so that all people will see God's salvation. We visited every country, moving so quickly that I hardly had time to take off my shoes. As we walked the path of True Parents, we did not waver. We have borne truly unbearable persecution. Not only political regimes but also religious believers defamed us. Looking neither to the left nor the right, we endured, persevered and shared God's word and God's Blessing. Following this way, the number of people who believe in and follow me as the True Mother is growing day after day in every nation.

Jesus said that God is his Father. John 3:16 refers to Jesus as the "only begotten Son." The only begotten Son is the fruit of Heavenly Parent's deepest love. The coming Lord is the bridegroom, and he came to receive the only begotten Daughter as his bride. The two must meet and marry. That is the marriage supper of the Lamb prophesied in the last book of the Bible. Then the two must form a family. Heavenly Parent's hope has always been for one thing: that His only begotten Son and only begotten Daughter form a true family.

To live as true people in this world and enjoy eternal life in the next, we need to meet True Parents. We need to meet them even while walking down the path of death. Even if we have lost all of history and our own descendants, when we meet True Parents, we will regain the past and the future. We will be the true family of the True Parents. True Parents embody the eternal word. The greatest gift of God is rebirth through His word. We can become true parents ourselves, perfected through love.

Jesus said, "I am the way, the truth, and the life." My husband added one more word: love. Without love, we cannot do anything. We need to add love to this biblical text and engrave it: "I am the way, and the truth, and the life, and the love. No one comes to the Father except through me."

We each need this love. Every one of the nearly eight billion people in the world needs to meet the True Parents on earth. That is the purpose of the marriage Blessing. The fact that True Parents are with us is the fearsome yet joyful truth. Happiness is when human beings, who have lost their parents, find them again. There is nothing more joyful.

As the True Mother, only begotten Daughter and Mother of the universe, I have completed all works of the providence and opened a new age. Now we need to engrave that truth in our hearts and act upon Heaven's will. Guided by the Mother of peace, the only begotten Daughter, we will receive True Parents' seal and achieve harmony on the path of life.

CHAPTER 10

THE CHALLENGE
OF REALIZING
A HEAVENLY WORLD

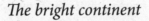

The bright continent

When you go to Africa, you will see it is rich in red and yellow hues. Some areas are covered in fertile, red soil, and others with ocher-colored sand. I have been told that Africa means "mother" or "sunlight" in different languages.

Unfortunately, multitudes of Africans still struggle to acquire the basic daily necessities. European colonizers exploited Africa's riches and did not invest effectively in its development. Even some who strongly believed in God enslaved and enchained their fellow human beings, considering them bereft of a soul. Too few lent a comforting hand or helped them find a way to live. And still fewer gave them words of Christ's love and hope of salvation.

The sense of profound grief I felt when I first stepped onto African soil in the 1970s remains in my heart. Over the years, my husband and I sent missionaries to Africa. Rather than invest in building our own churches, these missionaries worked to assist the local population by erecting schools, opening clinics and building factories. Their gallant efforts were humble contributions in helping to better the lives of others. Nonetheless, their altruistic endeavors did not answer the questions on everyone's minds. Africans would seek out Unification Church missionaries and pastors and ask:

"Why do we have to live in such misery?"
"When are True Parents coming to see us?"
"Do True Parents truly love us?
What do True Parents think about Africa?"

When these heartfelt words crossed oceans and reached my ears, I felt called, and I answered by going to Africa. However, despite my best efforts, it was difficult to meet and speak with everyone I wanted to see, and address the myriad complex circumstances afflicting each nation or tribe. Africa's complexity is evident in the multiplicity of faiths, ethnicities and languages throughout the continent—French-speaking Africa, English-speaking Africa, Islamic Africa, Catholic Africa, and more and more, overlaying the histories of conflicts among tribes. I prayed: How can I help heal this continent's wounds and bring harmony and oneness of heart? As the decades passed, we built the foundation to bring together public-sector and private-sector leaders of several nations, including traditional chiefs and religious leaders, to discuss interdependence, mutual prosperity and universal values.

I cannot forget the date, January 18, 2018, the day we held the inaugural 2018 Africa Summit at the Abdou Diouf International Conference Center (CICAD) in Dakar, Senegal. The theme and our hopes were ambitious: Building a Heavenly Africa through Interdependence, Mutual Prosperity and Universal Values. His Excellency Macky Sall, president of the Republic of Senegal, and several former heads of state and prime ministers, as well as current cabinet ministers, parliamentarians, religious leaders and leading figures from every sphere of society, attended the Summit. From Algeria in the north to South Africa in the south, 1,200 representatives from 55 nations gathered. The Universal Peace Federation was hosting its largest ever summit in Africa.

June 7, 2019: True Mother with former president Goodluck Jonathan and Dr. Thomas Walsh at the African Summit

While Koreans back home battled freezing winds and heavy snow, West Africa was blessed with warm breezes and the equatorial sun. When I stepped off the plane in Dakar, the sons and daughters of Africa welcomed me with great enthusiasm, holding my hands with tears of joy.

Following my keynote address at the Summit, many of our non-profit organizations' transformative initiatives that were actively underway in Africa were introduced, including the Sae-ma-eul (New Village) Movement, the International Peace Highway Project, and the Sunhak Peace Prize. Furthermore, through our sponsorship, the International Association of Parliamentarians for Peace, the Interreligious Association for Peace and Development, and the International Association of Traditional Rulers (Chiefs) for Peace and Prosperity were launched.

June 8, 2019: Presenting the FFWPU flag to
Prophet Samuel Radebe of South Africa

On the evening of the Summit's plenary, the Little Angels of Korea held a special congratulatory performance. Mesmerized by the songs and dances, the audience cheered and applauded throughout the performances of the Drum Dance, the Fan Dance, the Folk Wedding Dance and Arirang. People were moved to tears when the Little Angels sang the Senegalese National Anthem in their language and Senegal superstar Ismaël Lô's hit song "Dibi Dibi Rek." Everyone was uplifted, and a profound sense of brotherhood and sisterhood permeated the hall. Loud shouts and laughter heightened the sense of hope and joy felt by everyone.

It was just the next day that I took the ferry to Gorée Island, which lies off the coast of Dakar, to offer a prayer for the liberation of Africa from the historical pain and suffering caused by the scourge of slavery.

God's embrace ends all tears

Before 2018, I had never heard of Gorée, as it is located thousands of miles from Korea. However, as our World Summit Africa 2018 approached, I forged a profound relationship with the island and its history.

The bean-shaped island of Gorée is now a tourist attraction drawing visitors from all over the world. As the ferry sailed from Dakar Harbor across the azure sea, tourists from various countries, enthralled by the scenery and atmosphere, were chattering in wonder and taking photos. However, an intense pain arose in my heart. I already was feeling that the bitter tears of grief shed by thousands of captives in transit through that island could fill the world's oceans. The beautiful site that we were approaching must be the most sorrowful island in the world.

Dakar is located along a continental protrusion on the west coast of Africa. It is the closest point of transit from West Africa to North America and Europe. This geographical location may be used for good today, but for nearly 500 years it was a linchpin of the transatlantic slave trade, one of history's cruelest and most inhumane episodes.

When European missionaries came to Africa in the name of Christ, the great majority were righteous, but there were also people who failed to remain true to Christ's essence, who prioritized the monetary interests of their respective nations over Jesus' teachings. As European colonizers and their local collaborators exploited the God-given natural resources of Africa, they invested little in educating the people. Instead, they dehumanized and enslaved many of the indigenous people. From the fifteenth century on, European colonial powers flocked to Africa, plundering the continent's resources and enslaving the local populations. Men, women and children were placed in chains, forcibly taken to Gorée Island and shipped off to slavery in Europe and the Americas.

While at Gorée Island, captives were chained so heavily that it was nearly impossible for them to walk. They were starved until just before being sold at auction, when they were force-fed a diet of beans so they would gain weight. If they became seriously ill aboard the slave ship, they were thrown overboard into the ocean. The once-peaceful island of Gorée was a slave camp filled with screams, tears and grief.

The slave trade continued for hundreds of years, and it is estimated that more than 20 million Africans were sold into slavery, many passing through the House of Slaves on Gorée Island. No one knows how many innocent lives were lost at sea during the voyages. As the True Mother, it broke my heart to know that such atrocities were committed by many who prayed in the name of Jesus Christ. Knowing these things, I wanted to visit Gorée Island and liberate the historical agony and heartbreak of all the Africans who suffered due to the scourge of slavery.

The throngs of people taking photos of its historic sites easily overlook the reminders of this tragic past. Gorée is a small island, with the seaside easily reached by a 20-minute walk either to the east or west. During my tour, I saw that visitors were impressed by its many European-style buildings. One tourist remarked, "Walking along these cobblestone streets reminds me of European neighborhoods." Another said, "These European houses are so beautiful and full of character."

What is now a tourist site was the epicenter of the West African slave trade. I looked at the beautiful houses built for the European slave traders, and the contrast with the slave camp located barely a hundred feet behind them could not have been greater.

The House of Slaves is a two-story building. The slave traders lived on the second floor, while innocent Africans captured and brought there from throughout the continent were kept on the first floor while awaiting to be boarded onto slave ships. Most visitors and dignitaries tour the second floor, but I spent my time in the slave cells on the first floor.

The slave house was built with stones and contained cramped, gloomy holding cells. The cells were like caves—dark and damp, with no natural sunlight and ceilings so low that one could not stand up straight. At the end of a narrow corridor with cells on either side was the infamous Door of No Return. The men, women and children who went through this door onto slave ships sailing for the Americas never saw their families again.

Holding onto the frame of the Door of No Return, I shed tears, along with the mayor of Gorée and everyone in our party, as I prayed for Africa to be freed from the pain and resentment caused by slavery. As I stood at that door, I could hear the cries and weeping of countless Africans taken against their will.

My grief increased when I witnessed tourists laughing and joking as they passed by the slave cells. But I also saw families frown and sigh in sadness at the sight of these reminders of human cruelty. One mother leaned over a red brick staircase and offered a tearful prayer. She seemed hopeful that her prayer might contribute to healing centuries of cruelty and misery.

Liberating those who have ascended differs from comforting those who are alive on earth. Both are possible through the earnest prayer of God's only begotten Daughter, who carries the mission to save humanity. Facing the silent, grieving walls of the House of Slaves, I forever broke the miserable chains of Africa's oppression.

January 19, 2018: The Door of No Return at Gorée Island, Senegal

The anguished cries of Africans should be heard and their plight embraced. Humankind's long, painful history of exploitation and deprivation of freedom must come to an end. This was my motivation as I traveled thousands of miles to come to Gorée Island and walk in this still pitiable and sorrowful land of Africa. Having seen the slave cells and the Door of No Return on the first floor, I did not take the stairs going to the second floor where the slave owners lived. I instead made my way to the courtyard. There, together with Gorée Island Mayor Augustin Senghor and his wife, and many local officials, I offered a prayer for the liberation of all Africans who died as victims of slavery.

A short walk from there brought us to a small square. Along one of the yellow-painted walls were several small plaques honoring eminent leaders who had visited the island, including Nelson Mandela, Barack

Obama, Mother Teresa and John Paul II. As they unveiled a plaque with my name and read the inscription, Mayor Senghor said, "This doesn't fully embody how grateful and indebted we feel, but it will stand for eons as an enduring symbol of the precious heart you have brought here." Many among the crowd expressed their thanks to me for liberating Africa from the weight of 500 years of suffering. It was a heartfelt token of appreciation from the people of Senegal and, I felt, the continent.

Following the unveiling, the Little Angels moved everyone to tears with beautiful Senegalese songs they had learned and rehearsed over many hours. As we made our way to the pier to depart, I told the mayor I wanted to leave a gift behind that would benefit the whole island. When we reached the pier, we could hear the sound of a motorboat approaching. It was a water ambulance I had prepared as a gift to Gorée Island for passenger and emergency patient transport. Christened with the name Victoria, it reflected our common hope that, although innumerable lives have been lost over the centuries, no others will be lost for the lack of a medical boat.

In Africa, the plight of many remains bleak. Despite abundant natural resources and wondrous scenic beauty, poverty is rampant. Nevertheless, Africans are kind, compassionate and diligent. God has called the peoples of Africa to shine as bright, immutable, heavenly creations. Africans make me feel the heart of our Creator, our Heavenly Parent.

The mother nation

Whenever we hold an event at our Cheongpyeong complex in Korea, thousands of Japanese Unificationists participate. I am always concerned, because incredible logistical support is necessary to welcome and host anywhere from 3,000 to more than 6,000 members at this site, our original spiritual homeland. But from their side, Japanese members feel it is a joy to visit their spiritual homeland of Korea. They treasure prayer at holy grounds, such as Bomnaetgol in Busan, where Father Moon built his first church out of discarded military ration boxes and mud. They value the Cheongpa-dong Headquarters Church. For many, it is a once-in-a-lifetime opportunity and honor.

The sight of thousands of devout Japanese members coming to Korea provides a glimpse of a great spiritual wave that I believe will bring positive change to Asia. Asia is considered the continent of the future for many reasons, one of which is that it is where the Unification movement's revival and expansion are most dynamic. Japan was the second country in which the Unification movement developed. Mission work began in dramatic fashion when, in July 1958, Missionary Choi Bongchoon boarded a ship in Busan headed for Japan. His mission work was an endless marathon of hardships. Entering the country without a proper visa, he was arrested and incarcerated, then hospitalized. Finally gaining his freedom, Mr. Choi broke through when, at 7:15 p.m. on October 2, 1959 in a crumbling attic in Tokyo, he led the first public Unification Church of Japan Sunday Service. Over the 60 years since then, the Unification Church has expanded throughout Japan.

Nonetheless, theirs has been a tortuous course. Accusations of being a cult were incessant, and ferocious opposition from Japanese communists arose in reaction to our Victory Over Communism activities. When several celebrities participated in our marriage Blessing Ceremony, some in Japan felt threatened by the expansion of our movement, and they fiercely opposed us in the media. For decades, my husband could not enter Japan. Some of our beloved members even lost their lives. A major assault on religious liberty was allowed when Japanese authorities turned a blind eye to criminals kidnapping our members, holding them captive until they renounced their faith, and even committing them to mental hospitals. Despite such hardships, the Unification movement in Japan has grown steadily, and the society now is recognizing the wrongness of such treatment. Our movement is a shining light for Japanese society. It also has sent thousands of missionaries throughout the world. They have invested themselves wholeheartedly in teaching the Divine Principle and serving local communities.

～～

Prior to the 1990s, two groups of Korean immigrants living in Japan shunned each other over ideological differences. They coalesced into two organizations, Mindan, the pro-democracy Korean Residents Union in Japan, and Chongryon, the pro-Pyongyang General Association of Korean Residents in Japan. The fact that citizens belonging to the same "Korean people" separate themselves from each other like water and oil was a great shame. As we engaged in Victory Over Communism activities, we forged ties even with Chongryon and invited its members to visit South Korea. Initially they viewed us with suspicion, but when they saw the sincerity of our offer, they joined the tours. Many among them eventually distanced themselves from communism.

In the summer of 2018, at the Saitama Super Arena in Tokyo, we held the Rally of Hope and Resolve to Advance God's Providence in Heavenly Japan, to celebrate the 60th anniversary of the Japanese movement. During my address, I called Japan and Korea to go forward hand in hand for the sake of the future. I exhorted the two nations to unite in heart and complete the Korea-Japan undersea tunnel linking the two nations and the world through the International Peace Highway.

Since the 1960s, I have visited Japan whenever possible to meet members, share personal stories and encourage missionaries. I have spoken publicly at hundreds of gatherings in various cities, including Tokyo, Nagoya, and Hokkaido, sharing God's word.

Nagano, which once hosted the Winter Olympics, is a Japanese city that has touched me in a special way. The Nagano Unification Church initially consisted of a small church with a few dozen members. Through my constant encouragement, the church grew steadily. Next to the beautiful, cozy church building is a small training center that they named "Hwarang." The local members gave this name in honor of the noble spirit that guided elite young leaders of Korea's Silla Dynasty. Moved by the members' dedication, I visited the church, encouraged the members and asked them to bring God's will to fruition there. I also planted an apple tree in their backyard, and when I visited the church again a few years later, the tree had grown magnificently and was bearing delicious apples. Just like the apple tree, the words I have sown in Japan have multiplied and are now bearing many beautiful fruits.

I blessed Japan to now arise as "Heavenly Japan," a Japan in which society and culture are reborn. Tens of thousands of Japanese men and women have found new life in the bosom of God through True Parents. Every year, many of them cross the Korea Strait to visit the homeland of their faith. This convergence of members makes our HJ Cheonwon campus a bridge of harmony between two former enemy nations.

My heart is especially with Japan during natural disasters and other difficult times. During the great earthquake of Tohoku, the Kumamoto earthquakes and the floods in Okayama Prefecture, countless lives were lost and the damage was overwhelming. When such calamities occur, I offer my condolences and wholehearted support. In the context of God's global providence, True Parents blessed Japan as the mother nation. A mother gives everything to her children unconditionally. Just as a mother goes without sleep to take care of her children, Japan is walking the path of sacrifice with the heart of a mother for the sake of the world.

Love and service in South America

"We are probably worse off than Africa," lamented many of the locals in South America to whom I talked. "Even though we have many resources and so-called democratic institutions, our lives are very poor."

The continent of South America, like Africa, has a history of grief, exploitation and poverty. It was occupied for over 300 years by powerful European countries that subjugated its peoples and appropriated its gold, silver and other resources. Moreover, the Europeans introduced foreign diseases that decimated native populations that had no immunity to those germs.

In the early nineteenth century, South American countries fought for and finally attained their independence, and many sought to establish democracies. But too often, governments became riddled with corruption, and later communist and fascist movements arose and used people's resentments to prop up harsh dictatorships.

All of this meant that untold millions of people suffered and died through human cruelty. The first thing I did whenever I got off an airplane in South America was offer a prayer to liberate and comfort the anguish of those people in the spirit world.

Despite their miserable hardships, I have seen that the South American people lead decent and honest lives, working hard for even a little improvement. They also have a very strong faith in God. Much of the continent is rich with potential, as natural resources are abundant and the weather is temperate. Moreover, South America is a gift from God in that it possesses large areas of unspoiled nature. Anyone who goes to South America will feel a deep affinity for the vast land, abundant natural beauty, and the kind and pleasant people.

In South America, my husband and I offered continual prayer and devotions, which we call *jeongseong*. My husband's visit to five Latin American nations in 1965 were the first footsteps of the Unification Church on that continent. In the decades that followed, our missionaries established foundations throughout Central and South America, building churches, witnessing and increasing our membership, working for healthy marriages and families, and connecting these nations to global efforts for peace and reconciliation. Most South Americans are Catholic, while Protestantism is growing there as well. As with other peoples of the world, Latin Americans are open to exploring new pathways of relating to God, and we spread the Divine Principle teachings with all our heart.

The most influential project we invested in there was the educational project we named CAUSA. Father Moon and I created CAUSA in the 1980s because Marxist revolutionaries in Central and South America were gaining influence. For a time, it seemed the entire continent might become communist. We knew that if Mexico became communist, the United States would have to withdraw its troops from around the world to protect its southern border. This withdrawal of US troops would have allowed communism's evil influence to spread in many countries, including South Korea and Japan.

The CAUSA lectures provided a clear critique and counterproposal to communism to thousands of leaders and young people in Latin America and elsewhere in the world. Through this educational series, many former and current national leaders rejected communism's ideology and deceitful calls for revolution.

My husband and I conducted the "True Parents and the Completed Testament Age" speaking tour of six Latin American nations in 1993, and the "True Family and I" speaking tour of 17 Latin American nations in 1995. During those tours, we met the presidents of eight nations. Each one of them thanked my husband and me for halting the advance of communism in their country. On that foundation, we created economic projects to connect Paraguay, Uruguay, Brazil and Argentina, with the aim of bringing South America together as one family of nations.

The original beauty of Mother Nature

Our motorboat, which was basically a rowboat with an engine, noisily chugged its way across the deep, blue Paraguay River. Halfway across, one passenger suddenly stood up, and the boat rocked wildly from side to side. The other passengers cried out, fearing the boat would capsize. Just as everyone settled back down, someone yelled, "Ai! What's that?"

Before our eyes, a bizarre-looking fish jumped high out of the water and landed on the deck. There it flopped around in the hot sun, jerking its salmon-sized body and gnashing its dozens of razor-sharp teeth. The frightened passengers moved away from it, protecting their legs, as the boatman calmly picked it up with a long stick and tossed it back in the river.

"It looked scary. What is it called?" someone asked.

"It is a dorado," he said, "It's Spanish for 'golden.'"

The dorado is one of countless species of fish peculiar to the waters of Mato Grosso do Sul, one of the mid-western states of Brazil. The Paraguay River, which forms the border between that part of Brazil and Paraguay, is abundant not only in such fish but in every kind of living organism. In the regions of South America that are near the equator, the weather is either a warm springtime or hot summer. Flowers are constantly in bloom, and fruit is abundant for the picking. It is a pleasant land for human habitation in harmonious coexistence with the animal and plant life.

If paradise on earth is defined by having many different creatures living together in a lush, green garden, Mato Grosso do Sul belongs in that paradise. Its vast territory is covered by virgin forest and wetlands. It is ideal for cultivating a farm or caring for an orchard. Enormous trees provide shelter and sustenance for many kinds of birds, insects and animals. The rivers are clean, and some of them are quite clear. There are more than 20 waterfalls, including the famous Iguazú Falls that thunders where Brazil meets Argentina.

Even though it was South America's hottest season, in December of 1994 we brought our senior missionaries from around the world to experience a fishing workshop on the Paraguay River. As the sun blazed on those days, local people would wade into the river and lie in the water to cool off, watching us curiously while we fished.

As beautiful as the Pantanal was, one had to be careful at all times. We would take a boat up the river, dock it and explore the countryside. Sometimes we could barely get through tangles of vines hanging down from enormous trees, and we would have to crawl on our bellies. We often would not return to the boat until midnight. We would rely on a steel cable stretched out through the forest to guide us back in the dark.

When we rose before dawn every day to continue, we again would deal with sweltering heat and swarms of mosquitoes. It was a strenuous routine. My most difficult task was bathing. I would awkwardly put up a screen for privacy in the narrow boat, so I could wash myself with the murky river water. But in my heart I welcomed such primitive and natural conditions.

Near the Mato Grosso do Sul town of Jardim, we built a headquarters for global education, called the Headquarters for the Education of Ideal Families for World Peace, and set up the New Hope Farm to establish a foundation to build God's nation. The local townsfolk told us that an old prophecy predicted that Jardim was where the Lord will come.

The first time Father Moon and I went to Jardim was in late 1994. When we held our first leaders' workshop there, the training center was a rundown storehouse without even bathrooms or a kitchen. I cannot begin to describe how uncomfortable it was, but it was perfect for the experiential education we wanted to provide our leaders. It was a workshop of heart during which participants breathed the warm air and sweated without reserve as they read God's word in the early morning and fished in the midst of the unpolluted and pure original creation.

Over the years, we developed that Jardim site into a lovely family retreat center. We invested in the New Hope Farm that surrounded it. Unificationist missionaries and members from around the world moved there, with the vision of restoring the Garden of Eden that God created at the beginning. We built our community in Jardim with a school so that all these families from all over the world would be able to experience God's love while living in beautiful nature. We donated ambulances to the town, farmed and raised cattle and improved the livelihoods of local people. In the late 1990s, thousands of our members from around the world spent 40 days in study, prayer, and recreation in the natural beauty of New Hope Farm outside of Jardim.

The Pantanal, which Jardim borders, is the world's largest freshwater wetland area. Lying on both sides of the Paraguay River, it is a paradise on earth. Everything God created in the area has the appearance of the original creation. I am deeply impressed with the thought that this is what the Garden of Eden must have looked like, with the fish and all these animals and plants living exactly as they always have. There are capybaras, crocodiles, wild pigs, and birds such as rheas, all living freely in the wild. In the river you find surubi and pacu, and of course the piranhas that are dangerous even for humans. Many species considered endangered live here, including jaguars, pumas, deer, wolves, otters, armadillos and anteaters. There are also unique trees and cacti. It is the largest wetland in the world and, as a UNESCO world heritage site, it is protected. Thus it is a unique area in which to create an ideal village.

An extraordinary natural environment such as this has its dangers, but at the same time it could be a key region for solving food shortages in the future. We started farming and created a fish farm with a view to improving the local people's livelihoods. One of our ideas was to create a fish meal that could be supplied to boost people's nutrition in poorer areas. We made plans to raise cattle on our ranch and supply beef to as many as 160 countries. To protect the natural landscape, we planted a great number of trees in the land alongside the Paraguay River.

The second area in which we invested is called the Chaco. This remote area is part of the Gran Chaco region that covers parts of Bolivia, Paraguay and Argentina. In 1999, we encouraged our members to develop a settlement there called the Puerto Leda project. If you cross the Paraguay River at Puerto Leda, moving from Paraguay to Brazil, you're only a couple of hours by four-wheel-drive vehicle from Jardim.

Puerto Leda was the most difficult place to live in the Chaco, yet our Japanese brothers rolled up their sleeves and worked their hardest. In only a few years, they transformed the area into an ideal village where people and nature live in harmony, a place where anyone would enjoy living. They even built a swimming pool. It is a model ecological settlement, including water purification and fish farming, which was recognized by Paraguay's president, who personally visited the site. We prioritized these projects over building churches, but as the number of people who responded to our members' tireless devotion grew, our faith community also grew.

I wept many times over the pain of the people who lead arduous lives under those spacious skies in Latin America. My heart was torn for the children who craved to learn to write but could not. In the 1970s, when our missionaries from that area expressed how difficult it was to bring God's truth to people who struggle day to day to survive, all I could do was listen and silently pat their shoulders. We would pray together, "We will return here on another day and build a land of happiness. Heavenly Father, please don't forget these people." In the 1990s, God opened the door, and we began to fulfill those prayers.

When we arrived there, Puerto Leda lacked every basic facility. The nearby village needed a school as well as a hospital, and they urgently needed to secure an economic foundation to overcome hunger. Our members all over the world, especially Japan, responded to our call and donated in support of the Leda Project. Nothing can change in a day;

yet our members were comforted by the hope they saw in the eyes of the children, and by seeing changes emerge in the hearts of the youth. The new generation of Puerto Leda began to think, "We too can have a good life."

We keep in mind the need to stop the steady destruction of the ecosystem. We know that, in the name of economic development, we are losing the Amazon rainforest. Overfishing and the rapacious killing of valuable animals for monetary profit also are a serious problem. At the same time, more than 800 million people around the world regularly go hungry. Some South American countries have abundant stocks of beef and wheat, yet they cannot prevent malnutrition. In the midst of our education and community building in Latin America, we conduct plant and animal research on how to best utilize the local resources while protecting nature.

The wings of monarch butterflies span just a few inches, but they migrate 3,000 miles between Canada and Mexico every winter. No one taught them to do this; it is encoded in their nature. Human beings and nature have an inseparable relationship. We can be enlightened about God's act of creation and His mystical truth through nature, which represents Him, only when we live in it, invest in it, and study it. We can feel the infinite joy and love that God felt when He created the earth for us. When we do so, we can live each day with a heart of love and gratitude. The land in which we can learn this truth is Latin America. Through family-oriented love, as one family under God, we can discover our original homeland in this land, God's gift of nature.

The world's parliamentarians share one heart

Nepal has no seashore but having the world's tallest mountains makes up for that. Countless hikers and wealthy tourists visit Nepal, as it has eight of the world's 10 highest mountain peaks and its border passes over the very tallest peak, Mount Everest. But Nepal sits secluded between China and India, and the development of its largely agrarian economy is not keeping up with its neighbors.

When I arrived at the Kathmandu airport in the summer of 2016, two dogs were napping peacefully on the waiting-room floor and nobody was shooing them out. Cars and motorcycles came to a sudden stop because far ahead a cow was meandering along the road. Only after she moved off the road did the traffic start moving again. This is Nepal.

Nonetheless, large-scale changes have taken place since Nepal encountered our movement. For example, an amazing event took place in Nepal in 2016, which was an unforgettable year for our movement's peace efforts. In July, hundreds of leaders in the fields of politics, economics, religion and education arrived in Kathmandu from every nation in Asia. These distinguished men and women came to inaugurate the regional chapter of the International Association of Parliamentarians for Peace (IAPP), a project of the Universal Peace Federation.

Let me take a moment to introduce the IAPP. World peace cannot come about by human effort alone, nor by the efforts of just a few. Many people, from everyday citizens to high-ranking government officials, need to overcome social class divisions and actively take initiative. Every nation in the world, small or large, has a congress, a parliament or a national assembly. It represents the people of the nation.

Over the years, as I visited nations around the world, I repeatedly urged the parliamentarians who came to meet me to remember the precious mission bestowed upon them by their nation and its people. I said that when the people's elected representatives put their heads together and focus on what they can do to solve conflicts, peace will come quickly and naturally. I spoke of a world alliance of parliamentarians dedicated to the search for peaceful solutions. When I did so, parliamentarians would agree with me.

This vision from Heavenly Parent is the starting point connecting the world's parliamentarians as one body. Transcending nation, race and culture, by aligning with the only begotten Daughter, parliamentarians can work together to address the ills that bedevil human life.

As I shared this vision, people close to me tried to educate me about political infighting. They asked, "Will leaders of different parties be willing to gather and cooperate? Gathering influential people and peacemakers is not an easy task," they said, "All the nations' governments are fraught with conflict and strife caused by the divisions among opposing parties." I did not budge. I had not a shadow of a doubt that today's parliamentarians are ready, and I had faith that God would guide each of them to listen to me.

The launch of the International Association of Parliamentarians for Peace took place in February 2016 at the National Assembly of the Republic of Korea. The theme of the conference was "Addressing the Critical Challenges of Our Time: The Role of Governments, Civil Society and Faith-Based Organizations." This was the first of a series of such events, one held on each continent, about which I will now say a few words.

In Nepal in July 2016, under a hot sun, people gathered in great numbers to launch IAPP in the Asia-Pacific region. More than 166 parliamentarians and another 350 observers came from 29 nations. Many Nepalese citizens attended, and the Right Honorable President Bidhya Devi Bhandari personally conveyed her deep gratitude. Those who said it wouldn't work were wrong; the conference was a great success from the start, and many people later expressed their appreciation for IAPP as a much-needed organization.

Following the Nepal conference, we launched the West African regional IAPP in August 2016. More than 600 people from 24 nations came to Burkina Faso's National Assembly building and engaged in lively talks. A few weeks later, we opened the European regional IAPP in London with over 300 people from 40 nations in attendance. As the founder of IAPP, I sought to encourage them. "In building an eternal world of peace," I said at the London meeting, "each nation's political leaders must possess a moral character and follow ethical values and the voice of their conscience. The world will change when the world's parliamentarians unite and cooperate for the sake of peace."

Then in October, we launched IAPP chapters for Central America and South America in Costa Rica and Paraguay, respectively. Following those events, people gathered in Zambia in early November for the South and East African regional IAPP inauguration. In the northern climes, autumn was already well underway, but in parts of Africa, IAPP attendees had to endure sweltering heat. Still, we focused on our peace ideology and, in the end, resolved to find ways to cleanse our painful histories and work together.

The final IAPP events took place in Japan and the United States. In Japan, people were nervous about how many government officials would attend. These concerns were allayed when more than 200 Japanese leaders and allies, including 63 incumbent parliamentarians, attended the grand event. Regardless of political beliefs and cultural differences, they gathered without hesitation with the will to build a world of peace. In my remarks to the Japanese parliamentarians and key leaders, I conveyed my longing for peace and proposed a path by which to achieve it. They received my words with one heart.

Our final 2016 rally took place in Washington, DC. The choice of venue for this IAPP conference, which was the culmination of all previous efforts, was very important. In the end, members of the United States Senate offered the Kennedy Caucus Room, one of the Senate's most prestigious and historic rooms, as the event location. I was told by the Senate sponsors, "There are many rooms available for the launching ceremony. However, in view of this meeting's importance to us, we will prepare the Kennedy Caucus Room."

November 30, 2016: Establishment of the International Association
of Parliamentarians for Peace, Kennedy Caucus Room,
Russell Senate Office Building, Washington DC

The Kennedy Caucus Room is where John F. Kennedy declared his presidential candidacy in 1960. The Senate voted in 2009 to name the room in honor of the three Kennedy brothers. The room has seen numerous meetings on matters of great significance in United States and world history. It was a most fitting venue for the momentous launching in North America of the International Association of Parliamentarians for Peace.

On November 30, 2016, while a winter rain drizzled outside, the venue was filled with more than 300 US and foreign parliamentarians from 56 nations. Many participants had already met one another at previous IAPP events, and they happily embraced their colleagues from neighboring countries. The mood in this splendid venue was one of great joy and hope as people from nations large and small expressed their pleasure at participating in a global event for peace. The words of Hon. Gilbert Bangana, representing the president of the National Assembly of Benin, touched people's hearts: "When I was young, I learned Father and Mother Moon's principles of peace, and today I continue to practice their peace philosophy."

November 30, 2016: Mother Moon with US Senator Orrin Hatch at the United States Capitol

Many people expressed to me their gratitude for having introduced a new path toward peace. Republican US Senator, and Senate president *pro tempore*, Orrin Hatch, who assisted with and attended the inauguration, is a longtime friend. After I delivered my keynote address, he took the podium and kindly mentioned his appreciation for our unchanging movement for peace. Senator Hatch, who served in the

United States Senate from 1977 until 2019, has always offered strong support for our work. Senator Edward Markey, representing the Democratic Party, expressed his gratitude for our contributions toward environmental preservation and promised to support us.

With the conclusion of this final launch in Washington, DC, my course to inaugurate IAPP worldwide came to a close. For a year and more, I had traveled the globe, going to six continents to convene these events. More than 20,000 people, including 2,500 incumbent parliamentarians from 190 nations, had attended, making this initiative a great success.

Each IAPP regional inauguration marked a historic first for parliamentarians from so many nations to gather in one place. These men and women put aside differences of nationality, race and religious persuasion, and any sense of being from enemy nations. Spending several days in each other's company, they would always begin with the important question, "What can we do now for the sake of peace?"

The Cape of Good Hope and righteous hyojeong

On the southern tip of the African continent lies the Cape of Good Hope. My husband and I chose that as the starting point of our proposed International Peace Highway. As the Mother of peace, I need to give hope to the people of Africa and wipe away their tears. At the Holy Wedding of True Parents in 1960, I pledged to God, "I will accomplish Your will in my lifetime," and I have not forgotten this pledge for a moment. I have constantly spread God's word from east to west and south to north with a heart of filial piety for Heaven. In 2012, after my husband's ascension, I bade him farewell with the words "Please put all earthly work behind you and peacefully enter the heavenly gates to comfort our Heavenly Parent."

From that time, despite having to push myself beyond my limits, I took on an exhausting agenda, traveling the globe to fulfill the promise I had made to Heaven and my husband. With my husband's ascension, it was left to me to accomplish God's desire and ideal, and I have embarked on a tearful journey for that cause. For the past seven years, I have journeyed on.

Creating a heavenly tribe, a heavenly nation and a heavenly world centered on God is not simple. In my resolve to restore seven countries by 2020, I spent countless hours in prayer and devotion. My late husband lived by the mantra that "sincere devotion moves heaven" and we felt the results. Many received inspiration from Heaven, including Dr. Yun Young-ho, then secretary-general of FFWPU International Headquarters. On July 17, 2017, he received a revelation in which Father Moon gave him three golden keys.

At that time, Dr. Yun was preparing for several events simultaneously, including Europe's Peace Starts with Me Rally of Hope in Vienna, Austria, and the Latin America Summit 2018 in São Paulo, Brazil. After hearing his report about the dream, I invited three "golden keys," three religious leaders, to attend the upcoming Peace Starts with Me festival in the United States. The three were Sheikh Mansour Diouf of Senegal, Prophet Samuel Radebe of South Africa, and Archbishop Johannes Ndanga of Zimbabwe. During the festival in New York, we forged strong relationships that laid the foundation for what was to come.

In January 2018, as I have mentioned previously, I traveled to Senegal for the first Africa Summit. I held the Summit in Senegal because God had prepared a righteous man there, Sheikh Mansour Diouf, a distinguished Muslim leader. Through his efforts, numerous fellow leaders, some with millions of followers, heartily welcomed me. Impressed by our ideals and initiatives, Sheikh Diouf invested himself in preparing for the Summit. Putting his reputation on the line, Sheikh Diouf encouraged His Excellency President Macky Sall to co-host the Summit. "True Mother is coming to bring blessings to Africa," he told President Sall; "This Summit will be historic, and your support is essential."

President Macky Sall gladly welcomed me and provided the best venue in Senegal for the Summit, the Centre International de Conferences Abdou Diouf (CICAD). In addition to his generous support, President Macky Sall also generously offered his presidential vehicle and members of his security team to protect me wherever I went.

Nonetheless, one thing remained uncertain. Even as I landed in Senegal, I had not yet received confirmation of President Sall's participation in the Summit. On the eve of the Summit, President Sall kindly offered to have a private meeting. After receiving his warm welcome, I spoke about the history of God's providence, Heaven's providence in Africa, my identity as only begotten Daughter and my wish to bless the nation and continent. After hearing me, President Sall said, "I'll attend tomorrow's Summit."

Following our meeting, I was told that President Sall was moved by the sincerity with which I wished to bless Africa and bring salvation to humankind, and by my lack of desire for honor, power or profit. I cannot verify that anecdotal report, but it is consistent with my experience of President's Sall's exemplary leadership and gallantry. The government was mobilized for the Summit, and the Summit was broadcast live throughout the nation on national television and reported by national and international media. I spoke without a prepared speech on Heaven's providence and the African Continent, and concluded my address by proclaiming Heavenly Africa, a continent of hope blessed by Heaven, and inviting everyone present to join this initiative. President Sall later expressed his desire to work together.

The following summer, in June 2019, I visited Johannesburg, South Africa, to officiate at the 100,000 Hyojeong Family Blessing Festival.

Prophet Samuel Radebe's and my team worked together for this Blessing. More than 500 dignitaries—government officials, members of parliament and religious leaders from across Africa, including 12 current and former presidents and prime ministers—joined the event to support the True Family Movement. During the Blessing Prayer, I prayed that the continent of Africa, together with the 100,000 in attendance, would form a Heavenly Africa, a light unto the world.

Prophet Radebe is the founder of the Revelation Church of God and Inkululeko Yesizwe, both major religious organizations with millions of followers throughout Africa. Prophet Radebe comes from a long line of Prophets well known throughout Africa. During the Blessing, he testified to me, "South Africa, and Africa as a whole, welcomes Dr. Hak Ja Han Moon, who has devoted her whole life to the cause of peace as True Mother, the only begotten Daughter of God." The entire nation was in a festive mood as the South African public television network, SABC, broadcast the Blessing event.

I'll share some background on this Blessing. The previous November, as I mentioned earlier, I had hosted a Summit and Blessing in Cape Town to celebrate the centenary of Nelson Mandela's birth. At that time, Prophet Radebe was in Mozambique launching a new church. After Dr. Yun Young-ho spoke with him and expressed my heartfelt desire to meet him, Prophet Radebe immediately rented a plane and flew to Cape Town, arriving just in time for the Blessing. When we met in the green room, I poured out my heart, explaining God's ideal of creation and God's providence of salvation for humankind, including the Fall, the providence of True Parents and the only begotten Daughter. I felt that Prophet Radebe was moved by my words. He called me "True Mother" and during his keynote address, even though our theological frameworks are different, testified about me as the only begotten Daughter that Heaven has prepared.

After that Blessing, Dr. Yun laid out my vision to him: "True Mother would like to host a 100,000 Blessing Ceremony next year." Prophet

Radebe gladly replied, "Let's do it!" I felt that Prophet Radebe understood why I came to Africa: to give blessing. Eager to work together and help the flower of true love blossom in the continent, Prophet Radebe prepared meticulously for the June 2019 Blessing Ceremony at Orlando Stadium. From the hotel where I stayed to the airport welcome, Prophet Radebe invested himself and his entire foundation to welcome me and prepare for the Blessing Ceremony.

On June 7, 2019, on the eve of the Blessing, I visited the historic township of Soweto. Soweto is known throughout the world as the location of the first anti-apartheid uprisings in 1976. The home of global luminaries such as Nelson Mandela and Archbishop Desmond Tutu, its people played an important role in the civil rights movement in South Africa.

From 1948 until the 1990s, institutionalized racial segregation, known as apartheid, was enforced in South Africa. South Africa's minority white population dominated the nation's political, economic, and social institutions and actively discriminated against other races. The white government removed black people from their land, forced them to learn the Afrikaans language, and required them to have special permits to travel outside designated areas. They could not eat in the same restaurants or take the same buses as white people. Interracial marriage was illegal, and black people could not own land in white-designated areas.

In 1976, high school students in South Africa protested the forced introduction of Afrikaans as the official language through the Soweto Uprising and the many other protests that followed. Thousands of people were killed or injured during these uprisings, which became a major movement against apartheid. Archbishop Desmond Tutu and others denounced the law on learning Afrikaans, saying it forced children to learn the "language of the oppressor." The sacrifices young students made during the protests are truly heartbreaking. Police opened fire on the students and Hector Pieterson, a 12-year-old student, was killed. The photo of Hector carried by Mbuyisa Makhubo and his sister Antoinette weeping transformed South Africa and shook the world.

The day before the Blessing Festival, I visited the Hector Pieterson memorial in Soweto to pay my respects and offer a prayer for the victims of Apartheid and of all racial discrimination. I prayed to God, asking for the liberation of the black race from the painful history of racial discrimination, for the liberation of the students killed and deprived of their hopes and dreams, and for God's blessing on South Africa and Africa. I was particularly moved to see Antoinette, along with 400 youths from throughout South Africa, gather with me at the Hector Pieterson Memorial at Prophet Radebe's invitation. The youth danced and sang beautiful songs of hope. I felt that these young people were my children.

The events of June 2019 created the momentum upon which Prophet Radebe would prepare a Blessing Ceremony for 100,000 couples in South Africa that December.

Archbishop Johannes Ndanga of Zimbabwe is the Chairman of the Apostolic Christian Council of Zimbabwe (ACCZ), the largest Christian council in Zimbabwe with thousands of affiliated churches and millions of members. Dr. Yun recognized Archbishop Ndanga as the third righteous man Father Moon had indicated in his dream.

Archbishop Ndanga's relationship with our movement began when he came to Kenya to offer congratulatory remarks during an interfaith Blessing Ceremony. As he spoke, the Heavens opened and he heard, "Don't just offer congratulatory remarks, receive the Blessing as well!" Archbishop Ndanga promptly received the Blessing and joyfully came to participate in the 2017 Peace Starts with Me Festival in Madison

Square Garden. Archbishop Ndanga stated, "I recognized True Mother as the only begotten Daughter through Heaven's revelation. I am grateful to have received the Blessing and I am now sharing the gospel of True Parents wherever I go. I hope that True Parents' ideal of world peace can be realized."

On the eve of the Madison Square Garden festival, I invited the three "golden key" religious leaders to dine with me at our East Garden residence. There, Archbishop Ndanga said, "You are the True Mother humankind has eagerly been waiting and longing for." The following day, he testified to other religious leaders about his encounter with me, saying, "True Mother is our True Mother. I am her blessed son." Inspired by what he experienced in the US, Archbishop Ndanga returned to Zimbabwe, where he mobilized over 300 bishops from ACCZ and, together with FFWPU leaders, hosted a special Divine Principle workshop and Blessing for them. With the support of the government of Zimbabwe, each of those bishops educated and blessed 210 couples. In all, more than 60,000 couples received the Blessing.

On November 11, 2017, Archbishop Ndanga offered congratulatory remarks at the 80,000 Rally of Hope to Support the Peaceful Reunification of the Korean Peninsula at the Sangam World Cup Stadium in Seoul. As he was preparing to go home, he received the news that Zimbabwe was caught up in political upheaval and a change of leadership in government. The political turmoil was severe, with riots in the street and unrest throughout the nation. Archbishop Ndanga was apprehensive about the situation. When he arrived in Harare, he saw several ministers being apprehended and taken away. Yet it was as if no one recognized him. He passed swiftly through the airport and arrived home safely. Amid the turmoil engulfing the nation, as he was a prominent Christian leader, his life was certainly at risk. He firmly believes that I protected him from harm, testifying, "It was True Mother's miracle."

In 2018, I appointed Archbishop Ndanga to the position of Cheon Il Guk Special Envoy for Zimbabwe. He responded with determination, saying, "I will be a dutiful son who will testify throughout Zimbabwe and Africa to the True Mother as the only begotten Daughter of God."

All people are God's children. God does not discriminate based on skin color. True Parents have blessed Africa as Heavenly Africa and prayed for its liberation from past afflictions. A new history is being written, one where African families are being reborn as true families through the Blessing. This is initiating the change that will raise Africa to become the shining continent of hope for all humankind.

São Tomé and Príncipe, the model for national restoration

Following the inaugural Africa Summit held in January 2018, various nations throughout the African continent expressed a desire to host Summits and Blessings. After nearly four decades of mission work and on the foundation of the previous year's activities and World Summit 2019, the government of São Tomé and Príncipe expressed a strong desire to host initiatives throughout the country, including a Summit, a Blessing Festival and a Youth and Students for Peace Festival.

I sent my representative to São Tomé in the Spring of 2019 and, after he met the President, His Excellency Evaristo Carvalho, the Prime Minister, His Excellency Jorge Bom Jesus, and the President of the National Assembly, His Excellency Delfim Neves, a memorandum of understanding between UPF and the government of São Tomé was signed. Hearing about São Tomé's willingness to work together on several key initiatives, I was determined to bless it and lay the foundation for a Heavenly nation there, and I announced that I would hold the 2019 Africa Summit and the Hyojeong Family Blessing Festival in São Tomé and Príncipe.

This is a beautiful equatorial island nation in the Gulf of Guinea off the coast of Central Africa. It gained its independence from Portugal in 1975. After we had traveled for more than 40 hours, including two layovers, the government of São Tomé offered an extraordinary welcome. Cabinet ministers welcomed me warmly at the airport, and the next day His Excellency President Evaristo Carvalho welcomed me at the Presidential Palace for a private meeting. Following our cordial meeting, the presidential honor guard escorted me to the National Assembly building to open the Summit.

September 4, 2019: At São Tomé and Príncipe's presidential palace

More than 800 leaders from São Tomé and throughout Africa were in attendance. The National Assembly had generously offered the use of its premises for the Summit and Blessing, and by 9:00 a.m. the main hall and surrounding overflow rooms were full. In addition to His Excellencies President Carvalho, Prime Minister Jorge Bom Jesus and President of the National Assembly Delfim Neves, there were hundreds of parliamentarians, dozens of government ministers, hundreds of religious leaders and leaders of civil society, as well as several former heads of state from throughout Africa in attendance.

The Summit, Blessing and YSP festivals were all broadcast live on national television and the feedback from the viewers was overwhelmingly positive.

The Summit began, and after inspiring addresses by current and former heads of state, His Excellency Goodluck Jonathan, former president of Nigeria and the Africa chair of the International Summit Council for Peace (ISCP), introduced me. During my keynote address, I proposed that São Tomé and Príncipe work together with me in realizing the model of a heavenly nation. I blessed São Tomé and Príncipe as "Heavenly São Tomé," a nation blessed by God. Hearing this, the audience cheered.

Following my address, President Carvalho expressed his gratitude, sharing his profound appreciation for the various initiatives undertaken in the nation as well as the vision I had laid out during my address. President Carvalho also expressed a strong desire to forge an even stronger relationship and continue our work over the long term. He was particularly happy to hear the term "Heavenly São Tomé" and even referred to me as "Mother Moon."

That evening, President Carvalho invited me and other heads of state to a state dinner in a beautiful seaside restaurant reserved for state functions. The gentlemanly President Carvalho guided me as we made our way along the sumptuous buffet, recommending delicious local dishes. I was moved by the sincere desire of the São Tomé government to develop their nation in a polite and principled manner.

The following day, all government officers, including the President, the Prime Minister and the President of the National Assembly, as well as the former heads of state, gathered for the Blessing Festival. It was a beautiful sight to behold. Six hundred couples, most of them governmental leaders, religious leaders, and leaders of civil society from throughout São Tomé and neighboring Príncipe, gathered for the Blessing.

More than 10,000 couples had participated in a preliminary Blessing Ceremony and representatives were selected to attend this Blessing. I was moved by accounts of couples on the verge of divorce healing their differences and pledging to become ideal families through the Blessing. It was a magnificent family festival, and the eagerness of the families could be seen when at 8:00 a.m. the venue was full even though the Blessing was scheduled for 5:00 p.m. Several couples had come before dawn. The festive mood in the National Assembly was indeed unique. As the time for the Blessing drew closer, the anticipation and eagerness of the couples could be felt.

Fifteen current and former heads of state from throughout Africa were seated on the podium and I sprinkled holy water on 60 couples representing the realms of government, religion and civil society. It was a beautiful, solemn occasion. The enthusiastic participation of all three branches of the São Tomé government as well as the people meant this was truly a national Blessing Ceremony. During my Blessing prayer, I stated that São Tomé and Príncipe had earned the qualification of the first nation to be a model for national restoration.

One particularly moving part of the Blessing program was the purity pledge by representatives of São Tomé's youth.

As we prepared for these events, a local Catholic priest published a letter profoundly critical of the Unification Church, the Blessing Ceremony and the Universal Peace Federation. Nonetheless, the relationships we forged with the São Tomé government and people proved strong enough to bridge any theological differences. The government was firm in its commitment and the people were overjoyed to participate in the many programs that were held.

The day after the Blessing, IAYSP held what some said was the largest youth festival ever held in the nation.

As I was about to leave the country, the president of São Tomé and Príncipe bade me a sincere farewell with the kindest words: "São Tomé is your home and your country, so please come whenever you can."

Energy and optimism in Europe

I'm particularly fond of the small European nation of Albania. During the Cold War era, Albania was one of the most impoverished nations in the world, but in the last 20 years the Albanian people have made great strides in developing their country. Their energy and optimism reminds me of my own Korean people.

In 2005, President Alfred Moisiu gave my husband and me a state welcome as we were traveling the world to launch the Universal Peace Federation. He was the first sitting head of state to do so. I remember saying to President Moisiu, "If you give us 2,000 young people to educate, we can help you change this nation."

This challenge was fulfilled in October 2019 during the SouthEast Europe Peace Summit when 3,000 energetic school and college students gathered for the Youth and Students for Peace Rally in Tirana, followed by the launch of the Balkans Peace Road.

Earlier that same day, former President Moisiu, now a sprightly 90-year-old, and Senior Minister Elisa Spiropali welcomed me on behalf of the government to speak to the Albanian people at the Summit. We were joined on stage by President Hashim Thaçi of Kosovo and President Stevo Pendarovski of North Macedonia, and the event was broadcast live on national television.

I encouraged the Albanian people: "You do not need to be disappointed because you could not join the European Union. As you are the first, you need to embrace the people of Europe who are the last…. God will be with you wherever you go. From this point, if Albania overcomes all the pain of the past it is holding onto and is reborn as the heavenly nation of Albania attending God, it will not be a problem for Europe to become one."

October 26, 2019: SouthEast Europe Peace Summit 2019,
Palace of Congresses, Tirana, Albania

The following day, I conducted a Blessing Ceremony for 1,200 couples, representing 12,000 couples throughout Albania who had been blessed during 2018 and 2019. Albania is a moderate Muslim nation, and it is fortunate to house different religious traditions in harmony. Father Edmond Brahimaj, head of the World Bektashi Order, as well as imams and priests offered prayers of blessing in one accord.

In her congratulatory remarks, Monika Kryemadhi, the wife of Albanian President Ilir Meta, said it was the most beautiful event that had ever been held in the Palace of Congresses. On that day I declared that the nation had indeed become Heavenly Albania. I look forward to Albania becoming a great nation by living for the sake of other nations.

CHAPTER 11

THE RESTORATION OF CANAAN IN HEAVEN AND ON EARTH

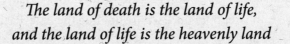

The land of death is the land of life,
and the land of life is the heavenly land

I was pushing beyond my limits to fulfill the promise I had made to Heavenly Parent, True Father and our global membership, to restore seven heavenly nations by our Foundation Day events in February 2020. The work of the seven years since True Father's ascension now was coming to its climax. To accomplish this, I dedicated a 40-day course, from mid-November to the year's end, as a course to restore Canaan in heaven and on earth.

In various parts of the world there are people who know me as the Mother of humankind, the Mother of peace, the universal Mother. Hence, despite tremendous challenges, my resolve for the sake of our Heavenly Parent, Heaven's providence and all humanity is steadfast. It is rooted in the pledge I made as I bowed my head before True Father's holy body: "I will establish Cheon Il Guk on earth."

The 40-day course began in Cambodia. On November 19, 2019, at the personal invitation of Prime Minister Hun Sen, which I gladly accepted, I flew into Phnom Penh. The Asia Pacific Summit was the first event that the government of Cambodia had ever co-hosted with a non-governmental organization. It was held in Phnom Penh at his office, which is known as the Peace Palace. At a reception prior to the Summit's opening, he gathered the participating world leaders.

The prime minister spoke about the importance of the Asia Pacific Summit, the necessity for harmony and cooperation among Asian nations, and the efforts he had made to help develop Cambodia. I then spoke about the significance of this event. "The purpose of this Summit," I said, "is to share that God the Creator, from whom we have been separated due to the human Fall, is humanity's Heavenly Parent. Our future is full of hope, since we are holding the Asia-Pacific Summit under God's guidance."

The participants expressed their support for the goals of the Summit and applauded the Cambodian government's groundbreaking initiative and cooperation with UPF. Prime Minister Hun also voiced support for my Asia-Pacific Union initiative as a path of cooperation that would lead to peace in Asia. Following our meeting, he escorted me into the main auditorium and the Asia Pacific Summit began.

More than 800 representatives from 46 nations, including several heads of state, were present. I spoke to them about our role in helping bring Heaven's providence to fruition and about the coming era of the

Pacific civilization, the final point of settlement in Heaven's providence. I stated that the Pacific civilization will be one of true love characterized by attendance to God as the Heavenly Parent. In the presence of several current and former heads of state and ambassadors, His Excellency expressed support for the vision of regional peace anchored in the Asia-Pacific Union initiative I had proposed.

November 19, 2019: The Asia Pacific Summit Opening Plenary, Phnom Penh Peace Palace, Cambodia

Jesus said that the first shall be last and the last shall be first. This sentiment could be felt as these delegates, though far from Jesus' homeland, signed the Phnom Penh Declaration and expressed active support for the vision of an Asia-Pacific Union. So much was accomplished for the providence; it seemed as if a thousand years had condensed into that one day. I felt that Heavenly Parent and True Father must have been very pleased with the outcome of the Summit.

The next day we convened the Youth and Family Festival for Nation-Building and Peace at the prestigious Koh Pich Theater in Phnom Penh. More than 4,000 participants attended, including heads of state from around the world as well as Deputy Prime Minister Bin Chhin, Chief Secretary Yim Nolla of the Ministry of Home Affairs, and numerous government officials. As I officiated the Blessing Ceremony, held as the culminating event of the Youth and Family Festival, I blessed the nation as "Heavenly Cambodia," a nation where our Heavenly Parent can dwell.

<hr />

In preparation for this historic event, I offered heartfelt prayers and devotion for the sake of Cambodia. Between 1975 and 1979, the blood of many innocent people was shed because of a wrong ideology. Some 2 million people were starved and slaughtered because of communism. Today, nearly 40 years later, Heavenly Parent sent the only begotten Daughter and Mother of peace to Cambodia to bless this land as a heavenly nation.

Heaven's providence has multiple dimensions. From the human perspective, my visit to Cambodia may have been a visit to a nation to host an event. However, Heaven's providence is not so one-dimensional. I had to liberate both the souls of the victims who had been unjustly killed and the souls of the young people whom the government had forced to commit murder and treat their fellow human beings with terrible cruelty.

During my benediction prayer, I first comforted Heavenly Parent, whose heart was torn to pieces by the massacres in Cambodia. I then liberated the souls of those who had died as a result of the atrocities. I blessed the past, present and future of Cambodia through the Blessing Ceremony so its young people of today can begin preparing for a hopeful future.

New hope for China

Since ancient times, in many cultures and traditions, the ocean has been seen as a mother. The Chinese characters for the Pacific Ocean translate as "great ocean of peace," and in English, "pacific" means "peaceful in character or intent." The Pacific civilization can become a great mother of peace by opening the era of a civilization characterized by filial piety for Heaven (*hyojeong*), and true love, living for the sake of others. It can do so by embracing and putting into practice the sacrificial and altruistic heart of the mother, and discarding our inherited fallen practices of seduction, conquest and exploitation.

The Pacific civilization arises in the latter stages of the providence centering on the True Mother of humankind, the only begotten Daughter. At this time, through the only begotten Daughter, the feminine aspect of God, the Heavenly Mother hidden throughout history, must be revealed. God can no longer be seen solely as the Heavenly Father; God is the Heavenly Parent, the harmonious, perfected union of Heavenly Father and Heavenly Mother. The Pacific civilization is defined by the ideal of one family of humanity, which manifests naturally when we attend Heavenly Parent as our vertical parent of humanity.

In 2017, I proclaimed this culture of heart based on true love at 12 Rallies of Hope held in Korea, Japan, the United States, Thailand and beyond. Hundreds of thousands of people attended these events. I continued to proclaim the Pacific civilization and the culture of heart throughout 2018, starting with the Africa Summit in Senegal and concluding with the Asia Pacific Summit in Nepal. But in order to firmly establish the age of the Pacific civilization, the participation of the Greater China region, with a population of 1.7 billion people, is essential.

Over the decades, the Unification movement in China has experienced challenges. Thus, we started preparations for the launch of the Chinese People's Federation for World Peace in 2017 by bringing together overseas Chinese and other ethnic Chinese. The former refers to those of Chinese lineage who have left the mainland and moved abroad while maintaining their cultural roots and connection to the mainland. The latter refers to Chinese emigrants who have lost their linguistic and cultural ties to China. When we say "Chinese People's Federation" we refer to both groups.

In 2019, the task at hand was to establish the Chinese People's Federation for World Peace (CPFWP) and the Asia-Pacific Union. Only after doing so can the age of the Pacific civilization be firmly established. In this historical context, the World Assembly of the Chinese People's Federation for World Peace was very significant. This World Assembly was hosted on November 22-23, 2019 in Taiwan after we had inaugurated the Chinese People's Federation for World Peace in eight nations, including Canada, Malaysia, Thailand and Indonesia.

It was truly a historic day. The opening ceremony was attended by more than 300 Chinese leaders. President Chang Po-ya of Taiwan's Control Yuan, who took the stage as the keynote speaker, introduced me with the following kind words: "True Mother is a great woman who has devoted her life for the sake of others, and we have been given a rare and precious opportunity to meet her in person."

Following the World Assembly, we held the Hyojeong True Love Family Blessing Festival at the Nangang Exhibition Center. The venue was packed with some 7,000 couples from throughout Taiwan. They were eager to participate in this uplifting festival and receive the marriage Blessing. Former Vice President Lu Hsiu-lien, who is widely respected in Taiwan, introduced me, saying: "Thanks to the Heaven-centered activities of Rev. Dr. Sun Myung Moon and Dr. Hak Ja Han Moon, we have now become one family transcending race, nationality and civilization. It is an honor for me to be a part of this wonderful event."

Two young Taiwanese siblings gave a beautiful testimony about their amazing experiences helping prepare for the event. The little

9-year-old girl named Jia-jen had publicized the festival by handing out pamphlets for 20 minutes after school every day. In her testimony, she mentioned not being able to remain idle when her True Mother was traveling all over the world to realize Vision 2020. One day, something very special happened to her: The 60-year-old owner of a restaurant, who often walked along that street, was moved to see the child's devotion in handing out pamphlets day after day at the same time and place. She stopped to talk. This little girl shared her heart with the much older lady, who ended up attending the festival.

Not to be outdone, her older brother Ding-jun also worked hard for the upcoming Blessing. Every day, he offered devotions, publicized the festival and searched for Blessing candidates. Because he invested so much time in public outreach, he had neglected his studies and received low grades during school exams. His worried parents came to him and asked, "As a student, shouldn't studies be your priority?"

"I will study after True Mother's visit to Taiwan," he replied and he concentrated even more on his outreach efforts. As a result, this young man brought 27 couples to receive the Blessing, including one village head and his wife. In Taiwan, village heads represent 5,000 to 10,000 residents. The young man was able to dedicate this amazing result to Heaven. He and his younger sister's achievements serve as truly moving examples of the beautiful tradition of filial piety.

The future of Cheon Il Guk is indeed filled with hope. The filial piety of the second and third generations for True Mother is akin to sunflowers following the sun's path across the skies. This filial devotion is truly a joyous gift. I was asked, "True Mother, how do you feel today at the conclusion of the Rally of Hope in Taiwan?"

"I feel so proud in my heart," I replied. "It was truly wonderful."

I was particularly moved by our Taiwanese youth who created a Hyojeong Cultural Performance. I pronounced great blessings upon them, knowing that the day is fast approaching when the Greater China region will attend Heavenly Parent and True Parents.

Through the marriage Blessing, the Greater China region can create harmony based on universal family values. The Blessing Ceremony for some 14,400 people could be considered a starting point to realize a unified world through harmonious families. Henceforth, all civilizations will bear fruits as the Pacific civilization. This is Heaven's trajectory. The Pacific civilization is not to be a self-centered civilization based upon conquest and plunder. Our task is to expand and firmly root the Pacific civilization in the culture of filial devotion for Heaven (*hyojeong*), characterized by true love, which is the heart of giving, giving again, forgetting that one has given, and wishing that one could give more.

With this in place, the Pacific civilization will bring about harmony and unity among the civilizations founded throughout human history: continental and oceanic, eastern and western, developing and developed. Centering on Korea, the homeland of God's providence, the Pacific civilization is being established.

The Mother of peace in the Muslim world

When I landed at the airport in Niamey, Niger, on November 27, 2019, government officials displayed their highest level of protocol as they received me. We had been told that the president and citizens in general were delighted that I was coming, and these words proved more than true. I truly enjoyed the warm welcome on the part of Prime Minister Brigi Rafini, his chief of staff, cabinet ministers and other high level representatives of this Muslim nation in Central Africa.

Our meeting had been long awaited. The prime minister and 10 cabinet ministers had scheduled to come to Seoul in February to attend World Summit 2019. Pressing state issues prevented the prime minister from making the trip, and he sent a ministerial delegation instead.

The officials whom he sent to Seoul were deeply moved. When they returned to Niger, they gave a detailed report about the World Summit 2019 and our activities. The prime minister agreed to attend the Africa Summit, which was being planned for September 2019 in São Tomé and Príncipe.

But once again, this time due to security issues caused by terrorist attacks in northern Niger, the prime minister could not attend the Summit. This time, he sent a special envoy, the Minister of Planning, with a personally signed message expressing his strong desire to host an African summit and Blessing Ceremony under True Mother's leadership.

Thus it was after initial setbacks that we finally met, and this made the meeting even more special and joyful. At the airport, the prime minister and the minister of foreign affairs accompanied me as I was saluted by an honor guard and received a welcome from their leading traditional dance troupe. I was particularly impressed by the honor guard and thought, "Niger's sons are so gallant, dashing and patriotic." As True Mother, I felt I wanted to adopt these young men of Niger as my sons.

The evening of my arrival, His Excellency President Mahamadou Issoufou kindly invited me to a Presidential Summit Welcoming Banquet. Three hundred current and former heads of state, parliamentary speakers, ministers and other VIPs attended the banquet. I fondly remember President Issoufou calling me the "Mother of peace" and expressing his sincere admiration and respect for the Republic of Korea.

Almost two years earlier, on January 18, 2018, I had proclaimed "Heavenly Africa" during my keynote address at the first continental-level Africa Summit, hosted in Dakar, Senegal. On the basis of this proclamation, beginning in June, the Universal Peace Federation and other organizations began working to secure the support and participation of

African governments in the "Heavenly Africa Project," a package of 10 projects aimed at promoting peace and development that includes the True Family Blessing Movement. At times, it took as many as 10 days for our delegates to meet with a head of state. As it wasn't unusual for meetings to be rescheduled, our delegation would skip meals and be on standby for many hours to ensure the meetings would take place.

November 29, 2019: The Family Renewal and
Blessing Festival in Niamey, Niger

On the foundation of such sincere investments of time and energy, 10 nations signed memorandums of understanding and agreements to participate in our Heavenly Africa Project. Niger, of course, was one of them. The ideal of one human family is Heavenly Parent's dream and humanity's wish. The president of Niger is a wise leader, especially with regard to realizing this dream. Through his active support and dedication, the 2019 Africa Continental Summit and Family Renewal Festival took place. These events involved pioneering a path that we had not previously trodden. It was a great challenge and a truly holy undertaking, conducted with the extraordinary support of the government, the nation and the continent. During the Summit, in front of some of the key stakeholders that move this continent, I proclaimed the truth that our Heavenly Parent had been unable to share for 6,000 years. The proclamation that Heavenly Parent's blessing comes when people are in unity with the only begotten Daughter resonated like rolling thunder not only across Niger but throughout Africa.

Following the Summit's opening plenary, President Issoufou and I signed the Niamey Resolution in the presence of the 2,000 leaders who were gathered there. Official representatives from 54 nations and many current and former heads of state came onstage. President Issoufou emphasized the importance of the Summit in promoting development in Africa, his admiration for Korea's growth after the Korean War, and his gratitude for co-hosting the Continental Summit and attending in person. I then offered the great victory of the Summit to Heaven.

I am fully aware of the dedication of the Prophet Muhammad in establishing the rich religious tradition of Islam and I regard many pre-eminent Muslim leaders I have met as my own sons. Through this event, heads of state and leaders from the Islamic realm came to know me on an entirely new level, as True Mother and the Mother of peace. The Summit was a miraculous event, unique in the history of the Unification movement.

The day after the Summit, the historic Family Renewal and Blessing Festival in Niger took place. Since this was the first Blessing Ceremony I had officiated in a Muslim nation, I prayed with a heart more serious than ever before.

On the morning of the Blessing, the president asked me if I had slept well in my new home of Niger. Happily, I responded that I had slept very well, thanks to the warm and comforting welcome I had received. After we had conversed briefly about the previous day's Summit, the presidential escort guided me to the Blessing venue.

Diplomatic protocol is sometimes referred to as "a war without weapons." That is why I call the protocol of Cheon Il Guk, "Heavenly

Protocol." Originally, the prime minister was scheduled to offer congratulatory remarks as the representative of the government during the Blessing. Hence, the protocol for that day was for me to enter the Blessing venue with the prime minister. However, the president of the National Assembly mentioned that, as representative of the people, he should enter the venue by my side together with the prime minister. Faced with this sudden request, the prime minister was taken aback. I decided to update the protocol by having both the prime minister, the representative of the government, and the president of the National Assembly, the representative of the people, stand on either side of me and enter the Blessing venue together. This was a special moment for me as I could feel how close in heart we had become.

The Blessing venue was filled with couples who had studied about the Blessing and were longing to receive it. The couples, beautifully dressed in white traditional garments, participated with dignity and grace. Dispelling earlier concerns, participating Muslim leaders solemnly accepted the holy Blessing Ceremony. Also in attendance were many current and former heads of state, parliamentary speakers, ministers, parliamentarians, religious leaders and other key leaders of civil society from throughout Africa.

The national Blessing began with the Holy Water Ceremony. To respect Muslim religious sensitivities, instead of sprinkling, I placed my two hands in a bowl of holy water and gently touched the backs of the crossed hands of each representative couple. The audience was moved and cheers and applause continued throughout the Holy Water Ceremony. The marriage Blessing is universal, transcending race, religion and nationality. Its bestowal in Niger, through heavenly actions that harmonized with their culture, brought closer the realization of one family of humankind under Heavenly Parent. I recalled that in 1991, when my husband was informed that Muslims are uncomfortable with the title "Reverend," he immediately responded, "No problem; call me Father Moon."

Eighty percent of Niger's land is desert. Within such a harsh environment, Heaven prepared for this nation to be blessed by raising righteous leaders. One of the righteous people who worked hardest to make the Summit possible was Kassoum Maiga, a member of parliament of Niger. He is a filial son among filial sons, and he testified that when he saw me alight from the plane, he shed tears of joy, as his dearest wish had finally been realized. He was the first person to offer me flowers to celebrate the victory of this first national-level Blessing Ceremony in an African Muslim nation. As soon as the Blessing Ceremony concluded, messages of gratitude and congratulations poured in from throughout the world. "True Mother, the Mother of peace, has embraced Islam."

The Family Renewal and Blessing Festival in Niger was an inspiring, even miraculous drama. As the event came to a close, Dr. Yun, Secretary-General of our Cheon Jeong Gung Headquarters, signed a memorandum of understanding as the Cheon Il Guk representative regarding the development of the Heavenly Africa Project with representatives of the African Union Commission, the Economic Community of West African States (ECOWAS) and the G5 Sahel.

Through these events, the African continent and the entire world were profoundly changed; this Summit will surely be remembered. Despite challenging circumstances, all those involved invested themselves with wholehearted unity. That is what set the condition; Heaven could not but support these events.

At the end of the day, I reflected that I am now nearly 80 years old, and there is a limit to how long one can live on earth. However, since I am the only begotten Daughter and the Mother of the universe, anywhere I am wanted, I plan to go. Heavenly Parent, once again I offer You my deepest thanks.

Torrential rain, tears of joy

In Africa, rain is considered a blessing.
The rain during today's Blessing Ceremony
was Heaven's tears of joy.

Torrential rains are common in South Africa. However, no one expected the rains to coincide with my entire stay in Johannesburg in December 2019. It rained for hours and days on end. Prior to my arrival, the thought had already come to me that the African Continental Blessing Ceremony will be unusually challenging. That thought turned out to have been prescient.

For years, we had planned to host a Continental Summit and Blessing Ceremony in South Africa. Unfortunately, Family Federation South Africa's foundation was not at a level where a Summit and Blessing could be co-hosted with the South African government. Finally, in 2018 we forged ties with the South African people and government when we co-hosted the celebration of Nelson Mandela's centenary in Mvezo, as well as the 2018 Cape Town Summit and Blessing. On that foundation, and energized by the ongoing initiatives of Prophet Radebe and other major religious leaders, we were ready to hold a continental-level Summit and Blessing.

Our blessed families and missionaries prepared more than 100,000 couples to attend in person, and we expected millions of African nationals and other people around the world to take part via the internet. Mobilization efforts had been successful, with the response overwhelmingly positive. Most of the participants were from Johannesburg, where the FNB Stadium is located, but there also were those who traveled for days to take part. All told, participants came from 54 countries, with the largest international contingents from Mozambique, Zambia and Zimbabwe. Furthermore, South Africa's state-run television and radio and other major media throughout Africa prepared for the live broadcast.

But Prophet Radebe and the hosts were nervous as they watched the skies. It had rained for eight days, and Johannesburg has a problem with flooding. On the day of the Blessing, the rain was continuous. At times it lightened up, but then it became heavy again. The roads in and around FNB Stadium were soaked; some areas were flooded. Most people in the government encouraged us to reschedule because they didn't believe anybody could come. Some 30 percent of the chartered buses realized that they could not reach their assigned pick-up points, and they simply cancelled.

The day before the Blessing, Prophet Radebe had told me that neither wind nor rain would deter the people from attending the Blessing. On the eve of the Blessing Ceremony, as the news of bus cancellations poured in like the rain, Prophet Radebe and his team went into emergency mode and somehow procured 500 more buses. The Prophet worked so hard, running here and there to fulfill what he knew was the people's great wish to attend the Blessing. As the day of the continental Blessing Ceremony arrived, the people acted on that great wish. Beginning at 5:00 a.m, couples entered the stadium. Long lines formed with everyone waiting patiently. When they entered, participants headed for the third floor, which provided shelter from rain.

Despite all this, a festive mood filled the venue. People danced and sang in gratitude for the historical Blessing they knew they would be receiving from God's only begotten Daughter. The atmosphere was like a festival. Their dedication was further on display when, at Prophet Radebe's request, participants on the third level made their way to the ground level and onto the field. Even with raincoats and umbrellas, most were soaked to the skin. Nevertheless, nothing could dampen their spirits. Once seated, the participants often rose to dance, sing or applaud. The commitment Prophet Radebe and the members of the Revelation Church of God showed was remarkable.

When I arrived at the stadium, I could see brides and grooms in their tuxedos and wedding dresses, waiting for the Blessing. Seeing me, a thunderous roar and loud shouts of "Mother Moon! Mother Moon!" and applause followed. I felt that the clouds were releasing showers of joy and blessing.

More drama ensued when, as I was about to leave the green room and enter the elevator, the electricity went out. Incredibly, even though the music stopped, the participants continued singing and cheering! Foregoing the elevator, I walked down three stories, determined not to let challenges, large or small, derail the Blessing Festival. When I arrived near the entrance tunnel, Prophet Radebe was waiting with a big, bright smile on his face. I was very pleased to see him and said, "Let's do our best today!"

He invited me to enter the stadium in an open car. The plan was for me to circle the stadium field, greeting the participants before making my way to the stage. Due to the rain, we adjusted the plan and closed the roof of the car. Even so, as we exited the tunnel onto the field, the crowds broke into a deafening roar. The participants rose, waved and shouted "Mother Moon!" as the vehicle made its way through an honor guard.

But after we had driven a few meters onto the field, a miracle occurred. The heavy rain suddenly stopped. The crowds moved into the unsheltered stands to see me and, and instantly we saw the stadium was packed. I once again felt gratitude for our joyful Heavenly Parent who is always working behind the scenes. We opened the roof of the car and Prophet Radebe and I waved and greeted the rapturous crowd. The cheers and shouts of the audience were incredible. It truly was an amazing sight. Prophet Radebe looked at me and proudly said, "Mother! The whole stadium is filled."

*December 7, 2019: Marriage Blessing Ceremony
for 200,000, Johannesburg, South Africa*

I went on stage to officiate the Blessing Ceremony. For the first time in human history, we held a continental Blessing Ceremony, with Africa the first continent to receive the honor. One hundred sixty two couples representing 54 countries, consisting of 54 newly-married, 54 already-married, and 54 religious, governmental or tribal leader couples, took the stage. Seated on the stage were more than 100 representatives, including five current heads of state and official government delegates. Among the Blessing participants and VIPs were six former heads of state, 12 parliamentary speakers, 140 parliamentarians, 219 traditional rulers, 127 major religious leaders, and more than 80 media representatives from 30 countries.

Among them was the king of South Africa's largest tribe, the Zulus. The Zulu tribe is famous for resisting conquest by European forces and for playing a key role in shaping the identity and tradition of modern-day South Africa. Assembling such a galaxy of distinguished couples and witnesses on stage added to the significance of the Blessing Ceremony.

I officiated the Holy Water Ceremony with the heart of blessing a reborn continent, "Heavenly Africa," a continent of hope and blessings. Prophet Radebe came onstage to receive the holy water bowl and assist me. Rather than emphasize protocol based on his position, Prophet Radebe gladly assisted me. I strongly felt that he was, indeed, a filial son whose only desire was to help his mother.

Following the Holy Water Ceremony was the proclamation of the Blessing and the Blessing Prayer. On this blessed day, I poured out my heart for Africa's sake: "The hope of countless prophets, kings and traditional rulers on this continent is to usher in the day of lasting peace by attending Heavenly Parent. I earnestly pray that this continent will be blessed by Heaven."

As I prayed, rain started again. We all felt that these were not tears of sorrow but God's tears of joy. Prophet Radebe later said, "The rain falling like a waterfall in South Africa during the Blessing symbolized Heaven's tears of joy. The rain washed away God's pain over Africa's misery." I was also moved by Prophet Radebe's testimony during his welcoming address:

"Today is a special day of Blessing for the African continent. We all extend our heartfelt welcome to True Mother, the only begotten Daughter of God, who brings together all the races and peoples of the world. Today, I believe a new future is opening for South Africa and Africa. She is indeed our True Mother."

The continental-level Blessing Ceremony was a great and historic triumph. What a perfect finale for 2019, opening the gates into 2020! When no one else believed in national restoration, we set the stage for the heavenly nation and the heavenly continent. We pioneered this uncharted course and gained a great victory for Heaven at the continental level. It was truly a miraculous day.

The Heavenly Unified World in Oceania

I wanted multiple generations of the True Family to take the lead in the 2019 model course of national restoration, so they could inherit this realm of victory and help prepare the gift of seven restored nations for Heavenly Parent and True Father. So I invited my family members to guide two Rallies of Hope as special emissaries, representing the heavenly world and the earthly world. The families of Moon Hyo-jin (Moon Yeon-ah) and Moon Heung-jin (Moon Hoon-sook) oversaw the events in Palau, and Moon Sun-jin and Park In-sup led the events in the Dominican Republic.

Palau lies in the western Pacific Ocean. It is made up of 340 beautiful islands that bring to mind God's original creation. My husband and I first visited Palau in 2005 to establish a branch of the Universal Peace Federation. I returned there in 2006 with some of my children and spoke to a large gathering.

When it came time to plan a "First Ladies Summit" in 2019, we decided that Palau would be the ideal hostess nation. Palau places the mother at the center of the family, society and traditional culture. The presidents and first ladies of Palau have actively supported our movement since 1992. I was particularly touched when Palau's first lady came to Korea to pay her respects when my husband ascended in 2012.

Considering how providentially appropriate it is for women to take the lead in establishing the Pacific civilization, it is truly meaningful that the Asia Pacific First Ladies Summit and Blessing Ceremony, marking the beginning of the Heavenly Unified World, was hosted in Oceania's matriarchal society of Palau. Nonetheless, our membership base in Palau is still somewhat small, so it was a challenge for us to host the Summit and Blessing Ceremony there, and I am grateful to all the local members and volunteers who made it happen.

On December 9, 2019, the eve of the main event, we held a welcoming banquet for more than 300 distinguished guests from 36 nations, including His Excellency President Thomas Remengesau Jr. and First Lady Debbie Remengesau of Palau, eight current and former first ladies, the speaker of the legislative assembly of Tonga and his wife, and parliamentarians from Bhutan and Sri Lanka. The welcoming dinner was held under a crystal-clear night sky filled with stars. In his greetings, the president said, "Though I am the president of this country, today I have come as a guest invited by my wife, the first lady, who is the hostess of this year's Summit." It was a festive and congenial gathering where every participant felt at home. At the same time, it was a banquet of longing, as many participants, including the president and his wife, kindly expressed how much they had longed to see True Mother.

The following day, December 10, attendees of the Asia Pacific First Ladies Summit 2019 gathered at the Ngarachamayong Cultural Center. The opening ceremony began with an address by the first lady. Then my emissary and daughter-in-law, Women's Federation for World Peace International President Moon Hoon-sook, read the founder's message on my behalf. Through her, I conveyed my love not only for Palau but for all of Oceania, the starting point of the Pacific civilization. In the past, Father Moon proclaimed the advent of "the Pacific Rim Era" and emphasized the providential importance of the Asia-Pacific region. In 1992, he wrote in his calligraphic Chinese characters, "The Unified World Will Begin in Oceania," and offered prayers and other spiritual conditions for the restoration of Oceania to God.

The 40-day Cosmic Canaan Course for the Settlement of Cheon Il Guk created the foundation for an "Asia-Pacific Union." I gained national-level support in November at the Cambodia Rally of Hope and the

Taiwan Rally of Hope, which connected with Chinese communities across the globe. At the Africa Summit in Niger, I won the support of Africa on the continental level. Palau's Rally of Hope Summit and Blessing Ceremony was the capstone of the Asia-Pacific Union.

The first ladies attending the Asia-Pacific First Ladies Summit resolved to address the fundamental problems of the world with a maternal heart. They called it "The Day of Women's Liberation" established by the True Mother of humankind. It was a true women's day for another reason also—in contrast to summits held elsewhere, it was women who were in charge of the preparations, assisted by men.

The next day, December 11, the government-sponsored Blessing Ceremony took place. Historic events always hit bumps in the road, and this one was no exception. As midnight approached on the day before the ceremony, the president's secretariat informed us that our schedule conflicted with a state budget meeting, so the president would not be able to attend. It was a bolt out of the blue that left us all deflated. Our spirits were revived, however, when, as the first lady of Palau and the other first ladies entered the Blessing venue the following morning, the emcee joyfully announced that the president had arrived and was making his way to the stage.

Palau's First Ladies Summit and Blessing was a milestone in God's providence. It marked Oceania as the starting point of the Pacific civilization, which unfolds around the maternal heart of giving and giving again. The Pacific Ocean is known as a symbol of peace and womanhood, especially motherhood. The victory was due not just to the leaders and people of that beautiful island nation, but also to my two daughters-in-law and Asia-Pacific Family Federation members, who united in earnest prayer offered with the heart to move heaven.

We are one family and one Holy Community of Heavenly Parent. With the conviction that "to stop is to fail; to persevere is to succeed,"

I keep moving forward undaunted, no matter what difficulties come. I need to be a mother of love and benevolence who can overlook faults and embrace all circumstances with a maternal heart as wide as the ocean. That is why, even today, I stay awake at night with the heart to cover all the world's children with blankets while they sleep.

Heavenly Latin America blooms flowers of hope

In my conversations with my husband, we often shared about Latin America. "It is a place we can never forget," he would say. "It is where we devoted a great part of our golden years," I would respond. It pains me now, for much remains to be completed. Compared with anywhere in the world, my husband and I offered our most devoted effort in Latin America. We offered devotions and conditions in the scorching sun, covered in dust from head to toe, to plow the fields of hope. Even now, I can close my eyes and vividly recall the scenes of the providence that unfolded in Latin America. That land is soaked with my husband's and my tears and sweat. Today, while that land sometimes seems like a wilderness of despair, we are once again cultivating flowers of hope.

In 2005, Father and I visited São Paulo to establish the Brazilian chapter of the Universal Peace Federation. That city served often as the site of regional peace council meetings. I chose São Paulo to host the Latin America Summit and Rally of Hope in August 2018. These events kindled the spirit of national restoration throughout Latin America. Building upon this spirit, it was the Dominican Republic in the Caribbean that hosted the Rally of Hope held December 14-15, 2019.

We convened the opening event, the Latin America and Caribbean Summit, at the Hodelpa Gran Almirante Hotel and the state government building in Santiago. More than 500 people attended from 43 nations, including Brazil, Mexico, Argentina, Colombia and Guatemala. His Excellency President Jimmy Morales of Guatemala and five former heads of state, from Trinidad and Tobago, Nicaragua, Ecuador, Bolivia and Haiti, were in attendance. From the Dominican Republic, President Danilo Medina appointed Governor Ana Maria Dominguez of Santiago as his official representative. Other guests included 10 current and former speakers of parliaments, 30 parliamentarians and dozens of interfaith, civil society, business and media leaders.

Former first lady of Nicaragua Maria Flores honored our ideals in her introductory remarks, after which my emissary and daughter, Women's Federation for World Peace International Vice President Dr. Moon Sun-jin, delivered my speech. "Ultimately, a true and lasting peace can only be achieved when we come to know and understand God, our Heavenly Parent," she said. "Only by connecting with God's will and providence can we expect to create lasting solutions."

Dr. Moon then presented awards to representatives from 15 countries, and received on my behalf a certificate recognizing me as "Mother of Peace" and making me an honorary citizen of the Dominican Republic.

The Summit concluded with the inauguration of the Latin America chapter of the International Summit Council for Peace. Universal Peace Federation International President Dr. Thomas Walsh introduced the purpose of the Council to serve as a forum in which heads of state and government, both current and former, can combine their unique expertise in addressing the most serious challenges to the realization of peace in our time. Four former presidents, their Excellencies Anthony Carmona of Trinidad and Tobago, Rosalía Arteaga of Ecuador, Jocelerme Privert of Haiti, and Jaime Paz Zamora of Bolivia, delivered speeches expressing their strong support. Former US Representative Dan Burton, co-chairman of the International Association of Parliamentarians for Peace (IAPP), officially proposed the initiative, and all current and former heads of state in attendance rose to affix their signatures.

After the conclusion of the Summit, its participants joined a crowd of 12,000 for the Family Peace Festival at the Gran Arena Del Cibao. The highlight of this beautiful event was the Blessing Ceremony of 6,000 couples. President Morales opened the ceremony, and my daughter and son-in-law, Park In-sup and Moon Sun-jin, officiated. The Dominican Republic Municipal Police co-sponsored this Family Peace Festival, and the families and friends of 4,000 city police and 600 national police came to uphold the ideal of "one family of humanity under our Heavenly Parent." In-sup and Sun-jin awarded prizes to 10 representatives of those stalwart citizens.

The Rally of Hope in the Dominican Republic succeeded due to the devotion of leaders and members throughout Latin America who pressed forward in a difficult environment. They brought the flower of hope to blossom in Heavenly Latin America, and I am confident that this flower will multiply blessings long into the future.

The course toward a Heavenly Unified World

At this point I realize that even if the entire sky were paper and all the seas were ink, there would not be enough to record this tearful course. We all overcame physical limits and continued on, even if we felt we might collapse. It was a victorious course through which our hopes and desires were fulfilled. At long last, the era of the Heavenly Nation and Heavenly Continent has arrived in providential history.

Every nation and continent has its unique path of restoration. The first seven nations to complete their path did so during the seven-year course after True Father's Holy Ascension in 2012. God re-created these seven nations as Heavenly Nations.

On the foundation of the substantial victory of seven Heavenly Nations and a Heavenly Continent, we have come to the historic day when, filled with determination, we can set out to reach the final objective of our journey, which is a Heavenly Unified World.

The United States is a Christian nation on a spirit-led continent. Let me explain about its course toward becoming a Heavenly Nation. The paths of Christianity and the United States are entwined. The Roman Empire legalized Christianity in 313 CE. From the Italian peninsula, Christianity leaped across the European continent to the British Isles, where it grew strong. But over the next millennia, Britain lost the ability to practice Jesus' teachings to "love your neighbor as yourself." She placed the monarch as ruler of the church and created a state monopoly on religion. By the seventeenth century, Great Britain was gaining power, but it was suppressing many sincere followers of Jesus. God's providence could no longer develop there, and it moved west with the Puritans who braved the treacherous ocean in search of religious freedom. The United States we see today was born of those sacrificial Christians.

My husband and I spent many decades in the United States. Because of its deep Christian roots and its people's devout faith in God, it has providential importance to Heaven. Nonetheless we encountered many difficult and heartbreaking ordeals on our path there. As I already discussed, in July 1984, the US government sent Father Moon to prison. As was the case in both North Korea and South Korea decades before, this was a story of communists and unknowing Christians finding common purpose in opposing God's work through True Parents. Fortunately, many fair-minded American Christians and political leaders, also from the left and right, spoke out against Father Moon's imprisonment. Some ministers marched in protest and set up makeshift jail cells behind the White House. Thousands of Christian leaders attended the Common Suffering Fellowship, a week-long seminar on religious freedom in Washington, DC, and joined Minority Alliance International and the Coalition for Religious Freedom. People of virtue within the American government, media and clergy decried Father Moon's imprisonment as a blatant assault on religious freedom. In 1987, these people coalesced through the American Constitutional Committee and its successor, the American Freedom Coalition.

In the three years following Father Moon's release from Danbury, we sponsored 7,000 members of the clergy to travel to Korea and Japan for the Advanced Interdenominational Conference for Clergy. Thousands of American pastors prayed at the Rock of Tears in Busan, just as Father Moon had prophesied would happen decades earlier. In 1996, we welcomed 5,000 members of the American Christian clergy to True Family Values seminars, and began the clergy Blessing movement. In November of 1997, ministers of all faiths prayed at the 40 Million Couple Blessing at RFK Stadium in Washington, DC. On that foundation, in the year 2000, at the border between North and South Korea, we established the American Clergy Leadership Conference (ACLC). The next year, ACLC organized the 50-state "We Will Stand" speaking tour, in which my husband and I declared in church after church the truth of Jesus and True Parents. The ACLC was the driving force behind the Middle East Peace Initiative, which in 2003 buried the cross of resentment between Jew, Christian and Muslim and crowned Jesus as the true King in Jerusalem.

On the foundation of these and more works over the following decade, at a major ACLC meeting in Las Vegas, 2015, I proclaimed for the first time, "I have come as the only begotten Daughter for God and humankind. Let's realize God's will together." The ministers welcomed my words with cheers. "Why have we not known of this truth until now?" some of them said. "Why has this obvious fact never crossed our minds?" I challenged those thousand ministers: "The 21st century is the era of

True Parents. Who are the chosen people of this age? The answer is, you! You are the chosen people centered on True Parents in the 21st century."

April, 2019, Mother Moon with Bishop Noel Jones
at the City of Refuge Church, Los Angeles

Meeting this challenge, at New York's Madison Square Garden in July 2017, at Long Island's Nassau Coliseum in November 2018, and in Los Angeles and Las Vegas in April and June of 2019, the Family Federation and ACLC sponsored Blessing Ceremonies and Peace Starts with Me Rallies of Hope for the Advancement of a Heavenly Unified World. In Los Angeles, inspired by not just ACLC but by the youth of Los Angeles CARP, Bishop Noel Jones of the City of Refuge Church, a former mentor of US President Barack Obama, testified that I am the Mother of peace.

"Dr. Hak Ja Han Moon was specially sent to unite humankind," he announced to an audience of 5,000, as he invited all couples to receive the marriage Blessing. At the end of the Rally, the City of Refuge Church raised our Family Federation's flag.

Six months later, on October 31, 2019, in the Lotte Hotel in Seoul, Korea, some 700 clergy members, including 40 Americans and 400 Koreans, attended the inaugural ceremony of the Korean Clergy Leadership Conference (KCLC). Then, on December 28, 2019, at the culmination of my 40-day Cosmic Canaan Course for the Firm Establishment of Cheon Il Guk, clergy gathered from all over the world to establish the World Clergy Leadership Conference (WCLC). At the Prudential Center, Newark, New Jersey, amid a crowd of 25,000 at the Peace Starts with Me rally, 400 American ministers were joined by more than 600 Christian ministers from 70 countries, including 160 pastors from South Korea, and prominent members of the clergy from Japan, Latin America, Asia and Africa. From Europe came ministers from the World Council of Churches, the world's largest council of Christians. In all, 1,000 Christian leaders united under the banner of a Heavenly Unified World centering on our Heavenly Parent.

I am deeply grateful to Heaven for the World Clergy Leadership Conference. Uniting Christianity was part of my resolution to bring True Father's work to its ultimate conclusion, and this was an important milestone in that providence. At that Rally, Rev. Paula White, a spiritual advisor to US President Donald Trump, spoke on the direction the United States should take for the sake of our Heavenly Parent. Six Christian clergy, representing the regions of the world, then spoke. Among them were Archbishop George Augustus Stallings, representing America, KCLC co-chair Rev. Kim Soo-man, representing South Korea, and Prophet Samuel Radebe, representing Africa.

December 28, 2019: World Clergy Leadership Conference (WCLC),
Rally of Hope, Newark, New Jersey

"We held two Blessings in South Africa this year alone," said Prophet Radebe. "In June, during a national Blessing Ceremony attended by more than 60,000 people, True Mother offered a prayer to liberate the young people who sacrificed their lives to fight against suppression and injustice. Following this, on December 7 at the FNB Stadium in Johannesburg, we held a Blessing Ceremony for 200,000 on the continental scale, and proclaimed Heavenly Africa. Africa is now a God-centered Africa."

Bishop Noel Jones then testified, "True Mother has given a special vision, not only to the American clergy but to all of us. Who can realize such a profound vision?"

On this foundation, I delivered my message. "Christians should not have put their focus only on the Second Coming of Christ but also on his bride, the only begotten Daughter. Heaven chose the Korean people at this historical time and brought forth not just the birth of Father Moon in 1920 but the birth of Mother Moon, the only begotten Daughter, in 1943. We must know that the Blessing officiated today by the only begotten Daughter, True Mother, is humanity's long-awaited dream of

6,000 years and the wish of our Heavenly Parent." As I uttered those words, I wept. The hearts of all those in attendance felt those tears.

At that event, many members of the clergy discarded their preconceived notions of our movement. I believe that Heaven can accept this one minister's words to represent all Christianity: "Through this event, I've found that the rumors about the Unification Church are far from the truth. I realize that I have blocked my eyes and ears to the truth of this group, having heard it was a 'cult' or 'heretical.' But when I listened to the introduction to the Family Federation, I received the powerful inspiration that without Heaven's guidance Rev. Sun Myung Moon and Dr. Hak Ja Han Moon could not have carried out such miraculous work."

Others shared similar words:

"Now my religious views have changed; I feel like a newborn Christian."

"Why did I oppose them? I regret opposing them without truly knowing who they are."

"I have been touched. I know that the Unification movement is doing the work of God, and from now on I will sincerely help in their activities."

"I was moved by the realization that Dr. Hak Ja Han Moon is the only begotten Daughter, and the promise to build the pure Garden of Eden through the principles of true family."

My husband, Father Moon, and I love America with our whole hearts and we live for its salvation. This love enabled us to endure years of criticism and persecution, including Father Moon's very unfair imprisonment, and offer it all for the sake of Heavenly Parent and humankind.

After True Father's Holy Ascension in 2012, I took upon myself a great responsibility. God led me through difficult circumstances and painful trials. I have now completed the seven-year course seeking the restoration of nations to God's embrace. The final 40-day course, at the end of 2019, was a path through a wilderness, uncharted in heaven and on earth. My objective was to settle God's kingdom of Cheon Il Guk in the worldwide Canaan. This path of restoration history was completed at the Vision 2020 Global Summit in Korea, February 2020, which was a beacon of hope lit on the eve of a global transformation.

Giving birth to the Heavenly World

Over the decades, I have kept a particular photograph close to my heart. When I close my eyes, I can clearly see it. It is of a woman, with a little girl on her back, holding the Korean flag. It was taken in the market of Anju, my hometown. The woman's face is flush with desperation, and it looks as if she wants to grab onto someone and plead her difficult situation.

The image is of my maternal grandmother, Jo Won-mo, carrying her daughter—my mother Hong Soon-ae—on her back, as she took part in the independence movement on the first day of March in 1919. My maternal uncle used to tell me stories as we looked at that photo. Unfortunately, we did not bring it with us when we fled the North. It is probably safe, somewhere in my hometown.

And there was a very similar photograph of grandmother Jo waving the Korean flag. But this one was taken August 15, 1945, and in that photo it is me she is carrying on her back. This time, her face is filled with joy, and she looks ready to embrace everyone she meets. Her expressions in those two photos contrast the sorrow of losing one's nation with the joy of gaining it back. Our sorrow over having lost God's world is soon to transform into the joy of gaining it back.

343

From the moment I could understand speech, my maternal grand-mother told me, "God is your Father." Her words formed the core of my faith. They set me on the course I had to walk. My husband, Father Sun Myung Moon, and I have lived our whole lives for the liberation of God's homeland. We have nothing to be ashamed of, nothing to hide. I have never looked back, nor to the left or the right; I have only looked at the path ahead. I never became attached to my circumstances. Night or day, there has never been a moment that I did not keep Heavenly Parent with me. In the Kremlin, we said to the leaders that they should remove the statues of Lenin and accept God. In the presidential residence in North Korea, we spoke out. On that foundation, President Mikhail Gorbachev and Chairman Kim Il Sung opened their hearts. We never wavered for the sake of the liberation of God's homeland. Whenever crises arose, Heavenly Parent guided us with pillars of fire and cloud.

September 15, 2012: Holy Seonghwa Ceremony for Father Moon,
who ascended September 3 at the age of 93. Some 250,000 people
from around the world came to pay their respects.

Standing before True Father's holy body in 2012, I promised in tears, "By the end of my days, I will absolutely bring about the settlement of Cheon Il Guk on this earth!" Whenever the opportunity arises, I repeat these words. After True Father's ascension, I set forth like a female Don Quixote spreading our teachings and embracing the world. I have lived every day with my promise to Father Moon in mind.

February 22, 2013: Mother Moon proclaiming the coming of God's kingdom of Cheon Il Guk at the Peace World Center, HJ Cheonwon, South Korea

The Republic of Korea did not honor True Father at his Seonghwa Ceremony. That is why I publicly committed to restore seven nations by 2020 and open the new Cheon Il Guk as a gift to True Father. With that accomplished, the providential opportunity has returned to Korea. The call of the Pacific *hyojeong* culture of giving and giving again must take root and show visible fruit in this nation. This door will not remain open forever.

In 2018 on New Year's Eve, members from all over Korea gathered at the Cheongshim Peace World Center to pray for the Settlement of the Era of a Unified Heavenly Korea. From the evening until the small hours in the morning of the new year, 2019, we beseeched God in tears to restore the Korean nation and liberate our Heavenly Parent's homeland.

That winter and spring I addressed five Rallies of Hope in South Korea. In Seoul, 100,000 people attended. We promoted the unification of North and South Korea under the theme, "Inherit Heavenly Fortune, Bring National Unity." We also held a rally in honor of the United Nations troops that came to Korea's aid during the Korean War. In Chungcheong Province, our rally was themed, "The 100th Anniversary of the March First Movement and the Movement for Peace between Korea and Japan." In Gyeongsang Province, we held a "Rally for Town and Community Leaders," and in the Honam region, the rally theme was, "New Life Centering on True Mother and the Settlement of the Era of the Pacific Civilization."

In Gangjin County, there were villages that had not heard the cries of new babies for many years. It is like that in all farming areas in Korea, because young women have moved to the cities. We held the "Gangjin County Rally of Hope for Childbirth and True Families" and conducted the Blessing Ceremony in three villages. The whole of Gangjin County was filled with a festive atmosphere. I sent holy robes that I had treasured as a gift to a slightly older couple that had been one of the representative couples during one of the Blessing Ceremonies. I later received a note of thanks: After wearing the robes, they had given birth—to twins! Amazingly, three couples that attended those Blessing Ceremonies gave birth to twins. In addition, as if caught up in the spirit, a local farmer's cow gave birth to twin calves.

The governor of the area sent a video of himself bowing to express his thanks. He said that Korea is on a demographic cliff—there have been too few marriages and births, and now the workforce is shrinking. He said that the Family Federation's Blessing Ceremony is the path of true patriotism, for only it can save the nation.

Sometimes I ask myself, "What will save the world for the sake of our Heavenly Parent?" Korea is not alone on the demographic cliff. Japan, China, Europe, Russia—the birthrate is in decline in many countries. The only solution is to bring joy through the Blessing of marriages in harmony with Heavenly Parent. The Blessing will bring peace within ourselves, within our families and communities, nation and world, heaven and earth—Heavenly Parent's Holy Community.

One hundred years ago, for the liberation of her homeland, my maternal grandmother waved the Korean flag that she had hidden in her bosom. Now, for the liberation of our global family's homeland, we must raise the Heavenly Parent flag that we have hidden in our bosom. Just like her, we must passionately live for God's kingdom of Cheon Il Guk.

The dawn of a new history is growing brighter. Through the manifestation of the only begotten Daughter in the providence of restoration, humanity has new hope. We are completing heaven's providence, reaching our global village with the message of the Mother of peace. Vision 2020 brought us to the mountain top. Now let us greet the rising sun with all our hearts. Let us advance together into the bright, new, hopeful era of the settlement of God's kingdom, Cheon Il Guk.

Thank you for reading
Mother of Peace, a Memoir by Hak Ja Han Moon.
Become part of the community and conversation.
Join our exclusive reader's list, and look for
our reader's guide and free offers at:

motherofpeace.com/readers

Did you like the book?
Spread the word and provide a quick review.
We appreciate you for helping us get the word out!

motherofpeace.com/reviews